readings for reflective teaching

in further, adult and vocational education

Edited by Margaret Gregson, Lawrence Nixon, Andrew Pollard and Patricia Spedding

BLOOMSBURY

LONDON • NEW DELHI • NEW YORK • SYDNEY

Bloomsbury Academic

An imprint of Bloomsbury Publishing Plc

50 Bedford Square	1385 Broadway
London	New York
WC1B 3DP	NY 10018
UK	USA

www.bloomsbury.com

BLOOMSBURY and the Diana logo are trademarks of Bloomsbury Publishing Plc

First published 2015

© Margaret Gregson, Lawrence Nixon, Andrew Pollard, Patricia Spedding and Contributors, 2015

Margaret Gregson, Lawrence Nixon, Andrew Pollard, Patricia Spedding and Contributors have asserted their right under the Copyright, Designs and Patents Act, 1988, to be identified as Authors of this work.

British Library Cataloguing-in-Publication Data
A catalogue record for this book is available from the British Library.

ISBN: HB: 978-1-4725-8650-6
PB: 978-1-4725-8649-0
ePDF: 978-1-4725-8652-0
ePub: 978-1-4725-8651-3

Library of Congress Cataloging-in-Publication Data
Readings for reflective teaching in further, adult and vocational education / edited by Margaret Gregson, Andrew Pollard, Lawrence Nixon and Patricia Spedding.
pages cm
ISBN 978-1-4725-8649-0 (paperback)-- ISBN 978-1-4725-8650-6 (hardback)
1. Adult education. 2. Reflective teaching. I. Gregson, Margaret.
LC5219.R38 2015
374--dc23
2014035138

Series: Reflective Teaching

Typeset by Fakenham Prepress Solutions, Fakenham, Norfolk NR21 8NN
Printed and bound in Great Britain

readings for reflective teaching

in further, adult and vocational education

Contents

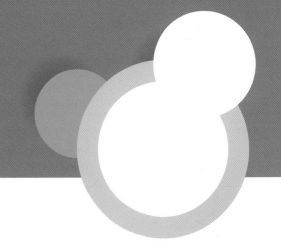

Part two Creating conditions for learning

Part four Reflecting on consequences

Part five Deepening understanding

Acknowledgements

A s editors of this book, one the most important decisions we have faced has been what should be included. Over the years that it has taken us to bring this book to publication, we have been fortunate in the advice we have had from many leading teachers, researchers and academics from across the Further Adult and Vocational Education (FAVE) sector as we explored possible selections for various chapters.

We have received a great deal of advice from colleagues in Scotland, England and Wales as well as from colleagues further afield in Australia, Luxemburg, the United States of America and Canada.

We would like to offer our particular thanks to Andrew Pollard as series editor, who was the first to recognize the need and potential for a book of this nature for the FAVE sector. Many thanks are also due to Yvonne Hillier who gave so generously of her time, experience and support throughout the production of this book.

Additional thanks are due to Sheila Kearney from the Education and Training Foundation (ETF) and Frank Coffield and Lorna Unwin (IOE) who have been a source of encouragement and support for the work of SUNCETT in developing practitioner research in the sector for so many years. Sincere thanks go to Gert Biesta (Luxemburg) for his advice in developing international perspectives regarding key ideas and issues raised in this book. Editors of other textbooks in the *Reflective Teaching* series also commented helpfully on the selection: Paul Ashwin (Lancaster) and Jen Colwell (Brighton).

Many thanks go to the student teachers and practitioners across the sector who have worked alongside us and contributed significantly to our understanding of teaching over the years, who may find echoes of the experiences and conversations they have shared with us in this book.

The administrative complexity of preparing the manuscript and obtaining permissions has been very considerable. This was helped enormously by Frances Moffatt and Andrew Buglass (Sunderland) and Miriam Davey (Bloomsbury). We are also extremely grateful to Frances Arnold, Ally Baker, Kasia Figiel, Rosie Pattinson and their colleagues at Bloomsbury for the contributions and advice they have given us on many occasions.

We would, of course, like to thank all the publishers' editors and other publishers' representatives, both in the UK and overseas, who were kind enough to grant permission for material to be reprinted. Some provided exceptional levels of support in respect of multiple readings. In particular, we acknowledge the generosity of IOE Press, Routledge, SAGE and Bloomsbury. A listing of permissions for the reproduction of extracts is formally provided at the end of this book. Attempts to trace permission-holders have been sustained, though a very few cases remain where replies to our enquiries have not yet been received; any enquiries on such matters should be sent in the first instance to the Permissions Manager at Bloomsbury Academic.

Finally, we would like to thank all the authors whose work features in this book – and apologize to the many other researchers and educationists whose high-quality material does not! Some, of course, may be delighted to have escaped, for word length constraints have occasionally forced detailed editing. We offer sincere apologies if any authors feel that their work has suffered in that process.

Having reviewed a wide range of publications for possible inclusion in this book, we remain enormously impressed by the richness of research and thinking which is available to teachers, mentors and student teachers across the FAVE sector. The collection can be seen as a representation of the work of several generations of educational researchers – though, even with so many readings, it has not been possible to include all the excellent material which is available. In a sense, though, the book remains a collective product and we would like to pay tribute to the many academic colleagues and educationalists who care enough to keep on trying to describe and understand education in so many diverse ways.

Margaret Gregson, Lawrence Nixon, Andrew Pollard and Patricia Spedding
February 2015

A note on citation

If you would like to quote from a reading within this book for coursework or for a publication, you will need to cite your source. Using the Harvard Convention and drawing only on this text, you should provide a bibliography containing details of the *original* source. These are provided in the introduction to each reading. You should then put: Cited in Gregson, M., Pollard, A., Nixon, L. and Spedding, P. (eds) (2015) *Readings for Reflective Teaching in Further, Adult and Vocational Education.* London: Bloomsbury.

If you are building up a substantial case around any reading, you are strongly recommended to go back to the original source to check your argument against the full text. Sources will be available through most colleges and universities with teacher education provision and most are available electronically. If using hard copy, you should then cite the full text only with the specific page numbers of any material that you quote. If using an online resource, you should cite page numbers as appropriate and the date on which the site was accessed.

Foreword

The Education and Training Foundation promotes high quality teaching and learning in England's further education and training sector. The new Professional Standards for Teachers and Trainers in our sector (see **http://www.et-foundation.co.uk/our-priorities/ professional-standards/professional-standards-2014/**) are at the heart of everything that we do, and are reflected in the design of every programme through which we support the sector and its workforce. The Standards emphasize the importance of professional reflection, of practitioners developing and refining their own expertise and judgement in applying theory to practice, and of identifying where practice needs to improve in order to ensure best outcomes for learners.

Those working in our sector cannot be expected to achieve these demanding standards on their own. Practitioners need time, space and support, including the support of their management and leadership, as well as their peers, in order to be able to operate at this level.

In our support for the sector we therefore design-in peer learning and practitioner-led activities, which legitimize practitioners' having time for reflection, trying things out, and sharing problems and learning with their colleagues. And we want to promote a culture that recognizes that learning also results from when things don't work out as expected.

This is why the Foundation is supporting the Joint Practice Development programme, which has been delivered by the University of Sunderland since 2009 and is integrated into these materials on reflective teaching.

JPD is based on mutual respect, a willingness to learn from each other, equality in argument, and a desire to improve everyone's practice for the sake of getting better at teaching so as to improve the quality of students' learning.

Since its inception we have seen this programme demonstrate the benefits of the JPD approach, and its impact on professional practices and on learner outcomes; these examples are drawn on throughout this volume.

I am very pleased that this new book of readings is now available to support practitioners in our sector. The appearance of this new textbook, along with the significantly revised edition of its companion volume and related website, is very timely. They demonstrate a practical and practitioner-led approach to professional development that is completely in tune with the new Professional Standards and also our vision at the Foundation for how we support education and training practitioners, whatever their role and position.

I thoroughly recommend these volumes and their website, and I'm delighted that the Foundation's investment in the JPD programme, and the work undertaken by its many participants over the years, have generated such rich material that can now be drawn on and support the broader workforce within further education throughout the UK and even beyond.

David Russell
Chief Executive Officer
The Education and Training Foundation
September 2014

Preface

This book is part of a set of professional resources. It links directly to the following textbook, *Reflective Teaching in Further, Adult and Vocational Education*, and to a website, reflectiveteaching.co.uk. They are part of a series with explicit provision for early years, schools, further, adult and higher education.

Reflective Teaching in Further, Adult and Vocational Education considers a very wide range of professionally relevant topics, presents key issues and research insights, suggests 'Reflective Activities' for classroom, workshop and studio work, and offers notes for selected 'Key Readings'. The text is used to support professional development for the initial and continuing professional development of teachers working in FE colleges, workplace learning, sixth form colleges and training consortia.

We hope that this will become the central textbook for supporting the development of professional practice for initial teacher education and the continuing professional development of teachers working in the FAVE sector across the UK and beyond. FAVE specialists from the University of Sunderland, the University of Brighton, Luxemburg University and the University of London Institute of Education have developed this unique companion book of readings to complement the *Reflective Teaching in Further, Adult and Vocational Education* textbook. This combination of a textbook and book of readings will support those engaged in teacher education in the UK and overseas.

Readings for Reflective Teaching in Further, Adult and Vocational Education contains some classic papers and new material from important recent research, drawing internationally as well as reflecting the unique character of the countries of the UK and Ireland. The balance of the book reflects current issues and concerns in education, and will support the development of a wide range of practitioners working in the FAVE sector and in university partnership arrangements.

reflectiveteaching.co.uk is a website supplementing the two books. For example, there are materials on mentoring which will be particularly helpful for teacher educators and teachers working across the wide variety of FAVE settings. It also offers ideas and resources on how to carry out teacher research and classroom enquiry as part of professional development. The web enables the Editorial Board to update material regularly. This is particularly relevant for 'Notes for Further Reading', a more extensive and current source of suggestions than is possible in a printed book. There is also a compendium of terms and additional 'Reflective Activities', download facilities for diagrams and supplementary resources of various kinds. The section on 'Deepening Expertise' offers access to more advanced features, including a framework linking research evidence to powerful concepts for the analysis of classroom practice.

Three major aims have guided the production of *Readings for Reflective Teaching in Further, Adult and Vocational Education.*

First, it is intended as a resource for busy teachers, mentors and trainee teachers in the FAVE sector who appreciate the value of educational thinking and research, and who wish to have easy access to key parts of important publications. There are illustrative readings from the UK, Ireland and mainland Europe, but the issues are of relevance anywhere.

Second, the book provides an opportunity to 'showcase' some of the excellent educational research from across the world which, in recent years, has been accumulating clear messages about high-quality teaching and learning. Readers may then wish to consult the full accounts in the original sources, each of which is carefully referenced.

Finally, these materials provide a unique resource for professional development activities and for initial teacher education courses. The structure of the three sources is identical, so that the chapters map across from one book to the other and to the web. Thus, whether used in classroom, workshop, workplace, studio activities, private study, mentoring conversations, tutorials, staff meetings, seminars or research projects, the materials should be easily accessible.

Reflective activity is of vital importance to the teaching profession:

- It underpins professional judgement and its use for worthwhile educational purposes;
- It provides a vehicle for learning and professional renewal – and thus for promoting the independence and integrity of teachers;
- Above all, it is a means to the principled development and improvement of teaching, the enhancement of learning and the steady growth in standards of performance across the FAVE sector.

We hope that you will find these materials helpful in your professional work and as you seek personal fulfilment as a teacher.

Margaret Gregson, Lawrence Nixon, Andrew Pollard and Patricia Spedding
February 2015

part one

Becoming
a reflective
professional

Identity

Who are we, and what do we stand for?

1

The readings in this chapter draw attention to the significance of values in education, different ways of looking at the purposes of education, and the development of teacher and student identity (who we are and what we stand for in education). We see how social expectations and contemporary change impact on our roles as teachers and learners and how we respond to them in deeply personal and professional ways. For both teacher and student in Further, Adult and Vocational Education (FAVE) it is important that we understand each other as persons as we explore what it means to become educationally wise together.

Regarding the purposes of education, Biesta (1.1) offers a helpful discussion of dimensions of education, how good judgement in education develops and how educational values are sustained and enacted in practice.

Coffield (1.2) challenges us to reconsider the ways in which government policy in England and elsewhere is influencing teaching, learning and assessment in ways that encourage 'teaching and learning to the test'. He points out that there is no such thing as best practice and argues (as we do [Gregson and Hillier, 2015]) that there are far more effective ways to improve teaching and learning. These include the use of joint practice development (JPD) as a model for improving teaching and learning and harnessing the potential power of formative assessment.

The parallel chapter of the companion textbook to this book of readings, *Reflective Teaching in Further, Adult and Vocational Education,* is structured in a similar way to this book. 'Knowing ourselves as teachers' presents ways of thinking about educational and personal values, the purposes and dimensions of education and how these influence teaching and learning. 'How can we understand student development' considers numerous factors which influence how our students learn, including their previous experiences of learning, current and potential levels of achievement, motivation, attitude, age, social and economic circumstances, employment status, physical and mental well-being and the time available for learning.

The website *reflectiveteaching.co.uk* supplements both books and contains materials on mentoring. These will be particularly helpful to student teachers and mentors engaged in teaching practice development and those interested in the enhancement of teacher expertise and identity across the spectrum of FAVE contexts. It also offers guidance on how to design and carry out practitioner research as part of the initial and continuing professional development of teachers.

Reading 1.1

What is education for? And what does that mean for teachers? On the role of judgement in teaching

Gert Biesta

This reading focuses attention upon the different purposes and dimensions of education and emphasizes the importance of teacher judgement. It comes from Gert Biesta's (2010) analysis of the particular nature of education practices and the role of purpose in such practices. Biesta then looks at the different judgements needed in education, what it means to judge and how we become better at making good educational judgements.

Edited from: Biesta, G. (2010) *Good Education in an Age of Measurement.* Boulder: Paradigm Publishers.

Introduction

It is often suggested that the main task of teachers and tutors is to deliver a curriculum that has been designed by others. In such a view – overstating it a little, but not that much – teachers and tutors should just 'do' (do as they are told, do as the curriculum tells them to do) without too much need for thinking, reflection and judgement. Such a view flies in the face of the idea of reflective teaching, that is, the idea that good teaching actually requires teachers to think about what they are doing, how they are doing it, and why they are doing what they are doing. In this chapter I argue that good teaching cannot do without *judgement* and that such judgement is fundamentally 'of the teacher.' I develop my argument in three steps. I first discuss the particular nature of educational practices and the role of purpose in such practices. I then look at the different judgements needed in education. And finally I reflect on what it means to judge and how to become better at making good educational judgements.

What is this thing called 'education'?

In recent years it has become popular to speak about what happens in schools, colleges, universities and life more generally in terms of *learning*. We have lifelong learning and the learning and skills sector, we speak about schools and colleges as learning environments, we call teachers and tutors as facilitators of learning, and we refer to students as learners. While learning is important in education, the language of learning is in a sense quite limited for understanding what education is about (see Biesta, 2004).

Perhaps the quickest way to highlight what the problem is, is to say that the point of education is *not* that students learn, but that they learn *something*, that they learn it for particular *reasons* and that they learn it *from someone*. Questions of *content*, *purpose and relationships* are precisely where we can find the distinction between (a general discussion about) learning and (a concrete discussion about) education. Education, to put it differently, is not designed so that children and young people might learn – people can learn anywhere and do not really need education for it – but so that they might learn particular things, for particular reasons, and supported by particular (educational) relationships.

Of these the question of purpose is the most important and most central one, because it is only when we know what we want to achieve with our educational endeavours – and when we know what we want our students to achieve – that we can make decisions about the content we need (the question of the curriculum) and about the kind of relationships (pedagogy) that are most conducive for achieving what we seek to achieve. Without a sense of purpose, there may be learning but not education. This is why we might claim that education is not just a practice that is *characterised* by the presence of purposes, but that it is a practice *constituted* by purpose(s).

The three functions of education and the three domains of educational purpose

This already provides one important reason why judgement is needed in education, as we need to come to some kind of understanding and a justification of what the purpose of our educational activities should be. But when we reflect on the purpose of our educational activities, we encounter something interesting, which is the fact that many – and in my view actually: all – educational activities do not function with regard to a single purpose but with regard to three different purposes (or to be more precise: three different domains of purpose – see below) (Biesta, 2010). Why is this so?

One way to understand this claim is by looking at the way in which education actually *functions*. One important function of education lies in the domain of *qualification*. Here education is concerned with the transmission and acquisition of knowledge, skills, dispositions and understandings that qualify children and young people to do certain things. Such doing can either be understood in a precise sense, for example becoming qualified to perform a certain task or job. Or it can be understood in a much wider sense, such as the idea that education qualifies children, young people and adults to live a successful and meaningful life in modern, complex societies.

Some would say that this is the only dimension in which education functions, that is, that education is only about getting knowledge and skills. Others highlight however that education is not just about qualification but also about *socialisation*. This has to do with the ways in which, through education, children, young people and adults become part of existing traditions cultures, ways of doing and ways of being. Education partly does this deliberately – for example when we want our students to become part of particular professional cultures and traditions. But research has also shown how education reproduces existing traditions and ways of doing and being 'behind the backs' of teachers and students, for example in the way in which education actually keeps existing social inequalities in place rather than that it provides everyone with the same opportunities – an idea known as the theory of the 'hidden curriculum'.

Whereas some would concede that education functions both with regard to qualification and socialisation, I wish to suggest that there is a third domain in which education always functions, and this has to do with the ways in which education impacts on our qualities as a person. Here we can think, for example, of the ways in which through the acquisition of knowledge, understanding and the ability to reflect and think critically, students can become empowered. Or how, through adopting particular cultural patterns and ways of being, they can become disempowered. In my own work I have referred to this domain as that of subjectification – as it has to do with how education contributes how we can be/ exist as human subjects.

If it is granted that qualification, socialisation and subjectification are three areas or dimensions in which education *functions* – which means nothing more that when we teach we always have some impact in each of these three domains – then it could be argued that as teachers we need to take responsibility for the potential impact of our educational actions in relation to these three domains. We need to think, in other words, what it is that we seek to achieve in relation to each of these three domains. That is why qualification, socialisation and subjectification are not only three domains in which all education functions or has an impact, but why we also can see them as three domains of educational purpose – three domains in which we need formulate an answer about what it is we seek to achieve with and for our students.

Before I discuss what this means for the role of judgement in our teaching, it is important to see that the three domains can be distinguished, but that they should not be thought of as separate. Perhaps the best way to think of them is in the form of a Venn diagram with three areas that are partly overlapping. The areas of overlap, as I will discuss in more detail in the next section, is that it is not always possible to separate the three domains, and this raises a further need for judgement in teaching.

Figure 1.1.1
The three functions of education and the three domains of educational purpose.

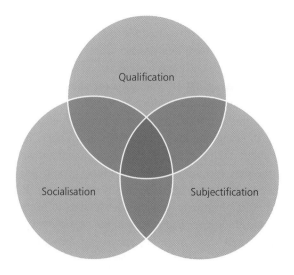

Three 'moments' of judgement in education

Against this background we are now in a position to answer the question why judgement is needed in education. The answer to this question is threefold, that is, there are three 'moments' in teaching at which judgement is needed. We first of all need judgement in relation to the question what the *purpose* of our educational arrangements and activities is to be – and this question, as mentioned, poses itself as a multi-dimensional question, so that we need to give an answer to what it is we wish to achieve and what we wish our students to achieve in relation to each of the three domains of educational purpose: qualification (the knowledge, skills, and attitudes we want our students to acquire); socialisation (the traditions and ways of doing and being we want our students to become part of); and subjectification (the qualities we seek to promote in them as persons).

Doing this also requires that we answer the question *why* it is that we want to achieve this, which is the issue of justification. The reason that we need judgement here, is because any answer to this question is not a matter of stating facts or referring to scientific evidence, but involves values and preferences. Scientific research can never provide an answer to the question what the purposes of education should be. What research can do, at most, is to provide information that might be relevant for understanding what is possible and feasible in each of the domains (see Biesta, 2007).

That is why at the very start of any educational endeavour we find a need for judgement. But it is not that we only need to come to a judgement about the purpose of our educational endeavours before we engage with them. The question of what it is we seek to achieve returns again and again as a very concrete question that needs to be answered in relation to concrete and, in a certain sense, always unique individual students in concrete and in a certain sense unique situations. It is therefore a question that lies at the heart of teaching and of what it means to be a teacher. Ongoing reflection on the purposes of our teaching is, in other words, at the very heart of what it means to be a reflective teacher.

A second 'moment' of judgement has to do with the ways in which we organise and enact education, that is, with regard to the *forms* of educational action. This has to do with another characteristic that makes education different from many other human fields and practices, namely the fact that in education there is an internal relationship between means and ends. The means of education – the ways in which we act, the things we say and how we say them, the ways in which we relate to our students and let them relate to each other – can never be thought of as mere instruments that should just effectively bring about certain 'outcomes'. And the reason for this is that students not only learn from what we say but also – and often more so – from how we say it and from what we do (see Carr, 1987). This means that our ways of doing in education do not just need to be effective (and sometimes that is not even a relevant criterion at all; see below). We always also need to judge whether they are educationally appropriate – which requires that we reflect on what our students might learn or pick up from the ways in which we do things and the ways in which we organise and arrange education.

This is not to suggest that question about how our educational actions might 'impact' in the different domains in which education functions are not relevant. On the contrary, there are important judgements to be made about that as well. But there is always the additional question whether our means, our ways of being and doing, are *educationally* appropriate, that is, whether the messages they convey – implicitly or explicitly – are indeed the messages we seek to convey. In addition to a technical judgement about the effectiveness of our actions and arrangements, there is therefore always also a need for a judgement about the educational desirability of our actions and arrangements. This shows another aspect of what it means to be a reflective teacher.

The third 'moment' of judgement in education follows directly from the multi-dimensional nature of educational purpose, because although there are interconnections between the three domains and there are, therefore, possibilities for synergy – to understand something, to gain knowledge about something can, after all, empower our students – the three domains are not seamlessly connected, which means that there is also the potential for tension and even conflict between the three domains. The three domains of educational purpose pull us as teachers in slightly (and sometimes significantly) different directions. Think, for example, of the way in which a constant emphasis on achievement in the domain of qualification can in the long run have quite damaging effects on the student as a person – for example those students who fail to achieve and thus are constantly being told that they are actually worthless. Also such an emphasis on achievement in the domain of qualification socialises students into a culture of competition rather than one of cooperation.

That is why in each educational situation – both at the general level of educational design and programming and at the concrete level of the encounter with each individual student – there is first of all judgement needed about what an educationally appropriate *balance* between the three domains might be. Secondly, and given the fact that such a balance can never be perfect, there is judgement needed about the inevitable *trade offs* between what can be achieved in each of the three domains in relation to each other. It is, after all, possible to achieve highly in each of the domains, but this often comes at a cost for what can be achieved in the other domains. And this is the third way in which within our teaching reflection needs to take the form of a judgement about what is an educational desirable way of doing and acting.

The final point I wish to make is that, given that education is a purposeful endeavour, all judgements we make about how to organise, conduct and give form to education have to be understood as entirely pragmatic. By this I mean to say that nothing in education is desirable in itself, but that it always depends on what it is we seek to achieve. Whether education should be flexible, student-led, personalised and transparent, or whether it should be structured, curriculum-led, and open-ended is not something we can decide in any general sense, but only in relation to what it is we seek to achieve. In some cases it can indeed be important to put our students at the centre of the educational process and make sure that they can express themselves or construct their own meanings and interpretations. But in other cases – for example when we want them to learn a particular skill and want to make sure that they get it right – flexibility and openness are actually counterproductive. The pragmatic nature of judgements about how to organise and conduct our educational efforts – that is, to repeat, the fact that what is desired always depends on what it is we seek to achieve – can help teachers not to fall for fashions, be they from policy makers or from researchers, that tend to suggest that all teaching should, for example, be personalised and flexible, or that all teaching should be strict and curriculum-led. Neither is in itself good or bad – it all depends on what we seek to achieve.

Becoming educationally wise

In the previous sections I have tried to provide a case why judgement in teaching is needed. This case mainly has to do with the fact that education is a purposeful endeavour, which partly means that we need to judge about the desired purposes of our activities, and that we partly need to make judgements about how to proceed in relation to these purposes. All this makes a strong case why teachers need to be reflective about their work. One interesting question this raises – both for teacher education and teacher professional development – is how teachers can become capable of making judgements about their work, and how, over time, they can become better at it. To answer this question we need to have an idea of what this ability to make judgements actually is. One interesting answer to this question can be found in the work of the Greek philosopher Aristotle (384–322 BC) who, in his time, was already interested in the question how we act in human domains such as education (for a detailed discussion of Aristotle's insights and their relevance for education see Heilbronn, 2009 (Reading 4.1); Biesta, 2014).

One thing Aristotle highlighted about a human domain such as education is that in such a domain things do not work in a mechanistic way – that is in terms of causes and predictable effects. This is because our students are not robots who simply obey what we tell them to do, but are human beings who can and need to make up their own minds, need to create their own understandings and interpretations. Education is therefore a 'variable' process – as Aristotle would call it – that works very differently from mechanical processes such as the movement of the planets or the behaviour of atoms. That is one reason why judgement is needed, because all the knowledge we have about how education might work can never totally predict what will happen in a concrete situation – we therefore constantly need to apply our general knowledge; we need to judge, in other words, how any general knowledge we may have might be applied to this concrete situation.

In this regard we can compare education to other fields of craft of art, where, although we may have a lot of general knowledge, there is always the question how this knowledge can be applied to concrete and unique situations. One example Aristotle gives of this is the art of saddle making, where we need to have knowledge about leather, about construction, about horses and horse riding, but where for each individual saddle we make we need to apply this general knowledge to this piece of leather, for this horse and this person riding the horse. In addition to making judgements about how to produce a saddle, Aristotle argues that in the practices of education we are not just producing 'things' – we are not producing our students but are educating them – which means that a different kind of judgement is needed, a judgement about what is to be done; which is the judgement about the purposes of our activities. Such judgements, Aristotle argues, are not technical judgements about how to do something or how to produce something, but are answers to the question 'What is to be done?' To be able to answer this question

Aristotle argues that we need a quality called 'phronesis' – usually translated into English as practical wisdom.

What is interesting and helpful about Aristotle's ideas concerning practical wisdom is that he does not think of this as a skill or a competency, but actually as a quality of the whole professional person – a way of acting and being, a way of being able to judge what is to be done, to judge what the right thing to do for this student (Reading 4.1) in this situation is. Practical wisdom is a kind of embodied quality that we can often see in experienced teachers who in a very practical way 'know' what is good for their actual students in real situations. Aristotle does indeed argue that practical wisdom is not something we can simply learn – but that it actually is something that we gain over time, through experience or, more precisely, through a constant engagement with this question, that is, the question What is to be done? To acquire this 'capacity' is therefore more like learning to play a musical instrument. It is a process that takes time, that requires practicing, and where over time we become more proficient at it, we get it 'in the fingers', so to speak. That is why we might say that good teachers, good reflective teachers, should over time aspire not simply to acquire practical educational wisdom as some kind of 'thing' they pick up. Rather they should, throughout their career, work on their ability to be educationally wise in their doing and being.

Reading 1.2

What is Further Education for? What freedoms do tutors have?

Frank Coffield

> Two main questions are addressed in this extract. The first discusses the future and purposes of Further Education (FE) and criticises the policies of successive governments, which, Coffield argues, are turning our FE colleges into *skills factories*.
>
> The second question is: what improvements can we make to the quality of teaching, learning and assessment in classrooms and to the culture of schools and colleges, irrespective of government policy?
>
> *Edited from:* Coffield, F. in Coffield, F. with Costa, C., Muller, W. and Webber, J. (2014) *Beyond Bulimic Learning.* London: Institute of Education Press, 1–21.

The instrumental attitude of politicians fails to capture the uniqueness of FE in the educational world in that it is *the* great transformer of the lives of people. Moreover, the relentless political pressure to improve standards, by which is meant test scores, is having a damaging effect on learning which is becoming 'bulimic'.

The parameters within which English educators currently work are being constantly tightened, so how much freedom is left to classroom teachers and senior management in colleges to enhance the quality of teaching and learning? We need to start behaving *as if* we lived in a democracy by exercising the freedoms we still possess. We need to act on the growing consensus, based on reasonably hard evidence among the research community, about the essential ingredients that make for effective teaching learning and assessment.

Let us begin by speculating about the future of Further Education (FE). Stephen Grosz has argued that "the future is not some place we're going to, but an idea in our mind now. It's something we're creating, that in turn creates us. The future is a fantasy that shapes our present" (Grosz, 2013: 157). I would add that any shaping of the future also needs to be based on an understanding of how the past is constantly recreated to justify a particular reading of the present. What is already clear is that we need a better future than the one we are currently hurtling towards.

What is the FE sector for? Over the last 20 years the language of learning and skills has eclipsed the language of education; the language of business so permeates the education system that every tutor has a "line manager", although there are no production lines; and the measurement of inputs and outputs has replaced dialogue about the aims and objectives of FE (see Biesta, 2010). Since incorporation in the early 1990s, when FE colleges became independent of local authorities, instead of being able to exercise that new freedom, the colleges have been turned through the policies of successive governments into skills factories, whose main and virtually sole aim has been to help British business compete in the 'global economic race'. The permanent revolutions which governments have introduced into structures, priorities and qualifications have sent pressures cascading down through every level within colleges. Students now resort to what I call 'bulimic learning' to cope with a testing regime that ministers would have you believe is robust and rigorous, but is in fact purgative and emetic: the outcome is *Bulimia Academica*, which is every bit as serious as its medical counterpart. Students are bingeing on large amounts of information and then, in government induced bouts of vomiting otherwise known as national tests, they spew it all out.

We need to return to the original purpose of FE. For me, the main purpose of FE is Further Education. The clue is in the name. FE does not stand for Further Employment or, that weasel term so beloved of the politicians, Future Employability, because that passes the responsibility for securing employment from governments and employers to individuals. The main purpose of education is not the wages students will earn but the quality of the life they will lead as parents, consumers and citizens as well as workers. In providing second chance education, vocational education and lifelong learning for all, FE fulfils a vital role not only for individuals but for society as a whole; and the wider benefits of education in terms of health, social cohesion and active citizenship enable adults to sustain and transform their lives and those of their communities through their interactions with committed tutors.

A sharper focus on Further *Education* will lead us to ask: are students leaving our colleges as educated people, prepared to take their place as skilled workers, wise parents, discriminating consumers *and* active citizens of a democracy? The Scottish government sets out clearly the aims for its Curriculum for Excellence, which are to create successful learners, confident individuals, responsible citizens and effective contributors to society (see MacLellan and Soden, 2012). Are we providing all FE students with the knowledge, skills and values and with the democratic experience of political action, which they will need to cope with the main threats to our collective wellbeing such as climate change (See Coffield and Williamson, 2012; Biesta, 2006). My answer to both questions is "No." FE students need not just highly relevant vocational training but also high quality general education; and in Germany, France and Scandinavia they receive it. That would prevent them taking out an action against their FE College for contravening the Trades Description Act – "you call yourself a Further Education college but you don't provide what it says on the tin."

Let me now turn to the second question I posed in the introduction to this extract: can we transform classrooms and colleges without transforming the role of the state? I refer readers to the final chapter of my book, *Beyond Bulimic Learning: Improving teaching in further education*, for a fuller answer to that question. I think some advances can still be made in classrooms by considered enactment and careful evaluation of the more effective interventions discussed in the chapters of that book such as harnessing the potential power of feedback or changing the model of professional learning (Reading 16.1). We all have far more freedom than we imagine but we must begin to exercise it. We are not living in a Stalinist or Fascist state; we need to start behaving *as if* we lived in a democracy. Tutors in FE need to become powerful, democratic professionals.

Over the last 25 years, government policies have become so numerous, invasive, ill-considered and short-lived that the freedom of action previously enjoyed by educators and Senior Management Teams has become seriously curtailed. In particular, the key resource in this sector, namely the *time* of tutors and managers, is increasingly taken up responding to the initiatives of ministers rather than to the needs of students. My own judgement is that the culture of fear, the constant raising of the barrier of minimal acceptable performance and the 'high stakes' testing regime which pits college against college and colleague against colleague will prevent the widespread emergence of communities of learning, which are again described fully in the final chapter of my book. My prediction is that this sick sector will get even sicker, if a total change of direction is not made.

The FE sector rightly prides itself on being infinitely resourceful and responsive, but Geoff Stanton (2008) was surely right to question whether it is not at times **too** responsive and he went on to argue that, before politicians embark on a radical reform, they should be obliged to state what steps they have taken to safeguard the interests of students during the transitional period. What employers, for example, can now be expected to remember the curriculum (or even the name) of Diplomas which the Conservative-led coalition dispensed with on coming to power in 2010? And yet hundreds of thousands of students/employees have Diplomas as their only qualifications.

When do we collectively say that we want to make some minimal demands upon government rather than always being on the receiving end of another wave of fundamental reforms? To ask, for example, for our representatives to be routinely consulted when policy is being formed. For tutors to be consulted about radical changes to the curriculum before those changes are made mandatory. Please do not tell me that the Department of Education routinely consults on all new proposals.

Democracy thrives on vigorous public debate. The education system in England has for some years been in crisis, and yet that great British institution, the BBC, has not one programme devoted to education and every time I turn on the television or radio the education correspondent is someone different. The current 'system' is failing because generations of students are leaving our schools, colleges and universities with a dangerously impoverished notion of education, and profoundly ignorant about the major threats to our collective being and what they could do about them. England does not have a high quality vocational path that could offer a prestigious alternative to the educational route so those students who do not sit A levels remain the forgotten 50%.

Educational policy in England becomes ever more extreme, divisive and inequitable, it is racing ever faster down the wrong road, reducing the professionalism of teachers to carrying out the detailed instructions of an opinionated politician, and the education of students to a narrow concentration on what can be measured and examined (see Coffield, 2007). The yearly application of more and more pressure for improved results is unsustainable. It is time to call a halt before any more damage is done.

What keeps me awake at night is not the hectoring demands of the market fundamentalists for more public assets to be turned into private profit, but the ghosts of those who built the sector we inherited, calling me to account: "What," I hear them ask, "did you do, Frank, to defend this sector? What will you do to defend those tutors now threatened with unemployment? Will you fight publicly for those who need a second, and yes, a third chance to transform their lives through Further Education? What action will you take to build a democratic education system in this country?"

How, may I ask, will **you** answer these questions?

Learning
How can we
understand learner
development?

2

The first readings in this chapter illustrate some major contributions to education and to learning theory from the field of psychology. The theory of behaviourism is represented by Skinner (2.1). In relation to modern theories of social cognition we owe much to the work of Vygotsky, as illustrated by his classic account of the Zone of Proximal Development (ZPD) (2.2). An extension of these ideas in relation to learning and culture is offered by Wells (2.3). Fisher (2.4) presents an argument on why thinking skills should be taught. Finally Nixon et al. (2.5) demonstrate how, in the absence of robust empirical evidence to support their use in FAVE contexts, the 'grip' of the intuitive appeal of the use of 'learning styles' remains strong.

The parallel chapter of *Reflective Teaching in Further, Adult and Vocational Education* reviews a similar range of issues and considers them in relation to practical teaching. The chapter begins with a discussion of behaviourist, cognitivist and what we call multidisciplinary theories of learning, including experiential learning, situated learning and social constructivist and sociocultural models of learning.

It then addresses a wide range of issues in relation to domains and taxonomies of learning. The final section of the chapter takes stock of current and key issues in the field of FAVE, including what Biesta (2009) describes as the 'learnification of education'. The chapter concludes by pointing to the importance of recognizing the need to understand the strengths and shortcomings of different theories of learning alongside the ability to strike a balance between them in pursuit of good educational practice.

Suggestions for further key readings and many other ideas for more detailed study can be accessed from *reflectiveteaching.co.uk*. You can do this by visiting the *reflectiveteaching.co.uk* website; navigate your way to this book and this chapter and the 'Notes for Further Reading'.

Reading 2.1

The science of learning and the art of teaching
Burrhus Skinner

B. F. Skinner made a very important contribution to 'behaviourist' psychology, a branch of psychology based on the study of the ways in which animal behaviour is shaped and conditioned by stimuli. In this reading, Skinner applies his ideas to the learning of pupils in schools. Taking the case of learning arithmetic, he highlights the production of correct 'responses' from children and considers the forms of 'reinforcement' which are routinely used in classrooms. He regards these as hopelessly inadequate. What do you see as the implications of behaviourism for the role of the teacher?

Edited from: Skinner, B. F. (1954) 'The science of learning and the art of teaching', *Harvard Educational Review*, 24, 86–97.

Promising advances have been made in the field of learning. Special techniques have been designed to arrange what are called 'contingencies of reinforcement' – the relations which prevail between behaviour on the one hand and the consequences of that behaviour on the other – with the result that a much more effective control of behaviour has been achieved. It has long been argued that an organism learns mainly by producing changes in its environment, but it is only recently that these changes have been carefully manipulated.

Recent improvements in the conditions which control behaviour in the field of learning are of two principal sorts. The Law of Effect has been taken seriously; we have made sure that effects do occur and that they occur under conditions which are optimal for producing the changes called learning. Once we have arranged the particular type of consequence called a reinforcement, our techniques permit us to shape up the behaviour of an organism almost at will. It has become a routine exercise to demonstrate this in classes in elementary psychology by conditioning such an organism as a pigeon. Simply by presenting food to a hungry pigeon at the right time, it is possible to shape up three or four well-defined responses in a single demonstration period – such responses as turning around, pacing the floor in the pattern of a figure-8, standing still in a corner of the demonstration apparatus, stretching the neck or stamping the foot. Extremely complex performances may be reached through successive stages in the shaping process, the contingencies of reinforcement being changed progressively in the direction of the required behaviour. The results are often quite dramatic. In such a demonstration one can see learning take place. A significant change in behaviour is often obvious as the result of a single reinforcement.

A second important advance in technique permits us to maintain behaviour in given states of strength for long periods of time. However it is important to note that long after an organism has learned how to do something, long after it has acquired behaviour, reinforcement continues to be important. Continuing reinforcement is necessary in order to maintain the strength of the learned response. We have learned how to maintain any given level of activity for daily periods limited only by the physical exhaustion of the organism and from day to day without substantial change throughout its life. Many of these effects would be traditionally assigned to the field of motivation, although the principal operation is simply the arrangement of contingencies of reinforcement.

These new methods of shaping behaviour and of maintaining it in strength are a great improvement over the traditional practices of professional animal trainers, and it is not surprising that our laboratory results are already being applied to the production of performing animals for commercial purposes.

From this exciting prospect of an advancing science of learning, it is a great shock to turn to that branch of technology which is most directly concerned with the learning process – education. Let us consider, for example, the teaching of arithmetic in the lower grades. The school is concerned with imparting to the child a large number of responses of a special sort. The responses are all verbal. They consist of speaking and writing certain words, figures and signs which, to put it roughly, refer to numbers and to arithmetic operations. The first task is to shape up these responses – to get the child to pronounce and to write responses correctly, but the principal task is to bring this behaviour under many sorts of stimulus control. This is what happens when the child learns to count, to recite tables, to count while ticking off the items in an assemblage of objects, to respond to spoken or written numbers by saying 'odd', 'even', 'prime' and so on. Over and above this elaborate repertoire of numerical behaviour, most of which is often dismissed as the product of rote learning, the teaching of arithmetic looks forward to those complex serial arrangements of responses involved in original mathematical thinking. The child must acquire responses of transposing, clearing fractions and so on, which modify the order or pattern of the original material so that the response called a solution is eventually made possible.

Now, how is the extremely complicated verbal repertoire set up? In the first place, what reinforcements are used? Fifty years ago the answer would have been clear. At that time educational control was still frankly aversive. The child read numbers, copied numbers, memorized tables and performed operations upon numbers to escape the threat of the birch rod or cane. Some positive reinforcements were perhaps eventually derived from the increased efficiency of the child in the field of arithmetic and in rare cases some automatic reinforcement may have resulted from the sheer manipulation of the medium – from the solution of problems or the discovery of the intricacies of the number system. But for the immediate purposes of education the child acted to avoid or escape punishment. It was part of the reform movement known as progressive education to make the positive consequences more immediately effective, but anyone who visits the lower grades of the average school today will observe that a change has been made, not from aversive to positive control, but from one form of aversive stimulation to another. The child at his desk, filling in his workbook, is behaving primarily to escape from the threat of a series of minor aversive events – the teacher's displeasure, the criticism or ridicule of his class-mates, an ignominious showing in a competition, low marks, a trip to the office 'to be talked to' by the principal, or a word to the parent who may still resort to the birch rod. In this welter of aversive consequences, getting the right answer is in itself an insignificant event, any effect of which is lost amid the anxieties, the boredom and the aggressions which are the inevitable by-products of aversive control.

Secondly, we have to ask how the contingencies of reinforcement are arranged. When is a numerical operation reinforced as 'right'? Eventually, of course, the pupil may be able to check his own answers and achieve some sort of automatic reinforcement, but in the early stages the reinforcement of being right is usually accorded by the teacher. The contingencies she provides are far from optimal. It can easily be demonstrated that, unless explicit mediating behaviour has been set up, the lapse of only a few seconds between response and reinforcement destroys most of the effect. In a typical classroom, nevertheless, long periods of time customarily elapse. The teacher may walk up and down the aisle, for example, while the class is working on a sheet of problems, pausing here and there to say right or wrong. Many seconds or minutes intervene between the child's response and the teacher's reinforcement. In many cases – for example, when papers are taken home to be corrected – as much as 24 hours may intervene. It is surprising that this system has any effect whatsoever.

A third notable shortcoming is the lack of a skilful program which moves forward through a series of progressive approximations to the final complex behaviour desired. A long series of contingencies is necessary to bring the organism into the possession of mathematical behaviour most efficiently. But the teacher is seldom able to reinforce at each step in such a series because she cannot deal with the pupil's responses one at a time. It is usually necessary to reinforce the behaviour in blocks of responses – as in correcting a work sheet or page from a workbook. The responses within such a block must not be interrelated. The answer to one problem must not depend upon the answer to another. The number of stages through which one may progressively approach a complex pattern of behaviour is therefore small, and the task so much the more difficult. Even the most modern workbook in beginning arithmetic is far from exemplifying an efficient program for shaping up mathematical behaviour.

Perhaps the most serious criticism of the current classroom is the relative infrequency of reinforcement. Since the pupil is usually dependent upon the teacher for being right, and since many pupils are usually dependent upon the same teacher, the total number of contingencies which may be arranged during, say, the first four years, is of the order of only a few thousand. But a very rough estimate suggests that efficient mathematical behaviour at this level requires something of the order of 25,000 contingencies. We may suppose that even in the brighter student a given contingency must be arranged several times to place the behaviour well in hand. The responses to be set up are not simply the various items in tables of addition, subtraction, multiplication and division; we have also to consider the alternative forms in which each item may be stated. To the learning of such material we should add hundreds of responses concerned with factoring, identifying primes, memorizing series, using shortcut techniques for calculation, constructing and using geometric representations or number forms and so on. Over and above all this, the whole mathematical repertoire must be brought under the control of concrete problems of considerable variety. Perhaps 50,000 contingencies is a more conservative estimate. In this frame of reference the daily assignment in arithmetic seems pitifully meagre.

The result of this is, of course, well known. Even our best schools are under criticism for the inefficiency in the teaching of drill subjects such as arithmetic. The condition in the average school is a matter of widespread national concern. Modern children simply do not learn arithmetic quickly or well. Nor is the result simply incompetence. The very subjects in which modern techniques are weakest are those in which failure is most conspicuous, and in the wake of an ever-growing incompetence come the anxieties, uncertainties and aggressions which in their turn present other problems to the school. Most pupils soon claim the asylum of not being 'ready' for arithmetic at a given level or, eventually, of not having a mathematical mind. Such explanations are readily seized upon by defensive teachers and parents. Few pupils ever reach the stage at which automatic reinforcements follow as the natural consequences of mathematical behaviour. On the contrary, the figures and symbols of mathematics have become standard emotional stimuli. The glimpse of a column of figures, not to say an algebraic symbol or an integral sign, is likely to set off – not mathematical behaviour – but a reaction of anxiety, guilt or fear.

The teacher is usually no happier about this than the pupil. Denied the opportunity to control via the birch rod, quite at sea as to the mode of operation of the few techniques at her disposal, she spends as little time as possible on drill subjects and eagerly subscribes to philosophies of education which emphasize material of greater inherent interest.

There would be no point in urging these objections if improvement were impossible. But the advances which have recently been made in our control of the learning process suggest a thorough revision of classroom practices and, fortunately, they tell us how the revision can be brought about. This is not, of course, the first time that the results of an experimental science have been brought to bear upon the practical problems of education. The modern classroom does not, however, offer much evidence that research in the field of learning has been respected or used. This condition is no doubt partly due to the limitations of earlier research, but it has been encouraged by a too hasty conclusion that the laboratory study of learning is inherently limited because it cannot take into account the realities of the classroom. In the light of our increasing knowledge of the learning process we should, instead, insist upon dealing with those realities and forcing a substantial change in them. Education is perhaps the most important branch of scientific technology. It deeply affects the lives of all of us. We can no longer allow the exigencies of a practical situation to suppress the tremendous improvements which are within reach. The practical situation must be changed.

There are certain questions which have to be answered in turning to the study of any new organism. What behaviour is to be set up? What reinforcers are at hand? What responses are available in embarking upon a program of progressive approximation which will lead to the final form of behaviour? How can reinforcements be most efficiently scheduled to maintain the behaviour in strength? These questions are all relevant in considering the problem of the child in the lower grades.

Reading 2.2

Mind in society and the Zone of Proximal Development

Lev Vygotsky

> Vygotsky's social constructivist psychology, though stemming from the 1930s, underpins much modern thinking about teaching and learning. In particular, the importance of instruction is emphasized. However, this is combined with recognition of the influence of social interaction and the cultural context within which understanding is developed. Vygotsky's most influential concept is that of the Zone of Proximal Development, which highlights the potential for future learning which can be realized with appropriate support.
>
> The influence of Vygotsky's work will be particularly apparent in **Reading 2.4** but it is also present in many other readings, particularly in Chapters 10, 11, 12 and 13.
>
> Thinking of a particular area of learning and a child you know, can you identify an 'actual developmental level' and a zone of proximal development through which you could provide guidance and support?
>
> *Edited from:* Vygotsky, L. S. (1978) *Mind in Society: The Development of Higher Psychological Processes*. Cambridge, MA: Harvard University Press, 84–90.

That children's learning begins long before they attend school is the starting point of this discussion. Any learning a child encounters in school always has a previous history. For example, children begin to study arithmetic in school, but long beforehand they have had some experience with quantity – they have had to deal with operations of division, addition, subtraction, and determination of size. Consequently, children have their own pre-school arithmetic which only myopic scientists could ignore.

It goes without saying that learning as it occurs in the preschool years differs markedly from school learning, which is concerned with the assimilation of the fundamentals of scientific knowledge. But even when, in the period of her first questions, a child assimilates the names of objects in her environment, she is learning. Indeed, can it be doubted that children learn speech from adults; or that, through asking questions and giving answers, children acquire a variety of information; or that through imitating adults and through being instructed about how to act, children develop an entire repository of skills? Learning and development are interrelated from the child's very first day of life.

In order to elaborate the dimensions of school learning, we will describe a new and exceptionally important concept without which the issue cannot be resolved: the zone of proximal development.

A well known and empirically established fact is that learning should be matched in some manner with the child's developmental level. For example, it has been established that the teaching of reading, writing and arithmetic should be initiated at a specific age level. Only recently, however, has attention been directed to the fact that we cannot limit ourselves merely to determining developmental levels if we wish to discover the actual relations of the developmental process to learning capabilities. We must determine at least two developmental levels.

The first level can be called the actual developmental level, that is, the level of development of a child's mental functions that has been established as a result of certain already completed developmental cycles. When we determine a child's mental age by using tests, we are almost always dealing with the actual developmental level. In studies of children's mental development it is generally assumed that only those things that children can do on their own are indicative of mental abilities. We give children a battery of tests or a variety of tasks of varying degrees of difficulty, and we judge the extent of their mental development on the basis of how they solve them and at what level of difficulty. On the other hand, if we offer leading questions or show how the problem is to be solved and the child then solves it, or if the teacher initiates the solution and the child completes it or solves it in collaboration with other children – in short, if the child barely misses an independent solution of the problem – the solution is not regarded as indicative of his mental development. This 'truth' was familiar and reinforced by common sense. Over a decade even the profoundest thinkers never questioned the assumption; they never entertained the notion that what children can do with the assistance of others might be in some sense even more indicative of their mental development than what they can do alone.

The zone of proximal development is the distance between the actual developmental level as determined by independent problem solving and the level of potential development as determined through problem solving under adult guidance or in collaboration with more capable peers.

If we naively ask what the actual developmental level is, or, to put it more simply, what more independent problem solving reveals, the most common answer would be that a child's actual developmental level defines functions that have already matured, that is, the end products of development. If a child can do such-and-such independently, it means that the functions for such-and-such have matured in her. What, then, is defined by the zone of proximal development, as determined through problems that children cannot solve independently but only with assistance? The zone of proximal development defines those functions that have not yet matured but are in the process of maturation, functions that will mature tomorrow but are currently in an embryonic state. These functions could be termed the 'buds' or 'flowers' of development rather than the 'fruits' of development. The actual developmental level characterizes mental development retrospectively, while the zone of proximal development characterizes mental development prospectively.

The zone of proximal development furnishes psychologists and educators with a tool through which the internal course of development can be understood. By using this method we can take account of not only the cycles and maturation processes that have already been completed but also those processes that are currently in a state of formation, that are just beginning to mature and develop. Thus, the zone of proximal development permits us to delineate the child's immediate future and his dynamic developmental state, allowing not only for what already has been achieved developmentally but also for what is in the course of maturing. The state of a child's mental development can be determined only by clarifying its two levels: the actual developmental level and the zone of proximal development.

A full understanding of the concept of the zone of proximal development must result in re-evaluation of the role of imitation in learning. Indeed, human learning presupposes a specific social nature and a process by which children grow into the intellectual life of those around them.

Children can imitate a variety of actions that go well beyond the limits of their own capabilities. Using imitation, children are capable of doing much more in collective activity or under the guidance of adults. This fact, which seems to be of little significance in itself, is of fundamental importance in that it demands a radical alteration of the entire doctrine concerning the relation between learning and development in children.

Learning which is oriented toward developmental levels that have already been reached is ineffective from the viewpoint of a child's overall development. It does not aim for a new stage of the developmental process but rather lags behind this process. Thus, the notion of a zone of proximal development enables us to propound a new formula, namely that the only 'good learning' is that which is in advance of development.

The acquisition of language can provide a paradigm for the entire problem of the relation between learning and development. Language arises initially as a means of communication between the child and the people in his environment. Only subsequently, upon conversion to internal speech, does it come to organize the child's thought, that is, become an internal mental function.

We propose that an essential feature of learning is that it creates the zone of proximal development; that is, learning awakens a variety of internal developmental processes that are able to operate only when the child is interacting with people in his environment and in cooperation with his peers. Once these processes are internalized, they become part of the child's independent developmental achievement.

From this point of view, learning is not development; however, properly organized learning results in mental development and sets in motion a variety of developmental processes that would be impossible apart from learning. Thus, learning is a necessary and universal aspect of the process of developing culturally organized, specifically human, psychological functions.

Reading 2.3

Learning, development and schooling
Gordon Wells

> Gordon Wells criticises three dominant views about the relationship between learning and development: behaviourism (**Reading 2.1**), constructivist psychology (**Reading 2.2**), and thinking conceptualized as computer information processes. However, he endorses and extends Vygotsky's social constructivism (**Reading 2.2**). In so doing, he is one of many contemporary educationalists who have been strongly influenced by versions of this approach because of the ways in which it links history and culture to personal learning through meaningful activity. For example, we inherit and use many cultural as well as material tools – such as language.
>
> Can you identify, in your own biography, some examples of how your learning was (or is) influenced by your cultural circumstances, social relationships and activities? And how might this apply to students you teach?
>
> *Edited from:* Wells, G. (2008) 'Dialogue, Inquiry and the Construction of Learning Communities'. In B. Lingard, J. Nixon and S. Ranson (eds) *Transforming Learning in Schools and Communities*. London: Continuum, 236–42.

For much of the twentieth century, three views about the relationship between learning and development predominated. The first is behaviourist in origin. It assumes that each individual has a fixed potential, often expressed as IQ, which is said to account for differences in educational achievement. The second view grew out of Piaget's early work on the universal stages of cognitive development, which led to an emphasis on readiness and child-centred discovery learning. The third is modelled on the mind as a computer with innately given cognitive modules. This latter view has tended to be expressed in terms of inputs and outputs, with thinking conceptualized as processing information that is stored in memory like files in a large computer.

However, none of these views does justice to the role of learning in human development. The first ignores what goes on in the mind, treating education as the reinforcement of associations and habits that can be assessed in purely quantitative terms. While the second view emphasizes the constructive nature of learning, it largely ignores the fact that human infants grow up as members of historically ongoing cultures, which strongly influence their development. Finally, the third view comes close to reducing the human mind to a machine and, in so doing, ignores the interdependence of bodily action, thinking and feeling and interaction with others in the activities through which learning occurs. It also has very little to say about development.

In the place of these three inadequate theories, I wish to describe an alternative view, which not only envisages development as ongoing transformation, but also treats it as involving a mutually constitutive relationship between the individual and the society in which she or he is growing up, and between biological endowment and the cultural practices in which, from birth, he or she is continuously involved. Known as cultural historical activity theory (CHAT), this explanation of the relationship between learning and development was first formulated by Vygotsky in Russia and has since been extended and refined by researchers and educators from many different countries. In summary form, the key points of CHAT can be stated as follows:

- The basic 'unit' of human behaviour is purposeful activity jointly undertaken with others in a particular time and place and in relation to a particular culture.
- In all major domains of human activity, goals are achieved by people carrying out actions mediated by tools, both material and symbolic, of which the most powerful and versatile is language.
- Individual development (cognitive, social and affective) results from participation in joint activity with more expert others, in which the individual masters the culturally developed tools and practices and 'appropriates' them as resources for acting and thinking, both alone and in collaboration with others.
- Learning is greatly facilitated by guidance and assistance that is pitched in the learner's 'zone of proximal development'.

While appropriating ways of acting, thinking and feeling from care givers and other community members, the child does not passively copy their knowledge and skills. In contrast, learning is an active and constructive process that involves a triple transformation: of the learner's repertoire for action; of the tools and practices involved, as the learner constructs his or her unique version of them; and of his or her relationship with others and thus of his or her identity. As a result of these transformations, all the individual participants, as well as the cultural situations in and on which they act, are in a constant state of change and development that is the continuously emergent outcome of their actions and transactions. In other words, the developmental relationship between society and its individual members is one of interdependence and co-construction.

Every occasion of joint activity provides a potential occasion for learning. By the same token, assistance given to a learner in his or her attempt to participate is an occasion of teaching. Most often, however, such teaching occurs incidentally and without deliberate intention – as in most parent–child conversations.

There are many occasions when an adult or a more knowledgeable sibling or peer deliberately helps a child with a task, particularly when they judge that the child cannot yet manage on his or her own. Vygotsky (1978) described assistance given in this way as working in the 'zone of proximal development'. In any task we undertake, there is frequently a limit to what we can achieve alone. In such situations, help from another with what is proving difficult both allows us to complete the task and models for us what we need to add to our resources so that, in the future, we shall be able to manage the task unaided. Indeed, in traditional cultures, this is how children learn most of what they know and are able to do.

This kind of situated learning 'on the job' has been described as 'cultural apprenticeship' (Lave and Wenger, 1991; Rogoff, 2003). However, while learning through apprenticeship provides an essential spur to development towards full membership in all cultures, on its own it is insufficient to equip young people today with all the knowledge and skills they need to participate fully in technologically advanced cultures (Lemke, 2002). It is to fulfil this role that educational institutions exist – as they have since it first became necessary to provide a setting for some members of each generation to learn to read and write (Cole, 1996). In the last few centuries, however, as written language and other semiotic systems, such as mathematics, scientific formulae and procedures, graphs, maps and diagrams of all kinds, have come to play an increasingly important role in the development and dissemination of 'formal' knowledge, schools, colleges, work places and universities have come to play a more and more significant role in the development of 'higher mental functions'. It is in this relatively novel context that we need to consider the part that deliberate teaching plays in young people's learning.

Schools, colleges and universities differ from settings for informal and spontaneous learning-and-teaching in several important ways. First, attendance is compulsory between certain ages (5 or 6 until 16–18 in most cultures); second, there is a prescribed curriculum that sets out – increasingly, in considerable detail – the knowledge and skills that students are required to learn in each year and for which they will be held accountable through tests and other forms of assessment; and third, in each age-based class there is typically a ratio of 25 or more students to each teacher. Furthermore, although the students are all approximately of the same age, they vary considerably in terms of their interests and aspirations, as well as in their physical and intellectual strengths and needs, as a result of their very different backgrounds and life trajectories. Every school class, therefore, is characterized by diversity on a variety of dimensions that need to be taken into account.

Throughout most of the history of schooling, this combination of constraints has led to a transmission approach to education, aimed at ensuring that all students acquire the same set of knowledgeable skills that are considered most useful and important for their future roles in the workforce. With this end in view, the goals of teaching have been those of organizing what is to be learned into appropriately sized and sequenced chunks and of arranging optimal methods of delivery, together with opportunities for practice and memorization. In this approach, little or no attention is given to students' diverse backgrounds, interests and expertise, nor are they encouraged to show initiative and creativity in formulating questions and problems and in attempting to solve them in collaboration with their peers and teachers. Instead, students' success is largely evaluated in terms of their ability to recall what they have been taught and to reproduce it on demand in response to arbitrary questions, often divorced from any meaningful context.

If this pattern was not so historically engrained, its inappropriateness would surely have led to its demise long ago, given the high proportion of students who, each year, fail to master the required curriculum and how little the remainder remember of what they learned a few months after the test (Reading 1.2). Its one merit is that, from an administrative point of view, both teacher and students can be held accountable for what has to be 'covered', whether or not the actual teaching-and-learning is of long-term value to the learners. With the current preoccupation with efficiency, it is perhaps this administrative convenience that ensures the continuation of practices that, if considered in terms of their effective contribution to student development, would be clearly seen to be unacceptable.

However, these criticisms of the prevailing organization of schooling are not intended to suggest that there should be no guidance given as to what activities students should engage in and as to what they are expected to learn; nor is it intended to suggest that there is no role for deliberate teaching. But teaching certainly cannot be reduced to telling and testing and to maintaining the control necessary to keep students to this externally imposed agenda.

What, then, is the alternative?

I suggest that learning-and-teaching should be seen as complementary aspects of a single collaborative activity we may refer to as 'dialogic inquiry' in a community of learners. In this approach, the teacher has two important roles: as leader, to plan and organize the community's activities; and as facilitator, to provide contingently appropriate assistance to individuals and groups to enable them to achieve goals that they cannot achieve on their own. At the same time, there is a third role that is equally important. As the more expert member of the community, the teacher should also model the dispositions and actions of learning by conducting his or her own inquiries aimed at improving the quality and effectiveness of the community's activity (Wells, 2001).

Reading 2.4

Why thinking should be taught

Robert Fisher

In this reading Fisher defines a range of thinking skills and makes a strong case for the educational value of philosophical enquiry per se. He argues that 'thinking' can certainly be taught in the classroom. School education can, in other words, not only impart knowledge but also teach powerful capabilities for evaluating and applying such knowledge. In later life, independent thinkers are likely to lead innovation in spheres such as the arts, economy and society, but in a democracy this is a capability we should encourage for all our citizens.

How can the development of thinking skills be promoted in your classroom?

Edited from: Fisher, R. (2013) *Teaching Thinking: Philosophical Enquiry in the Classroom.* London: Bloomsbury, 2–26.

'Thinking skills' is a generic description of the human capacity to think in conscious ways to achieve certain purposes. Such processes include remembering, translating thoughts into words, questioning, planning, reasoning, analysing, hypothesising, imagining, forming judgements based on reasons and evidence, and so on.

However, a focus on thinking does not mean ignoring the role of knowledge. Knowledge is necessary. But simply knowing a lot of things is not sufficient if children are to be taught to think for themselves. Children need knowledge but they also need to know how to acquire it and use it.

It is true then, that thinking must be about something – but people can do it more or less effectively. The capacity, for example, to assess reasons, formulate hypotheses, make conceptual links and ask critical questions is relevant to many areas of learning. As Gemma, age 10 put it: 'To be a good learner you need to practice training your mind.' Indeed, we want our children to use their skills on a regular basis and get into the habit of thinking critically, creatively and with care. Good thinking requires that cognitive skills become habits of intelligent behaviour learned through practice. We know, for example, that children tend to become better at giving reasons or asking questions the more they practise doing so.

Psychologists and philosophers have helped to extend our understanding of the term 'thinking', by emphasising the importance of dispositions. This has prompted a move away from a simple model of 'thinking skills' as isolated cognitive capacities.

If we can systematically cultivate better thinking then we should surely do so.

One reason frequently advanced for the teaching of thinking is that thinking is intrinsic to human development, and that every individual has a right to have their intellect developed. Teaching thinking becomes an end in itself by the very fact that we are thinking animals, and have a right to the education of those faculties that constitute what it is to be human.

Another justification is that we gain pleasure from the right sort of intellectual stimulus and challenge. The Greeks argued that the exercise of the human intellect produced both virtue and satisfaction. In the nineteenth century John Stuart Mill developed this idea further by distinguishing what he called the 'higher' and the 'lower' pleasures of human existence. The higher pleasures of the mind, he said, were more profound and satisfying than the lower pleasures of the body.

Many of the reasons for seeking to develop thinking and learning skills are instrumental or pragmatic, and are to do with the success of individuals and of society. The most important resource any society has is the intellectual capacity of its people. A successful society will be a thinking society in which the capacities for lifelong learning of its citizens are most fully realized. Critical and creative thinking is needed to make sense of knowledge in any subject area.

Another perceived need to teach thinking skills comes from a growing awareness of the rate of change within society. This is accelerating so rapidly that it is difficult to assess what factual knowledge will be needed in the future, and this means that schools, colleges, universities and workplaces should be less focused on imparting information than on teaching students to learn and to think for themselves. (Reading 11.1)

Exercising the mind through intellectual challenge can also promote moral qualities and virtues. Intellectual virtue can be seen as a complex set of attributes including curiosity, thoughtfulness, intellectual courage and perseverance in the search for truth, a willingness to speculate and analyse, to judge and self-correct, and openness to the views of others. Such qualities need to be practised through thinking for oneself and thinking with others. Philosophical enquiry can be a means whereby such qualities can become embedded in human character.

Teaching people to be better thinkers is thus both a rational and a moral enterprise. These processes require more than an isolated set of thinking skills. They are also a matter of developing attitudes and dispositions. Teaching thinking cannot be simply a matter of imparting certain skills, for if skills are not used they are redundant. All the finely-honed thinking skills in the world will be for naught if they are not used for positive purposes.

A good thinker displays a number of intellectual virtues. These include:

1 *Seeking truth*
They care that their beliefs are true, and that their decisions are as far a possible justified. They show this by:

- seeking alternatives (hypotheses, explanations, conclusions, plans, sources, ideas)
- supporting views only to the extent that they are justified by available information
- being well informed, including being informed by the views of others.

A good thinker is someone who is always trying to find out new things. (Rachel, aged 9)

2 *Being honest*
They care that their position and the position of others are represented honestly: They show this by attending, i.e.:

- being clear about what they mean

- maintaining a focus on the issue in question

- seeking and offering reasons

- considering all factors relevant in the situation

- being aware of their own point of view

- considering seriously other points of view.

To be a good thinker you have to be honest with yourself, and with other people. (Brian, aged 9)

3 *Respecting others*
They care about the dignity and worth of every person. They show this by:

- attentive listening to the views of others

- avoiding scorn or intimidation of others

- showing concern about the welfare of others.

A good thinker listens to what others say, even if you don't agree with them. (Nicholas, aged 9)

Being a person means having a sense of oneself, including oneself as a thinker and learner, and a sense of others through our interaction with them. A broad view of the purposes of education (Reading 1.1) would include developing such intellectual virtues and dispositions as to attend, concentrate, cooperate, organize, reason, imagine and enquire. We need to develop the virtues of seeking truth and being honest, and of respect for others.

Democracy is the political expression of the human urge for freedom, freedom of thought and freedom of expression (Reading 2.2). Education should be a process whereby people are gradually helped to recognize the nature of human freedom and of human responsibility. We need to encourage people to think in ways which express their authentic individuality.

Reading 2.5

Challenging the intuitive appeal of learning styles

Lawrence Nixon, Margaret Gregson and Patricia Spedding

This extract argues that teachers in the FAVE sector should resist the temptation to use learning styles models to differentiate learning. First, concerns are raised about the lack of robust evidence to support claims to effective practice (LSRC report 2004). Second, the ways in which learning styles instruments describe differences between students are questioned because they offer decontextualized descriptions of human types that are unable to acknowledge the actual situated lives and needs of students.

This piece was presented at the Philosophy of Education Society UK Conference, 2006, New College, Oxford. It was subsequently published: Nixon, L., Gregson, M. and Spedding, P. (2007) 'Pedagogy and the intuitive appeal of learning styles in post-compulsory education in England'. *Journal of Vocational Education and Training* 59 (1), 39–50.

Learning styles tools have been widely used across the FAVE sector over the last twenty years. It is asserted that the use of learning styles assessment instruments will promote student achievement. They typically aim to achieve this end by shaping pedagogy into a form that lets tutors and learners see more clearly who they are and what they need to do to thrive. In other words, learning styles tools quantify the essential differences between the ways students learn. This clear view of types of learner then allows teachers to plan for and address these different types of learning need. We challenge the claim that these tools are effective and appropriate to the task of identifying and addressing individual needs. First, with reference to the LSRC report of 2004 we raise concerns about the lack of robust evidence warranting the claims to efficacy. Second, we criticise the descriptions of types of learners for being decontextualised pictures of human types that appeal to the imagination but make it difficult to see and engage with richness and complexity of students' lives.

Learning style models, and there are many variations, all tend to share three core features. The first feature claims that an individual's behaviour demonstrates a pattern of preferences or habitual ways of acting. Second, these patterns of preferences can be identified and then organised into a classificatory scheme. Finally, it is claimed that reliable and insightful diagnostic tools can be devised to link students to these different sets of preferences. In short, they offer a strategy that helps us to see more clearly who we are, who they are and how the pedagogical relationship ought to be organised. One assumption here is that when we see more clearly who our students are in terms of their preferred learning styles, we will be better able to address their real needs.

The way in which these features work in practice can be illustrated with reference to the learning styles model offered by Dunn and Dunn who discuss types of learners in terms of a set of preferences that are manifest in behaviour in a particular context (Coffield et al., 2004). For Dunn and Dunn the concept of learning styles marks the preferences individuals demonstrate in the ways in which they concentrate, process, internalize and retain academic information. This positing of distinct sets of preferences lends credibility to the idea that learners should be divided into distinct groups. Dunn and Dunn also offer us a taxonomy of kinds or types. They begin with the assumption that our shared world is best described in terms of a set of external stimuli. For example, environmental stimuli are described only in terms of sound, temperature, light and seating in the classroom. Building upon this premise, Dunn and Dunn identify four types of learners, who are identified in terms of their habitual patterns of responding to these stimuli. These modalities of response are famously identified as the visual, auditory, kinaesthetic and tactile (Coffield et al., 2004), the simplified triptych of visual, auditory and kinaesthetic (VAK) learners is probably familiar to nearly all tutors in the FAVE sector. It is the identification of these three or four kinds of learners that plays a key role in orientating tutor and learner relations. (Reading 1.1, Reading 2.1)

Finally, Dunn and Dunn claim that their model formally develops the soft evaluations of learners already made by tutors through the introduction of diagnostic instruments (Coffield et al., 2004). A typical example of these instruments would be a questionnaire that asked learners to rate statements on a 1–5 scale, from 'strongly agree' to 'strongly disagree'. Examples of these stimulus statements would be: 'I like to listen to music while I'm studying', 'I study best when the lights are dim' (Dunn and Dunn quoted in Coffield et al., 2004: 23). The test results are then scored according to a marking regime which ensures that subjects are identified predominantly with one strong preference and the resulting description of the student's learning character can then be used to match student preferences to the appropriate teaching method (Coffield et al., 2004).

From the perspective of Dunn and Dunn the paramount pedagogical concern becomes that of *how* content is to be taught (Coffield et al., 2004). One of the tutor's primary duties is then to match classroom practice to the preferences of the individual learners within the class. Illustrative examples would include: auditory learners preferring the lecture format, visual learners preferring reading, tactile learners preferring to use their hands and kinaesthetic learners preferring real-life visits, acting and interviewing (Coffield et al., 2004) … It is, as Dunn states, 'inconceivable … that communities, parents and the judiciary … would permit schools to function conventionally and continue to damage global, tactual, kinaesthetic children' (Dunn quoted in Coffield et al., 2004: 34).

Coffield, in the 2004 LSRC report, identifies two possible explanations for the popularity of learning styles methods and practices: first, evidence of effectiveness and second, intuitive appeal. Coffield et al. concentrate on evaluating the evidence claims made in support of learning styles models and practices. With regard to the broad field of learning styles, as we have already noted, Coffield et al. express serious concerns regarding the lack of independent robust studies that offer reliable and valid evidence for the effectiveness of these models and instruments. In relation to Dunn and Dunn's model, Coffield et al. note that the model is often promoted as if it were scientifically robust and supported by research but they point out that to date no detailed and comprehensive, *independent* evaluative research into the effectiveness of this model has been conducted. At the very least these conclusions suggest that the claim that this model will bring about improvements in student performance remain, as yet, an unsubstantiated assertion. Interestingly, Coffield et al. also note that sometimes the comments of those promoting this model have the appearance and status of a total belief system (Coffield et al., 2004).

The second explanation of the popularity of these learning styles models and instruments is suggested when Coffield et al. observe that there is 'a strong intuitive appeal in the idea that teachers and course designers should pay closer attention to students' learning styles' (2004: 1). The idea that these ways of seeing and dealing with learners has a strong intuitive appeal points to the possibility that these pictures of human types can easily grip our imagination. On this account their appeal is based upon our shared ability to be gripped by such abstract pictures of what human beings are like. It is the ability of these pictures to grip us, to give us a shared view, that is the key to understanding their popularity rather than their effectiveness in guiding teaching and learning. It is *normal* for people like us to see the sense in such pictures, and this appeal has nothing to do with evidence. The point here is that these pictures will be sustained in their popularity, up to a point, simply by the fact that they are capable of making an appeal that can grip imaginations. History is littered with these pictures that grip the imagination and seek to orientate us toward ourselves and others, for example, Lavater's discussion of physiognomy (2002) and Gall and Spurzheim's phrenological accounts of human nature (1810–19).

When we put these pictures of types of learner into a FAVE context we can see how for teachers they could fit well with other aspects of their working environment. First, these models would sit comfortably with the plethora of 'recipes for teachers' that swirl around the FAVE sector. Second, in a context where much of their energy is consumed by providing evidence of their compliance with externally set standards, regulations and centrally prescribed curricula (Ainley and Bailey, 1997; Keep, 2003; Ball, 2004), learning styles offer a novel way to demonstrate compliance that difference is addressed. (Ball, 2003) Third, the tutor's ability to get a quick intuitive hold of the 'issues' may be valuable to a stressed, often novice (even 'casualised') workforce. Here these models may even appear as 'guild knowledge'…

Learning styles inventories offer a simplified list of the ways that a human being can 'be' and think and act in a landscape where all boundaries are known and must simply be accepted. Against this model of clarity we wish to situate an alternative approach to pedagogy and the issue of difference, one that invites and encourages conversation and learning together (Reading 2.2). In this alternative context possible solutions to real problems are jointly decided in full realisation that further problems will be encountered and the enacted solution revised. We argue that learning styles theory and practice reflect the deep confusion of thought concerning the aims and purposes of education (Reading 1.1) and the nature of the relationship between pedagogy and identity formation and development. Learning styles inventories limit, decontextualise and depoliticize experience and identity. We argue for a form of pedagogy that encourages us all to listen seriously to the different voices that make sense of life together across difference. These different claims on identity enrich our conversation even as they remain as 'tension points between past and future lives' (Bernstein, 2004).

Reflection
How can we develop the quality of our teaching?

3

The readings in this chapter illustrate key ideas about the meaning of reflective practice and its relationship with the professional development of teachers. First Calderhead demonstrates the complexities and multiple dimensions of teaching (3.1). Dewey (3.2) contrasts routinized and reflective thinking and suggests that 'to be genuinely thoughtful we must be willing to sustain a state of doubt'. The readings of Stenhouse (3.3) and Pring (3.4) present classic arguments about why teachers can and should engage in educational research and enquiry in the contexts of their practice.

The parallel chapter of *Reflective Teaching in Further, Adult and Vocational Education* emphasizes the importance of the processes of reflection in the development of practical wisdom. The chapter clarifies the meaning of reflective teaching by identifying seven key characteristics of reflective practice, including the use of evaluative evidence and collaborative learning with other practitioners and with your students (Pollard, 2013). A recurring theme in *Reflective Teaching in Further, Adult and Vocational Education* and indeed throughout this book is that professional development which aims to improve practice often works best when conducted with others.

There are also suggestions for further reading on the *reflectiveteaching.co.uk* website as well as additional reflective activities and resources which are relevant to the development of reflective practice in a wide range of educational contexts.

Reading 3.1

Competence and the complexities of teaching
James Calderhead

In this reading James Calderhead identifies five distinct areas of research on teaching and learning to teach and provides a concise overview of the main issues which have been considered. He summarizes by highlighting the complexity of teachers' work and warning against partial and oversimplified conceptions.

How do you feel this analysis relates to the dimensions of education listed in **Reading 17.4**?

Edited from: Calderhead, J. (1994) 'Can the complexities of teaching be accounted for in terms of competences? Contrasting views of professional practice from research and policy'. Mimeo produced for an Economic and Social Research Council symposium on teacher competence, 1–2.

Within recent policy on teaching and teacher education, there has been a popular trend to consider issues of quality in teaching in terms of competences that can be pre-specified and continuously assessed. In particular, the competences that have received most attention have related to subject matter knowledge and classroom management skills, a view which might be simplistically matched to the different responsibilities of higher education institutions and schools as closer working partnerships are formed in initial training. Such a view of teaching, however, is in sharp contrast to the complexity of teachers' work highlighted by empirical research on teaching over the past decade.

Research on teaching and learning to teach falls into several distinct areas, each exploring different aspects of the processes of professional development amongst teachers, and each highlighting some of the influential factors involved.

Socialisation into the professional culture

The material and ideological context in which teachers work has been found to be one of the major influences upon the ways in which teachers carry out their work. New teachers are greatly influenced by traditions, taken-for-granted practices and implicit beliefs within the school, and a powerful 'wash out effect' has been identified (see Zeichner and Gore, 1990). Socialisation studies on professional development have succeeded in highlighting some of the complex interactions that occur between an individual's values, beliefs and practices and those of the school, and also the importance of the individual's capacity to negotiate and manoeuvre within a social system where there may well be several competing professional cultures. This raises issues concerning how student teachers might be appropriately prepared to work as members of teams or as individuals within institutions.

The development of knowledge and skills

This is perhaps the most often cited perspective on learning to teach which emphasises the knowledge and skills that contribute to classroom practice. Studies comparing experienced and novice teachers have demonstrated how the experienced teacher often has a much more sophisticated understanding of their practice. The experienced teacher appears to have access to a wide range of knowledge that can be readily accessed when dealing with classroom situations and which can help in interpreting and responding to them. Recent research on teachers' subject matter knowledge also indicates that teachers, for the purposes of teaching, relearn their subject and also develop a new body of knowledge concerning the teaching of the subject – Shulman's 'pedagogical content knowledge'. Studies of novice and experienced teachers suggest that there is an enormous diversity of knowledge that the experienced teacher possesses, and that acquiring appropriate professional knowledge is often a difficult and extremely time-consuming process for the novice.

The moral dimension of teaching

Teaching as well as being a practical and intellectual activity is also a moral endeavour. Teaching involves caring for young people and adults, considering the interests of children, preparing people to be part of a future society, and influencing the way in which they relate to each other and live. The ethic of caring has been claimed to be a central facet of teaching, often valued by teachers, parents and children, but frequently unacknowledged in discussions of professional development. Teaching in schools inevitably presents several moral dilemmas (Reading 1.1) in the form of decisions about how to allocate time in the classroom, how to cater for individual needs, and how to maintain principles such as 'equality of opportunity'. How are teachers to be prepared for this?

The personal dimension of teaching

Several different aspects of the personal dimension have been emphasised in the research literature. First of all, teachers bring their own past experiences to bear on their interpretation of the teacher's task. Individual past experiences of school, of work, or parenting have been found to provide teachers with metaphoric ways of thinking about teaching that shape their professional reasoning and practice. Secondly, teachers' personalities are themselves an important aspect of teachers' work. In order to establish working relationships with children and adults, to command their attention and respect and to ensure the smooth running of their classes, teachers' personalities are intrinsically involved. Part of the professional development of the novice teacher requires teachers to become aware of their personal qualities and how other people respond to them, so that they can take greater control in their interactions with others. Thirdly, evidence from research on teachers' life cycles suggests that people pass through different phases in their lives in which they adopt different perspectives on life and work, and experience different needs in terms of inservice support.

The reflective dimension of teaching

Notions of reflection have become extremely popular in recent discussions of teacher education. What reflection actually amounts to, however, is considerably less clear. Several notions of reflection are identifiable in the literature – reflection-in-action, reflection-on-action, deliberative reflection, etc. Attempts to generate greater levels of reflection amongst student teachers have taken many forms – reflective journals, action research, the use of theory and research evidence as analytical frameworks, etc. Creating a course that helps students to become more analytical about their practice and to take greater charge of their own professional development is a task with a number of inherent difficulties. For instance, how does the teacher educator reconcile their traditional role as a gatekeeper to the profession with that of mentor and facilitator of reflection? How is reflection fostered when in schools a much higher priority is given to immediate, spontaneous action rather than analysis and reflection? Efforts in this area, however, have stimulated enquiry into identifying the cognitive, affective and behavioural aspects of reflection: what are the skills, attitudes and conditions that promote reflection and enable greater levels of learning from experience to be achieved?

Research on teaching and teachers' professional development points towards the complexity of teachers' work. Each of the dimensions discussed above identifies an important set of variables and provides a partial picture of the whole professional development process. Learning to teach involves the development of technical skills, as well as an appreciation of moral issues involved in education, an ability to negotiate and develop one's practice within the culture of the school, and an ability to reflect and evaluate both in and on one's actions.

Such a view of teaching is in sharp contrast to that promulgated in the current language of 'competences' and 'subject matter knowledge'.

Reading 3.2

Thinking and reflective experience

John Dewey

The writings of John Dewey have been an enormous influence on educational thinking. Indeed, his distinction of 'routinised' and 'reflective' teaching is fundamental to the conception of professional development through reflection. In the two selections below Dewey considers the relationship between reflective thinking and the sort of challenges which people face through experience.

Do you feel that you are sufficiently open-minded to be really 'reflective'?

Edited from: Dewey, J. (1933) How We Think: A Restatement of the Relation of Reflective Thinking to the Educative Process. Chicago: Henry Regnery, 15–16; and Dewey, J. (1916) Democracy and Education. New York: Free Press, 176–7.

The origin of thinking is some perplexity, confusion, or doubt. Thinking is not a case of spontaneous combustion; it does not occur just on 'general principles'. There is something that occasions and evokes it. General appeals to a child (or to a grown-up) to think, irrespective of the existence in his own experience of some difficulty that troubles him and disturbs his equilibrium, are as futile as advice to lift himself by his boot-straps.

Given a difficulty, the next step is suggestion of some way out – the formation of some tentative plan or project, the entertaining of some theory that will account for the peculiarities in question, the consideration of some solution for the problem. The data at hand cannot supply the solution; they can only suggest it. What, then, are the sources of the suggestion? Clearly, past experience and a fund of relevant knowledge at one's command. If the person has had some acquaintance with similar situations, if he has dealt with material of the same sort before, suggestions more or less apt and helpful will arise. But unless there has been some analogous experience, confusion remains mere confusion. Even when a child (or grown-up) has a problem, it is wholly futile to urge him to 'think' when he has no prior experiences that involve some of the same conditions.

There may, however, be a state of perplexity and also previous experience out of which suggestions emerge, and yet thinking need not be reflective. For the person may not be sufficiently critical about the ideas that occur to him. He may jump at a conclusion without weighing the grounds on which it rests; he may forego or unduly shorten the act of hinting, inquiring; he may take the first 'answer', or solution, that comes to him because of mental sloth, torpor, impatience to get something settled.

One can think reflectively only when one is willing to endure suspense and to undergo the trouble of searching. To many persons both suspense of judgment and intellectual search are disagreeable; they want to get them ended as soon as possible. They cultivate an over-positive and dogmatic habit of mind, or feel perhaps that a condition of doubt will be regarded as evidence of mental inferiority. It is at the point where examination and test enter into investigation that the difference between reflective thought and bad thinking comes in.

To be genuinely thoughtful, we must be willing to sustain and protract that state of doubt which is the stimulus to thorough inquiry.

The general features of a reflective experience are:

- perplexity, confusion, doubt, due to the fact that one is implicated in an incomplete situation whose full character is not yet determined;

- a conjectural anticipation – a tentative interpretation of the given elements, attributing to them a tendency to effect certain consequences;

- a careful survey (examination, inspection, exploration, analysis) of all attainable consideration which will define and clarify the problem in hand;

- a consequent elaboration of the tentative hypothesis to make it more precise and more consistent, because squaring with a wider range of facts;

- taking one stand upon the projected hypothesis as a plan of action which is applied to the existing state of affairs; doing something overtly to bring about the anticipated result, and thereby testing the hypothesis.

It is the extent and accuracy of steps three and four which mark off a distinctive reflective experience from one on the trial and error plane. They make thinking itself into an experience. Nevertheless, we never get wholly beyond the trial and error situation. Our most elaborate and rationally consistent thought has to be tried in the world and thereby tried out. And since it can never take into account all the connections, it can never cover with perfect accuracy all the consequences. Yet a thoughtful survey of conditions is so careful, and the guessing at results so controlled, that we have a right to mark off the reflective experience from the grosser trial and error forms of action.

Reading 3.3

The teacher as researcher

Lawrence Stenhouse

> Lawrence Stenhouse led the Humanities Project during the late 1960s – curriculum development work that revolutionized thinking about professional development. One of his central concerns was to encourage teachers as 'researchers' of their own practice, thereby extending their professionalism. There is a strong link between the argument of this reading and Dewey's conception of 'reflection'.
>
> *Edited from:* Stenhouse, L. (1975) *An Introduction to Curriculum Research and Development.* London: Heinemann, 143–57.

All well-founded curriculum research and development, whether the work of an individual teacher, of a school, of a group working in a teachers' centre or of a group working within the co-ordinating framework of a national project, is based on the study of classrooms. It thus rests on the work of teachers.

It is not enough that teachers' work should be studied: they need to study it themselves. My theme is the role of the teachers as researchers in their own teaching situation. What does this conception of curriculum development imply for them?

The critical characteristics of that extended professionalism which is essential for well-founded curriculum research and development seem to me to be:

The commitment to systematic questioning of one's own teaching as a basis for development;

The commitment and the skills to study one's own teaching;

The concern to question and to test theory in practice.

To these may be added as highly desirable, though perhaps not essential, a readiness to allow other teachers to observe one's work directly or through recordings – and to discuss it with them on an open and honest basis. In short, the outstanding characteristics of the extended professional is a capacity for autonomous professional self-development through systematic self-study, through the study of the work of other teachers and through the testing of ideas by classroom research procedures.

It is important to make the point that teachers in this situation are concerned to understand better their own classroom. Consequently, they are not faced with the problems of generalizing beyond his or her own experience. In this context, theory is simply a systematic structuring of his or her understanding of such work.

Concepts which are carefully related to one another are needed both to capture and to express that understanding. The adequacy of such concepts should be treated as provisional. The utility and appropriateness of the theoretical framework of concepts should be testable; and the theory should be rich enough to throw up new and profitable questions.

Each classroom should not be an island. Teachers working in such a tradition need to communicate with one another (Reading 16.1). They should report their work. Thus a common vocabulary of concepts and a syntax of theory need to be developed. Where that language proves inadequate, teachers would need to propose new concepts and new theory.

The first level of generalization is thus the development of a general theoretical language. In this, professional research workers should be able to help.

If teachers report their own work in such a tradition, case studies will accumulate, just as they do in medicine. Professional research workers will have to master this material and scrutinize it for general trends. It is out of this synthetic task that general propositional theory can be developed.

Reading 3.4

Action research and the development of practice
Richard Pring

Richard Pring, a leading educational philosopher, builds on the Stenhouse tradition to take stock of some key characteristics of 'action research'. The reading makes useful comparisons with the characteristics of conventional academic research. Although there are important differences in key objectives, there are also many similarities in the issues that must be faced in any classroom enquiry. Pring emphasizes the need for openness, the importance of dialogue with colleagues and of critical reflection on practice. Action research may thus involve scrutiny of values, including those which might be embedded in centrally prescribed curricula, pedagogies or forms of assessment.

Edited from: Pring, R. (2000) *Philosophy of Educational Research.* Continuum: London, 130–4.

Respect for educational practitioners has given rise to the development of 'action research'. This may be contrasted with conventional research. The goal of research is normally that of producing new knowledge. There will, of course, be many different motives for producing such knowledge. But what makes it research is the systematic search for conclusions about 'what is the case' on the basis of relevant evidence. Such conclusions might, indeed, be tentative, always open to further development and refinement. But the purpose remains that of getting ever 'nearer the truth'. Hence, it makes sense to see the outcomes of research to be a series of propositions which are held to be true.

By contrast, the research called 'action research' aims not to produce new knowledge but to improve practice – namely, in this case, the 'educational practice' in which teachers are engaged. The conclusion is not a set of propositions but a practice or a set of transactions or activities which is not true or false but better or worse. By contrast with the conclusion of research, as that is normally conceived, action research focuses on the particular. Although such a practical conclusion focuses on the particular, thereby not justifying generalisation, no one situation is unique in every respect and therefore the action research in one classroom or school can illuminate or be suggestive of practice elsewhere. There can be, amongst networks of teachers, the development of a body of professional knowledge of 'what works' or of how values might be translated into practice – or come to be transformed by practice. But there is a sense in which such professional knowledge has constantly to be tested out, reflected upon, adapted to new situations.

Research, as that is normally understood, requires a 'research forum' – a group of people with whom the conclusions can be tested out and examined critically. Without such openness to criticism, one might have missed the evidence or the counter argument which casts doubt on the conclusions drawn. Hence, the importance of dissemination through publications and seminars. To think otherwise is to assume a certitude which cannot be justified. Progress in knowledge arises through replication of the research activity, through criticism, through the active attempt to find evidence against one's conclusions.

Similarly, the growth of professional knowledge requires the sympathetic but critical community through which one can test out ideas, question the values which underpin the shared practice, seek solutions to problems, invite observation of one's practice, suggest alternative perspectives and interpretation of the data.

This is an important matter to emphasise. The temptation very often is to seek to justify and to verify, rather than to criticise or to falsify, one's belief, and to protect oneself by not sharing one's conclusions or the way in which one reached them.

With action research, reflection upon practice with a view to its improvement needs to be a public activity. By 'public' I mean that the research is conducted in such a way that others can scrutinize and, if necessary, question the practice of which it is part. Others become part of the reflective process – the identification and definition of the problem, the values which are implicit within the practice, the way of implementing and gathering evidence about the practice, the interpretation of the evidence. And yet teacher research, in the form of action research, is so often encouraged and carried out as a lonely, isolated activity. Those who are concerned with the promotion of action research – with the development in teachers of well-tested professional knowledge – must equally be concerned to develop the professional networks and communities in which it can be fostered. (Reading 16.1)

There is a danger that such research might be supported and funded with a view to knowing the most effective ways of attaining particular goals – goals or targets set by government or others external to the transaction which takes place between teacher and learner. The teacher researches the most efficient means of reaching a particular educational objective (laid out, for instance. in the National Curriculum or a skills-focused vocational training). But this is not what one would have in mind in talking about research as part of professional judgement or action research as a response to a practical issue or problem. The reflective teacher comes to the problem with a set of values. The problem situation is one which raises issues as much about those values as it does about adopting an appropriate means to a given end. Thus, what makes this an educational practice is the set of values which it embodies – the intrinsic worth of the activities themselves, the personal qualities which are enhanced, the appropriate way of proceeding (given the values that one has and given the nature of the activity).

One comes to science teaching, for example, with views about the appropriate way of doing science – evidence based enquiry, openness to contrary evidence, clarity of procedures and conclusions. The practice of teaching embodies certain values – the importance of that which is to be learnt, the respect for the learner (how he or she thinks), the respect for evidence and the acknowledgement of contrary viewpoints. Therefore, when teacher researchers are putting into practice a particular strategy or are implementing a curriculum proposal, then they are testing out the values as much as the efficaciousness of the strategy or proposal. Are the values the researchers believe in being implemented in the practice? If not, does this lead to shifts in the values espoused or in the practice itself? Action research, in examining the implementation of a curriculum proposal, involves, therefore, a critique of the values which are intrinsic to the practice. Such a critique will reflect the values which the teacher brings to the practice, and those values will in turn be refined through critical reflection upon their implementation in practice. 'Action research' captures this ever shifting conception of practice through the attempt to put into practice certain procedures which one believes are educational.

However, such constant putting into practice, reflecting on that practice, refining of beliefs and values in the light of that reflection, subjecting the embodied ideas to criticism, cannot confine itself to the act of teaching itself. It cannot but embrace the context of teaching – the physical conditions in which learning is expected to take place, the expectations of those who determine the general shape of the curriculum, the resources available for the teachers to draw upon, the constraints upon the teacher's creative response to the issues, the scheme of assessment. It is difficult to see how the clash between the 'official curriculum' and the 'teacher researcher' can be avoided when the latter is constantly testing out the values of the teaching strategies. One can see, therefore, why the encouragement of teacher research is so often defined within official documents in a rather narrow sense.

Action research, therefore, is proposed as a form of research in which teachers review their practice in the light of evidence and of critical judgement of others. In so doing, they inevitably examine what happens to the values they hold, and which they regard as intrinsic to the transaction they are engaged in. Such critical appraisal of practice takes in three different factors which impinge upon practice, and shape the activities within it – the perceptions and values of the different participants, the 'official expectations and values' embodied within the curriculum, and the physical conditions and resources. To do this, various methods for gathering data will be selected – examination results, classroom observation, talking with the pupils. And the interpretation of what is 'working' will constantly be revised in the light of such data. But, of course, others too might, in the light of the data, suggest other possible interpretations. Thus, the dialogue continues. There is no end to this systematic reflection with a view to improving practice.

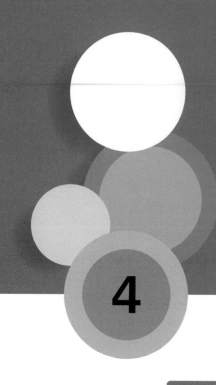

Principles

What are the foundations of effective teaching and learning?

4

The readings in this chapter illustrate knowledge and understanding developed to date regarding good pedagogic practice. Research from across the world provides helpful insights into strategies and methods that have been found to support good teaching and learning in different educational contexts (see James and Pollard, 2012). While there are variations in different countries and in respect of different cultures and policy environments, there are also considerable overlaps in the learning and teaching strategies which have been found to be helpful in supporting good teaching and learning. Ruth Heilbronn (4.1) draws attention to the importance of the development of practical judgement and the 'eye' to know what is the right thing to do at the right time when faced with complex, unexpected or difficult situations. As teachers share these ideas and practices with each other, we begin to develop incremental understandings of good pedagogic practice. Each of the remaining readings in this chapter draws upon what is known about good pedagogic practice in Finland (4.2), New Zealand (4.3) and England (4.4).

The TLRP's principles for effective teaching and learning could have provided a further reading but are the subject of the parallel chapter in *Reflective Teaching in Further, Adult and Vocational Education*. There, the rationale for 'evidence informed principles' to inform teaching and learning is presented, together with a discussion of each principle in turn.

The relevant parts of the *reflectiveteaching.co.uk* website maintain this focus and provide links to further work across the world. On the site navigate your way to the FAVE book and then to this chapter.

Reading 4.1

Practical judgement and evidence-informed practice

Ruth Heilbronn

This reading explains the deep roots of 'practical judgement' in Aristotle's philosophy and thus confirms the enduring qualities which are required in combining experience and analysis in practical contexts. Interestingly, Bennett writes on managing behaviour (**Reading 7.3**) from a similar position.

Heilbronn identifies three dimensions of practical judgement: ethics; flexibility; personal rootedness. In this way she affirms that teaching has moral purposes which always require personal judgement from the person who is the teacher. This is what makes it so interesting, and such a responsibility.

What forms of evidence could help you in making practical judgements?

Edited from: Heilbronn, R. (2011) 'The Nature of Practice-based Knowledge and Understanding'. In R. Heilbronn and J. Yandell (eds) *Critical Practice in Teacher Education: A Study of Professional Learning.* London: IOE Press, 7–9.

Practical judgement might be characterised as a capacity 'to do the right thing at the right time': to respond flexibly and appropriately in particular situations, whose unique correlation of variables could not be known in advance. (**Reading 1.1**) Training for professional practice is designed to enable such expert decision making and action.

The concept of 'practical judgement' goes back to Aristotle's concept of phronesis. Although this rich notion has been interpreted in a variety of ways, a relevant understanding for teachers is found in Dunne's statement that phronesis is: 'an eye for what is salient in concrete situations' (Dunne, 1993: 368). Expert practitioners know what to do in specific situations. They have what seems to be 'an intuitive sense of the nature and texture of practical engagement' (Dunne, 1993: 8).

> Phronesis does not ascend to a level of abstraction or generality that leaves experience behind. It arises from experience and returns into experience. It is, we might say, the insightfulness – or using Aristotle's own metaphor, 'the eye' – of a particular type of experience, and the insights it achieves are turned back into experience, which is in this way constantly reconstructed or enriched. And the more experience is reconstructed in this way, the more sensitive and insightful phronesis becomes. (Dunne, 1993: 293)

In the above quotation the key term is 'experience'. There can be no split between elements encountered in reading, research, university and schools, because these elements make no sense, have no meaning, bear no significance to the practitioner, until and unless they are integrated and able to be applied. Understanding develops through the practical situations in which novices are placed, and with which they grapple. This is true for many kinds of workplaces, where novices may be changed by experience into highly proficient practitioners (Hogan, 2003).

It is possible to outline some characteristics of practical judgement in three main dimensions.

First, there is an ethical dimension to 'the right' response. Professional practices have their codes of ethics and it is expected that practitioners follow these codes and uphold the values of the profession. If we try to think of an example of practitioner action that seems 'value free' we soon give up the attempt. Teaching, nursing, social work, are thoroughly relational practices. They have 'the other', the client, the learner, the patient, whose welfare is inextricably linked to choices and actions. So the right action at any time needs to draw on ethical considerations: a good practitioner will be someone whose actions we can trust as 'wise' or 'judicious'. In acting seemingly spontaneously practitioners draw on their own values, qualities and dispositions, as well as on technical know-how and information based on previous, relevant experiences.

Having professional values and living by them in practice are an essential part of being a practitioner involved with others. The capacity for trustworthiness is fundamental to teaching. The practice of teaching involves the ability to see things from the learners' perspective, to show 'pedagogical thoughtfulness' (van Manen, 1991) and to make adjustments accordingly. Van Manen has described 'tactful' teaching, as that which 'locates practical knowledge not primarily in the intellect or the head but rather in the existential situation in which the person finds himself or herself' (van Manen, 1995: 45–6).

Practical judgement is connected to 'virtue', in the sense that such a practitioner exercises qualities of 'practical wisdom' (Reading 1.1). A good teacher could be said to be a wise person, someone who exercises an ethical sense of doing what is right, of acting for the good. An example would be a teacher who rejects a strategy for gaining order in the classroom which would involve humiliating pupils, in favour of another, involving more effort based on developing trusting relationships. As Smith (2003) has stated the importance of relationships between pupils, and between them and their teacher cannot be over-emphasised. Teaching is 'thoroughly relational' (Noddings, 2003: 249) and many of the virtues are exercised in relation to others in a pedagogical space of trust (van Manen, 1991).

A second dimension of practical judgement is its flexibility. Expert practitioners can respond flexibly to changing situations. We cannot know in advance what individual situations will throw up in the way of stimuli requiring response. Experts respond flexibly. Since there cannot be a definitive, right way to respond in every circumstance, it follows that any expert response might not be the best one for the circumstance. Therefore, reflecting on practice, interrogating aims, purposes and outcomes of particular choices in particular situations, can be a fruitful source of knowledge and understanding, and can support the development of practical judgement. It follows too that there can be no universally applicable, infallible theory or pedagogical intervention, given the contingency of individual situations of practice. This is significant if there are government promoted pedagogical strategies and educational changes and control over the school or college curriculum.

A third feature of judgement is its rootedness within an individual person, with a particular character, dispositions and qualities. When a teacher decides what is to be done in any situation, for example with a recalcitrant pupil, even if her decisions seem intuitive they are informed by the teacher's prior experiences and values. There is always more than one available course of action and individual teachers make choices of what they consider the right action in the circumstances. These choices may be based on a number of different factors, involving practical and ethical considerations. A teacher's character, dispositions and capacities underlie the exercise of practical judgement.

Good teachers can be said to exercise sound practical judgement, which involves exercising virtues such as justice, tolerance and courage, and qualities such as patience and optimism. We think of good teachers as acting with integrity and trustworthiness, being open-minded and able to learn from experience. It is an interesting exercise to think of all the qualities required, desired and expected, an exercise fruitfully revisited at various points in a teaching career (Burbules, 1997).

Reading 4.2

Learning from Finland

Pasi Sahlberg

> Finland's educational system is often compared with that of the countries of the UK, and Sahlberg considers what others can learn from the Finnish experience. Some particular characteristics of Finnish society are apparent, but so too is the 'main message' that improvement comes from enhancing teacher quality, limiting student testing to a necessary minimum, placing responsibility and trust before accountability, and handing over school- and district-level leadership to education professionals. Finland's comprehensive school system is explicitly contrasted with market models for improvement.
>
> Sahlberg offers Finland as a model in which public policy 'builds on teacher strengths' and offers 'fear-free learning for students'. Although the reading is set in the schools sector, it is not difficult to see its relevance for teachers and education managers in the FAVE sector.
>
> *Edited from:* Sahlberg, P. (2011) *Finnish Lessons: What Can the World Learn from Educational Change in Finland.* New York: Teachers College Press, 1–6, 140–5.

The demand for better quality teaching and learning, and more equitable and efficient education is universal. Indeed, educational systems are facing a twin challenge: how to change schools so that students may learn new types of knowledge and skills required in an unpredictable changing knowledge world, and how to make that new learning possible for all young people regardless of their socioeconomic conditions. To be successful with these challenges is both a moral and economic imperative for our societies and their leaders.

At the beginning of the 1990s, education in Finland was nothing special in international terms. All young Finns attended school regularly, the school network was wide and dense, secondary education was accessible for all Finns, and higher education was an option for an increasing number of upper secondary school graduates. However, the performance of Finnish students in international assessments was close to overall averages, except in reading, where Finnish students did better that most of their peers in other countries. The unexpected and jarring recession of that time brought Finland to the edge of a financial breakdown. Bold and immediate measures were necessary to fix national fiscal imbalances and revive the foreign trade that disappeared with the collapse of the Soviet Union in 1990. Nokia, the main global industrial brand of Finland, became a critical engine in boosting Finland from the country's biggest economic dip since World War II. Another Finnish brand, peruskoulu, or the 9-year comprehensive basic school, was the other key player in the turnaround of the Finnish economy and society. Interestingly, both Nokia and the Finnish public educational system have their origins in the same time period in Finnish history: the golden years of building the Finnish national identity in the mid-19th century.

Finland as an example

Public educational systems are in crisis in many parts of the world. The United States, England, Sweden, Norway and France, just to mention a few nations, are among those where public education is increasingly challenged because of endemic failure to provide adequate learning opportunities to all children. Tough solutions are not uncommon in these countries. Tightening control over schools, stronger accountability for student performances, firing bad teachers, and closing down troubled schools are part of the recipe to fix failing education systems.

The main message from experience in Finland is that there is another way to improve education systems. This includes improving the teaching force (Reading 4.3), limiting student testing to a necessary minimum, placing responsibility and trust before accountability, and handing over school- and district-level leadership to education professionals. These are common education policy themes in some of the high performing countries – Finland among them – in the 2009 International Programme for International Student Assessment (PISA) of the OECD (2010a, 2010b). I offer five reasons why Finland is an interesting and relevant source of ideas for other nations that are looking for ways to improve their education systems.

One, Finland has a unique educational system because it has progressed from mediocrity to being a model contemporary educational system and 'strong performer' over the past three decades. Finland is special also because it has been able to create an educational system where students learn well and where equitable education has translated into small variations in student performance between schools in different parts of the country at the same time. This internationally rare status has been achieved using reasonable financial resources and less effort that other nations have expended on reform efforts.

Two, because of this proven steady progress, Finland demonstrates that there is another way to build a well-performing educational system using solutions that differ from market-driven education policies. The Finnish way of change is one of trust, professionalism and shared responsibility (Hargreaves and Shirley, 2009). Indeed Finland is an example of a nation that lacks school inspection, standardized curriculum, high-stakes student assessments, test-based accountability, and a race-to-the-top mentality with regard to educational change.

Three, as a consequence of its success, Finland can offer some alternative ways to think about solutions to existing chronic educational problems in the United States, Canada and England (such as high school drop-out rates, early teacher attrition an inadequate special education) and emerging needs to reform educational systems elsewhere (such as engaging students in learning, attracting young talents into teaching, and establishing holistic public sector policies). The Finnish approach to reducing early school leavers, enhancing teacher professionalism, implementing intelligent accountability and student assessment in schools, and improving learning in mathematics, science and literacy can offer inspiration to other school systems looking for a path to success.

Four, Finland is also an international high performer in commerce, technology, sustainable development, good governance, and prosperity and thus raises interesting questions concerning interdependencies between school and other sectors in society. It appears that other public policy sectors, such as health and employment, seem to play a role also in long-term educational development and change. In Finland, this holds true as well regarding income parity, social mobility, and trust within Finnish society.

Finally, we should listen to the story of Finland because it gives hope to those who are losing their faith in public education and whether it can be changed. This case reveals that the transformation of educational systems is possible, but that it takes time, patience and determination. The Finnish story is particularly interesting because some of the key policies and changes were introduced during the worst economic crisis that Finland has experienced since World War I. It suggests that a crisis can spark the survival spirit that leads to better solutions to acute problems than a 'normal situation' would. This speaks against those who believe that the best way to solve chronic problems in many educational systems is to take control away from school boards and give it to those who might run them more effectively, by charters or other means of privatization.

Although there are limits to the ideas that can be transferred from Finland to other nations, certain basic lessons may have general value for other educational systems, such as the practice of building on teacher strengths, securing relaxed and fear-free learning for students, and gradually enchanting trust within educational systems.

There is no single reason why any educational system succeeds or fails. Instead, there is a network of interrelated factors – educational, political and cultural – that function differently in different situations. I would, however, like to cite three important elements of Finnish educational policies since the early 1970s that appear to transcend culture.

The first one is an inspiring vision of what a good public education should be: Finland has been particularly committed to building a good publicly financed and locally governed basic school for every child. This common educational goal became so deeply rooted in politics and public services in Finland that it survived opposing political governments and ministries unharmed and intact. Since the introduction of peruskoulu in the early 1970s, there have been 20 governments and nearly 30 different ministers of education in charge of educational reform in Finland.

The second aspect of educational change that deserves attention is the way Finland has treated advice offered externally vis-à-vis its own educational heritage in educational reforms. Much of the inspiration in building independent Finland since 1917 has come from its neighbours, especially from Sweden. The welfare state model, health care system, and basic education are good examples of borrowed ideas from our western neighbour. Later, Finnish education policies were also influenced by guidance from supranational institutions, especially the OECD (which Finland joined in 1969) and European Union (which Finland joined in 1995). And yet, despite international influence and borrowing educational ideas from others, Finland has in the end created its own way to build the educational system that exists today. Many pedagogical ideas and educational innovations are also initially imported from other countries, often from North America or the United Kingdom.

The third aspect of change is a systematic development of respectful and interesting working conditions for teachers and leaders in Finnish schools. This raises an important question that is repeated in almost any situation when whole-system educational reforms are discussed: How do we get the best young people into teaching? Experience from Finland suggests that it is not enough to establish world-class teacher education programs or pay teachers well. The true Finnish difference is that teachers in Finland may exercise their professional knowledge and judgement (Reading 1.1, Reading 4.1) both widely and freely in their schools.

The future of Finnish education

The Big Dream in the early 1990s was to make the educational system serve the social cohesion, economic transformation and innovation that would help Finland to be a full member of the European Union and remain a fully autonomous nation.

The Big Dream for the future of Finnish education should be something like this: Create a community of learners that provides the conditions that allow all young people to discover their talent. The talent may be academic, artistic, creative, or kinesthetic or some other skill set. What is needed for each school to be a safe learning community for all to engage, explore and interact with other people. School should teach knowledge and skills as before but it must prepare young people to be wrong too. If people are not prepared to be wrong, as Sir Ken Robinson says they will not come up with new ideas that have value (Robinson, 2009). That is the only way that we in Finland will be able to make the best use of our scarce human resources.

Many changes are required to the existing format of schooling. First and foremost, Finnish schools must continue to become more pupil-friendly so that it allows more personalized learning paths. Personalization doesn't mean replacing teachers with technology and individualized study. Indeed, the new Finnish school must be a socially inspiring and safe environment for all pupils to learn the social skills that they need in their lives. Personalized learning and social education lead to more specialization but build on the common ground of knowledge and skills. The following themes of change would emerge:

1 Development of a personal road map for learning
It is important for each young person to acquire certain basic knowledge, such as reading, writing, and using mathematics. In the future, it will be important that students have alternative ways to learn these basic things. Children will learn more and more of what we used to learn in school out of school, through media, the Internet, and from different social networks to which they belong. This will lead to a situation in which an increasing number of students will find teaching in schools irrelevant because they have already learned what is meaningful for them elsewhere.

A good solution to address this is to rethink schools so that learning in them relies more on individual customized learning plans and less on teaching drawn from a standardized curriculum for all. The art of future education will be to find a balance between these two.

2 Less classroom-based teaching
Developing customized and activity-based learning eventually leads to a situation in which people can learn most of what is now taught in schools through digital devices wherever

and whenever. Hand-held portable devices will provide online access to knowledge and other learners. Shared knowing and competences that are becoming an integral part of modern expertise and professional work will also become part of schools and traditional classrooms. Finland and some other countries have shown that it is not the length of the school year or school day that matters most. Less teaching can lead to more students learning if the circumstances are right and solutions smart. Such circumstances include trust in schools, adequate support and guidance for all students, and curriculum that can be locally adjusted to meet the interests and requirements of local communities.

3 Development of interpersonal skills and problem solving
In the future people will spend more time on and give more personal attention to media and communication technologies than they do today. It means two things from the educational point of view. First, people in general will spend less time together in a concrete social setting. Social interaction will be based on using social networking and other future tools that rely on digital technological solutions. Second, people will learn more about the world and other people through media and communication technologies. Especially expanding engagement in social media and networks will create a whole new source of learning from other people who have similar interests.

Schools need to rethink what their core task in educating people will be. It cannot remain as it is today: to provide the minimum basic knowledge and skills that young people need in the future. The future is now and many young people are already using those skills in their lives today. Schools, and colleges need to make sure that all students learn to be fluent in reading, mathematics, and science concepts, and possess the core of cultural capital that is seen as essential. Equally important, however, is that all students develop attitudes and skills for using available information and opportunities. They will also need to develop better skills for social interaction, both virtual and real, learn to cooperate with people who are very different from themselves, and cope in complex social networks.

4 Engagement and creativity as pointers of success
Current education systems judge individual talent primarily by using standardized knowledge tests. At worst these tests include only multiple choice tasks. At best they expand beyond routine knowledge and require analytical, critical thinking, and problem solving skills. However, they rarely are able to cover the non-academic domains that include creativity, complex handling of information, or communicating new ideas to others.

Conventional knowledge tests will gradually give space to new forms of assessment in schools. As schools move to emphasize teaching skills that everybody needs in a complex and unpredictable world, the criteria of being a successful school will also change. People will learn more of what they need through digital tools and media, and therefore it will become increasingly difficult to know what role schools have played in students' learning (or not learning if you wish) of intended things. Two themes will be important as we move toward the end of this decade.

First, engaging all students in learning in school will be more important than ever. Lack of engagement is the main reason for the challenge that teachers face in schools and classrooms today. It is well known from research and practice that as children get older their interest in what schools offer declines. By the end of peruskoulu a growing number of young people find school learning irrelevant, and they are seeking alternative pathways to fulfil their intentions. Therefore, engagement in productive learning in school should become an important criterion of judging the success or failure of schools.

Second, students' ability to create something valuable and new in school will be more important than ever – not just for some students, but for most of them. If creativity is defined as coming up with original ideas that have value, then creativity should be as important as literacy and treated with the same status. Finnish school have traditionally encouraged risk taking, creativity, and innovation. These traditions need to be strengthened. When performance of students or success of schools is measured, the creative aspect of both individual learning and collective behaviour should be given. In other words, a successful school is able to take each individual – both students and teachers – further in their development that they could have gone by themselves.

The Finnish way of educational change should be encouraging to those who have found the path of competition, choice, test-based accountability, and performance- based pay to be a dead end. It reveals that creative curricula, autonomous teachers, courageous leadership and high performance go to together.

Reading 4.3

Visible learning: A global synthesis

John Hattie

> As this reading points out, many teaching strategies do work – but some work better than others. Hattie used statistical techniques to compare measurements of the effects of teaching strategies and harvested findings from across the world. The result is a synthesis of over 800 meta-analyses relating to achievement – and it is possible to 'read off' the most effective strategies. But by offering an explanation, Hattie tries to do more than this. The key themes, 'visible teaching, visible learning', have many resonances with the other readings presented in this chapter, and are developed further throughout *Reflective Teaching in Further, Adult and Vocational Education.*
>
> How do you feel about your own practice and experience in relation to the 'six signposts towards excellence' which Hattie identifies?
>
> *Edited from:* Hattie, J. (2009) *Visible Learning: A Synthesis of Meta-Analyses Relating to Achievement.* Abingdon: Routledge, 1–3, 236–40, 244.

In the field of education one of the most enduring messages is that 'everything seems to work' to some extent. However, a lot is also known about what makes a major difference in the classroom. A glance at the journals on the shelves of most libraries, and on web pages, would indicate that the state of knowledge in the discipline of education is healthy.

Why does this bounty of research have such little impact? One possible reason is the past difficulties associated with summarizing and comparing all the diverse types of evidence about what works in classrooms. In the 1970s there was a major change in the manner we reviewed the research literature. This approach offered a way to tame the massive amount of research evidence so that it could offer useful information for teachers. The predominant method has always been to write a synthesis of many published studies in the form of an integrated literature review. However, in the mid-1970s, Gene Glass (1976) introduced the notion of meta-analysis – whereby the effect in each study, where appropriate, are converted to a common measure (an effect size), such that the overall effects could be quantified, interpreted, and compared, and the various moderators of this overall effect could be uncovered and followed up in more detail. The method soon became popular and by the mid-1980s more than 100 meta-analyses in education were available. My book is based on a synthesis of more than 800 meta-analyses about information on learning that have now been completed, including many recent ones. It demonstrates how the various innovations in these meta-analyses can be ranked from very positive to very negative effects on student achievement.

An explanatory story, not a 'what works' recipe

Figure 4.3.1 provides examples of effects associated with teaching methods and working conditions.

Figure 4.3.1 Examples of effects associated with teaching methods and working conditions

Teaching	d	Working Conditions	d
Quality of teaching	0.77	Within-class grouping	0.28
Reciprocal teaching	0.74	Adding more finances	0.23
Teacher-student relationships	0.72	Reducing class size	0.21
Providing feedback	0.72	Ability grouping	0.11
Teaching students self-verbalization	0.67	Multi-grade/age classes	0.04
Meta-cognition strategies	0.67	Open vs. traditional classes Summer vacation classes	0.01 −0.09 −0.16
Direct Instruction	0.59	Retention	0.08
Mastery learning	0.57		
Average	0.68		

There are many teaching strategies that have an important effect on student learning. Such teaching strategies include explanation, elaboration, plans to direct task performance, sequencing, drill repetition, providing strategy cues, domain-specific processing, and clear instructional goals. These can be achieved using methods such as reciprocal teaching, direct instruction, and problem solving methods. Effective teaching occurs when the teacher decides the learning intentions and success criteria; makes them transparent to the students; demonstrates them by modelling; evaluates if they understand what they have been told by checking for understanding; and re-tells them what they have been told by tying it all together with closure. These effective teaching strategies involve much cooperative pre-planning and discussion between teachers, optimizing peer learning, and require explicit learning intentions and success criteria.

Peers play a powerful role, as is demonstrated in the strategies involving reciprocal teaching, learning in pairs on computers, and both cooperative and competitive learning (as opposed to individualistic learning). Many of the strategies also help reduce cognitive load and this allows students to focus on the critical aspects of learning, which is particularly useful when they are given multiple opportunities for deliberative practice.

The use of resources, such as computers, can add value to learning. They add a diversity of teaching strategies, provide alternative opportunities to practice and learn, and increase the nature and amount of feedback to the learner and teachers. They do, however, require learning how to optimize their uses.

It is also clear that, repeatedly, it is the difference in the teachers that make the difference in student learning. Homework in which there is no active involvement by the teacher does not contribute to student learning, and likewise the use, or not, of technologies does not show major effects on learning if there is no teacher involvement. Related to these teacher influences are the lower effects of many of the interventions when they are part of comprehensive teaching reforms. Many of these reforms are 'top down' innovations, which can mean teachers do not evaluate whether the reforms are working for them or not. Commitment to the teaching strategy and re-learning how to use many of these methods (through professional development) seems important.

Any synthesis of meta-analyses is fundamentally a literature review, and thus it builds on the scholarship and research of those who have come before. My major purpose has been to generate a model of successful teaching and learning based on the many thousands of studies in 800 and more meta-analyses. The aim is not to merely average the studies and present screeds of data. This is not uncommon; so often meta-analyses have been criticized as mere number crunching exercises, and a book based on more than 800 meta-analyses could certainly have been just that. That was not my intent. Instead, I aimed to build a model based on the theme of 'visible teaching, visible learning' that not only synthesized existing literature but also permitted a new perspective on that literature.

The conclusions are recast here as six signposts towards excellence in education:

1 Teachers are among the most powerful influences in learning.

2 Teachers need to be directive, influential, caring, and actively engaged in the passion of teaching and learning.

3 Teachers need to be aware of what each and every student is thinking and knowing, to construct meaning and meaningful experiences in light of this knowledge, and have proficient knowledge and understanding of their content to provide meaningful and appropriate feedback such that each student moves progressively through the curriculum levels.

4 Teachers need to know the learning intentions and success criteria of their lessons, know how well they are attaining these criteria for all students, and know where to go next in light of the gap between students' current knowledge and understanding and the success criteria of: 'Where are you going?', 'How are you going', and 'Where to next?'.

5 Teachers need to move from the single idea to multiple ideas, and to relate and then extend these ideas such that learners construct and reconstruct knowledge and ideas. It is not the knowledge or ideas, but the learner's construction of this knowledge and these ideas that is critical.

6 School leaders and teachers need to create schools, staffroom, and classroom environments where error is welcomed as a learning opportunity, where discarding incorrect knowledge and understanding is welcomed, and where participants can feel safe to learn, re-learn and explore knowledge and understanding.

In these six signposts, the word 'teachers' is deliberate. Indeed, a major theme is the importance of teachers meeting to discuss, evaluate and plan their teaching in light of the feedback evidence about the success or otherwise of their teaching strategies and conceptions about progress and appropriate challenge (Reading 16.1). This is critical reflection in light of evidence about their teaching.

Note what is not said. There are no claims about additional structural resources, although to achieve the above it helps not to have the hindrance of a lack of resources. There is nothing about class size, about which particular students are present in the school or class, or about what subject is being taught – effective teaching can occur similarly for all students, all ethnicities, and all subjects. There is nothing about between-school differences, which are not a major effect in developed countries. There is little about working conditions of teachers or students – although their effects, though small, are positive and positive means we should not make these working conditions worse.

Teachers and principals need to collect the effect sizes within their schools and ask 'What is working best?', 'Why is it working best?', and 'Who is it not working for?'. This will create a discussion among teachers about teaching. This would require a caring, supportive staffroom, a tolerance for errors, and for learning from other teachers, a peer culture among teachers of engagement, trust and shared passion for improvement.

Reading 4.4

The Nuffield Review of 14–19 Education and Training Summary

Richard Pring

This extract picks out key questions and themes from the detailed, six-year study (2003–9) that involved many of the leading academics working with the FAVE sector, including: Richard Pring, Geoffrey Hayward, Ann Hodgson, Jill Johnson, Ewart Keep, Alis Oancea, Gareth Rees, Ken Spours, Stephanie Wilde.

The report is written in a way that inspires and focuses collaborative discussion. It identifies a set of core questions and themes that should be at the heart of any discussion about current and future 14–19 provision.

Use the questions and findings from this extract to help you identify the strengths and challenges associated with the 14–19 provision you help to deliver.

Use the questions and findings from this extract to help you discuss how 14–19 provision should be further developed and to help you work out how you can contribute to this development.

Where to find out more:

http://www.nuffieldfoundation.org/14-19review
Nuffield Review of 14–19 Education and Training, England and Wales: Summary, Implications and Recommendations (from which this extract comes)
The full report *Education for All: The Future of Education and Training for 14–19 year olds* was published by Routledge in June 2009.

Extract from: Nuffield Review of 14–19 Education and Training, England and Wales

The key question

One criticism of policy, frequently met during the course of the Review, was that there have been too many fragmented and disconnected interventions by government which do not cohere in some overall sense of purpose. There is a need in policy, and in the provision and practice of education, for a clear vision of what all these interventions and investments of money and effort are for. What is the overall purpose?

The Review addressed this concern from the beginning. It was, therefore, shaped throughout by the answers to the following question:

What counts as an educated 19 year old in this day and age?

Values shape all that we do and decide, not least in education. The values we hold affect our opinions – and ultimately our decisions on such questions as:

- whether or not to select by ability
- whether to make the arts compulsory or optional in the 14–19 curriculum
- whether to build on or to ignore the experiences young people bring into school
- whether to reward academic achievement rather than practical capability
- whether to encourage young people to progress to higher education rather than to sign up for apprenticeships

We could go on. The point is that all such decisions embody values which constitute, in practice and for better or worse, the underlying and implicit aims of education.

The Review, therefore, argues for an understanding of education *for all* which would provide:

- the knowledge and understanding required for the 'intelligent management of life'
- competence to make decisions about the future in the light of changing economic and social conditions
- practical capability – including preparation for employment
- moral seriousness with which to shape future choices and relationships
- a sense of responsibility for the community.

Such knowledge, capability and qualities are potentially important for, and (in different degrees) accessible to, all young people, irrespective of social, religious and cultural background. All learners will have to become more rounded, resilient, creative and social, if they are to help shape an increasingly unpredictable and demanding world.

Therefore, what matters, as argued in the Review, is how these essential knowledge, capabilities and qualities are translated into the learning experience of young people, into the curriculum, into the role and training of teachers, into the 'indicators' by which schools and colleges are judged, into the qualifications framework, and into further training, employment or higher education.

The Review applauds the considerable achievements in England and Wales. However, there is not the progress which one might expect from so much effort and investment. Perhaps the government is trying to do too much – bearing in mind that educational failure cannot be totally disconnected from the wider social and economic context. Or perhaps there is something wrong in both the policies and the implementation of those policies.

The Review, in looking to the future and in the light of accumulated evidence, makes five over-arching demands:

1 *The re-assertion of a broader vision of education* in which there is a profound respect for the whole person (not just the narrowly conceived 'intellectual

excellence' or 'skills for economic prosperity'), irrespective of ability or cultural and social background, in which there is a broader vision of learning and in which the learning contributes to a more just and cohesive society.

2 *System performance indicators 'fit for purpose'*, in which the 'measures of success' reflect this range of educational aims, not simply those which are easy to measure or which please certain stakeholders only.

3 *The re-distribution of power and decision-making* such that there can be greater room for the voice of the learner, for the expertise of the teacher and for the concerns of other stakeholders in the response to the learning needs of all young people in their different economic and social settings.

4 *The creation of strongly collaborative local learning systems* in which schools, colleges, higher education institutions, the youth service, independent training providers, employers and voluntary bodies can work together for the common good – in curriculum development, in provision of opportunities for all learners in a locality and in ensuring appropriate progression into further education, training and employment.

5 *The development of a more unified system of qualifications* which meets the diverse talents of young people, the different levels and styles of learning, and the varied needs of the wider community, but which avoids the fragmentation, divisiveness and inequalities to which the present system is prone.

However, behind such over-arching demands, there is a more detailed story to be told and many recommendations, which are listed at the end of this summary.

Fresh thinking and new policies

Aims and values

As indicated above, *education and training should be guided and inspired by aims and values which are relevant to all young people, irrespective of background, ability and talent.* Such aims respect the young person as a whole, in need not only of intellectual development, but also of a wider sense of fulfilment, self-esteem and hope. They recognise and nurture 'moral seriousness' – a sense of responsibility for their future lives, for others and for the wider community.

Language matters

The words we use shape our thinking. The Orwellian language (seeping through government documents) of 'performance management and control' has come to dominate educational deliberation and planning – the language of measurable 'inputs' and 'outputs', 'performance indicators' and 'audits', 'targets' and 'curriculum delivery', 'customers' and 'deliverers', 'efficiency gains' and 'bottom lines'. There needs to be a return to an educational language. (Reading 1.1)

Reflecting the social and economic conditions of education and training

Social and economic conditions inevitably impact upon the attempts of schools, colleges and work-based training providers to raise standards, to develop citizens and to mitigate the ill-effects of disadvantaged circumstances. History shows, however, the limits of educational reform in attempting to solve problems which have a deeper social and economic source.

Those *social and economic conditions* make many schools, colleges and work-based trainers the main providers of that care for the well-being, resilience and self-esteem of young people. This broader responsibility of educational institutions, though recognised in theory and though pursued by countless teachers, too often goes unrecognised in the narrow 'performance indicators' by which schools, colleges and work-based training providers are made accountable by government.

Overall performance and its measurement

Poor rates of participation, high rates of attrition and low levels of attainment characterise the English and Welsh systems and are reflected in the relatively large NEET (Not in Education, Employment or Training) category of young people. Furthermore, there is a continuing divide in attainment between socially advantaged and disadvantaged groups. Successive initiatives to increase participation and progression have not had the hoped-for impact. But three cautionary notes: first, fault lies not so much with the education and training programmes (constantly blamed and then 'reformed'), as with other factors within the wider social and economic context; second, present performance indicators are no longer 'fit for purpose' – failing to reflect the broader aims and values; third, performance indicators also need to take into account the different social circumstances of schools and colleges – and their different missions within that context.

The variety of institutional arrangements sustained in England, though not in Wales, makes serving the needs of all the learners in a locality difficult. Policy has encouraged institutional complexity – comprehensive alongside grammar; local community schools alongside academies, specialist and trust schools; school sixth-forms alongside sixth-form and FE colleges; tertiary alongside 11–18 school systems – all governed and funded differently and often inequitably. In particular, three points stand out. First, the negative effect of this diversification is to be found in the so-called 'sixth-form presumption'; expansion of post-16 provision in schools through the development of small sixth-forms reduces choice, lowers attainment and raises costs. Second, the most needy learners – the NEETs – and the voluntary and community sector that helps them (e.g. 'detached youth workers') receive least money, typically in the form of short-term initiative-led funding. Third, the FE sector, despite its crucial role in giving a 'second chance' to those who have not succeeded earlier, rarely gets due recognition or (in England) equitable funding.

Learning, teaching and assessment

A broader vision of learning is needed. Learning programmes are too often purely 'academic', failing to acknowledge practical and experiential learning. The Review discovered many initiatives building on a broader vision of learning and valuing practical and experiential learning – though struggling to reconcile this with an assessment regime which prioritises 'transmission of knowledge' and attainment of pre-conceived objectives.

A broader vision of assessment (Reading 13.3) follows from a broader vision of learning. The system fails to reflect the totality of learning and achievement, and focuses on that which is more easily measureable. (Reading 17.4) It encourages 'teaching to the test', thereby impoverishing the quality of learning. There is a failure to utilise the full range of assessment tools that recognise different dimensions of learning. Moreover, the same assessments are used for distinct purposes: finding out what has been learnt, selecting for different progression routes and providers, and accounting for the performance of the school, college or system. These all require different assessment tools.

Teaching quality and the relationship between teachers and learners are central to successful education. This requires a respect for the profession of teaching – for the role of teachers as the custodians of what we value and as the experts in communicating that to the learners. Teachers should be central to curriculum development, not the 'deliverers' of someone else's curriculum.

An agreed curriculum framework for the 21st Century should be sufficiently broad as to recognise the expertise of teachers in adapting teaching to the circumstances of the learners – taking account of their experiences and responding to their needs and aspirations. Such a flexible national framework would include: the forms of intellectual enquiry which enable learners to make sense of the physical and social worlds they inhabit; opportunities to gain a sense of achievement; development of practical and economically relevant capabilities; introduction to issues of profound social concern; information, advice and guidance; and relevance to the wider community into which the young people are entering.

Qualifications and progression

The framework of qualifications should reflect rather than shape what is learnt, build on successful features of existing awards, move towards a more unified approach, and facilitate flexible routes into higher education, further training and employment.

Advanced Apprenticeships provide excellent pathways into employment, generating wage premiums as large as degrees in some cases. Apprenticeship is a tradition worth much greater promotion as an alternative to higher education.

Progression from 14–19 into employment. Level 1 and 2 qualifications are not the passports to employment they are made out to be. And the possibilities of work-based learning are fewer. Lack of opportunities for entry into further training and employment will be exacerbated by the present recession. Clear, well-funded policies, involving further education and public and private employers, are required so that otherwise disengaged young people might be trained for future employment and remunerated during that training.

Smooth and clear progression from 14 into higher education has been a priority. But getting that progression right is not easy. Higher education complains that young people are not well prepared for the more independent study of university. Applicants are faced with an increasing number of Entry Tests, not subject to regulation and quality control. Despite efforts on the part of HE, entrance requirements and procedures for many courses need to be more transparent – particularly where vocational qualifications are concerned.

Institutional collaboration

Organisational arrangements for 14–19 in England are complex and, as a result of competition for learners, collaboration is fragile. Young learners' entitlement to different kinds of course and training requires, as the respective governments recognise, partnership between schools, colleges, training providers, employers, voluntary bodies and social services. There is a need to create strongly collaborative local learning systems, building on the experience of the highly successful ones already established. These local learning systems' will involve schools, colleges, work-based learning providers, higher education, the youth service, voluntary organisations and employers. These local learning systems will be faced with negotiating a range of different perspectives, understandings and priorities. For example, very few schools are aware of the full range of apprenticeships available or of the different demands of different university departments (special entry tests). They will therefore need the support of a well-informed and professionally run and independent Information, Advice and Guidance Service. Such re-organisation could include development of 'federations' or re-organisation into tertiary systems, in order to ensure equity and value for money, as well as learner choice.

Policy development

A more integrated and responsive 14–19 education and training system requires a different approach to policy and policy-making. This would encourage the sustained commitment and involvement of key partners, viz. learners, education professionals, parents, employers and higher education. Decisions should be made as close to the learner as is practically possible, taking into account local conditions and local histories. This will mean a slower pace for national policy development so that all partners can be meaningfully involved at all stages of the policy process.

part two

Creating conditions for learning

Contexts
What is, and what might be?

5

These readings address the broad contexts in which teachers work. The first draws upon a classic text in which Mills (5.1) analyses the relationship between individuals and society. He accounts for social change in terms of a continuous interaction between biography and history. This brings to the fore how an awareness of the interplay between biography and history can help us to develop a reflective and questioning attitude towards taken-for-granted social and political power structures, policies and assumptions as well as how 'personal troubles' can often be seen in relation to 'public issues'.

Green and Janmaat (5.2) demonstrate how public policies vary in particular countries and highlight the underlying assumptions upon which taken-for-granted thinking is based. International comparisons help us to see how education and the purposes of education can be thought about in different ways.

The reading from Bruner (5.3) suggests that knowledge and development can be brought together through *appropriate* curriculum design. Jameson and Hillier (5.4) show how policy in the FAVE sector is influencing the work of teachers in the sector in less than helpful ways.

The parallel chapter in *Reflective Teaching in Further, Adult and Vocational Education* engages with additional issues in relation to the 'social context' of education in terms of the concepts of ideology, culture, opportunity, accountability as these inevitably influence FAVE in each country in the UK and elsewhere. Extensive 'Notes for Further Reading' on such factors are available on *reflectiveteaching.co.uk*.

The social context within which teachers and students work is a topic with many avenues for exploration in sociology, economics, history, politics, cultural studies, anthropology, comparative education, etc., therefore available literature is very extensive indeed. The readings in this chapter are also related to the readings in Chapter 17 of this book – for example, there are echoes of Mills's analysis in the discussion of the 'transformative teacher' in the reading by Menter et al. (17.2) and in the discussion of *subjectification* and the role of assessment by Hodgson and Spours (17.4).

Reading 5.1

The sociological imagination
C. Wright Mills

This reading comes from a classic sociological text. Mills focused on the interaction between individuals and society, and thus on the intersection of biography and history. Teachers have particular responsibilities because, though acting in particular historical contexts, we shape the biographies of many children, young people and adults and thus help to create the future. Mills poses several questions which can be used to think about our society and the role of education in it.

How do you think what you do today may influence what others may do in the future?

Edited from: Mills, C. W. (1959) *The Sociological Imagination*. New York: Oxford University Press, 111–13.

The sociological imagination enables its possessor to understand the larger historical scene in terms of its meaning for the inner life and the external career of a variety of individuals. It enables him [sic] to take into account how individuals, in the welter of their daily experience, often become falsely conscious of their social positions. Within that welter the framework of modern society is sought, and within that framework the psychologies of a variety of men and women are formulated. By such means the personal uneasiness of individuals is focused upon explicit troubles and the indifference of publics is transformed into involvement with public studies.

The first fruit of this imagination – and the first lessons of the social science that embodies it – is the idea that the individual can understand his own experience and gauge his own fate only by locating himself within his period, that he can know his own chances in life only by becoming aware of those of all individuals in his circumstances. In many ways it is a terrible lesson; in many ways a magnificent one. We do not know the limits of man's capacities for supreme effort or willing degradation, for agony or glee, for pleasurable brutality or the sweetness of reason. But in our time we have come to know that the limits of 'human nature' are frighteningly broad. We have come to know that every individual lives, from one generation to the next, in some society; that he lives out a biography, and that he lives it out within some historical sequence. By the fact of his living he contributes, however minutely, to the shaping of this society and to the course of its history, even as he is made by society and by its historical push and shove.

The sociological imagination enables us to grasp history and biography and the relations between the two within society. That is its task and its promise. To recognize this task and this promise is the mark of the classic social analyst. And it is the signal of what is best in contemporary studies of man and society.

No social study that does not come back to the problems of biography, of history, and of their intersections within a society, has completed its intellectual journey. Whatever the specific problems of the classic social analysts, however limited or however broad the features of social reality they have examined, those who have been imaginatively aware of the promise of their work have consistently asked three sorts of questions:

- What is the structure of this particular society as a whole? What are its essential components, and how are they related to one another? Within it, what is the meaning of any particular feature for its continuance and for its change?

- Where does this society stand in human history? What are the mechanics by which it is changing? What is its place within and its meaning for the development of humanity as a whole? How does any particular feature we are examining affect, and how is it affected by, the historical period in which it moves? And this period – what are its essential features? How does it differ from other periods? What are its characteristic ways of history-making?

- What varieties of men and women now prevail in this society and in this period? And what varieties are coming to prevail? In what ways are they selected and formed, liberated and repressed, made sensitive and blunted? What kinds of 'human nature' are revealed in the conduct and character we observe in this society in this period? And what is the meaning for 'human nature' of each and every feature of the society we are examining?

Reading 5.2

Regimes of social cohesion

Andy Green and Jan Janmaat

This reading is based on analysis of data on inequality and social attitudes in over 25 developed countries. The study shows how educational inequality undermines key aspects of social cohesion, including trust in institutions, civic cooperation and the rule of law. The authors argue that more egalitarian education systems tend to promote both economic competitiveness and social cohesion. The work highlights the significance for social cohesion of the distribution of opportunities and the nature of the values that people acquire.

Through its work with young people, education influences the future and is infused with moral purpose. We must recognize 'What is', but may also ask 'What should be?'. How do you feel that the policy context in which you work affects educational provision?

Edited from: Green, A. and Janmaat, J. G. (2011) *Education, Opportunity and Social Cohesion. Centre for Learning and Life Chances in Knowledge Economies and Societies.* London: Institute of Education, 2–5.

Regimes of social cohesion

Different traditions of thought and policy on social cohesion have evolved within the western world. Comparative analysis identifies three distinctive types of social cohesion in contemporary states. These can be characterised as 'liberal', 'social market' or 'social democratic'. We refer to these as 'regimes of social cohesion' to emphasise their systemic properties, which are relatively durable over time.

Liberal (English-speaking countries, e.g. particularly the UK and the USA)

In liberal societies, such as the United Kingdom and the United States, social cohesion has traditionally relied on the triple foundations of market freedoms, an active civil society, and core beliefs in individual opportunities and rewards based on merit. A wider set of shared values has not been regarded as essential for a cohesive society – and nor, in the British case at least, has a tightly defined sense of national identity. The state was not, historically, considered the main guarantor of social cohesion, beyond its role in the maintenance of law and order.

Social Market (NW continental Europe, e.g. Belgium, France, Germany and the Netherlands)

The social market regime, by contrast, has relied on a strong institutional embedding of social cohesion. Solidarity has depended relatively more on the state and less on civil society, and rates of civic participation have generally been lower. Trade union coverage and public spending on welfare and social protection are high. These factors, along with concerted and centralized trade union bargaining, have helped to reduce household income inequality. Maintaining a broad set of shared values – and a strong national identity – has also, historically, been considered important for holding societies together.

Social Democratic (The Nordic countries, e.g. Denmark, Finland, Norway and Sweden)

The social democratic regime, like the social market regime, institutionalises social solidarity. However, here, egalitarian and solidaristic values make a greater contribution to social cohesion. Levels of social and political trust are also much higher. This cannot be attributed solely to greater ethnic homogeneity in these societies, although this may have once played a part in Denmark and Norway. Sweden is both ethnically diverse and highly trusting.

Social cohesion during economic crisis

Every country is affected by the challenges of globalisation and particularly so during periods of economic crisis. However, societies differ in what holds them together.

The core beliefs of liberal societies, such as the UK (e.g. active civil society and individual opportunities), are seen to be embodied in the 'free market' which has become more dominant under globalisation. However, social cohesion in such societies is likely to be undermined by the rapid erosion of people's faith in individual opportunity and fairness.

The UK has high levels of income inequality and relatively low rates of social mobility. Inequality and lack of mobility are likely to grow due to the disproportionate effects of the economic crisis (in unemployment and public expenditure cuts, for example) on young people, women, the low paid and those in areas of socio-economic disadvantage. As the prospects of secure jobs and home ownership diminish for many people, belief in the core unifying values of opportunity, freedom and just rewards are likely to decrease, causing social and political trust to diminish further.

Education, inequality and social cohesion

Education systems play a key role in determining future life chances and in mitigating or exacerbating social inequalities. These have been linked with various negative health and social outcomes, including high rates of depression, low levels of trust and cooperation, and high levels of violent crime.

We found that education systems which select students to secondary schools by ability and make extensive use of ability grouping within schools tend to exhibit more unequal educational outcomes than non-selective comprehensive systems with mixed ability classes.

The four education systems in the UK perform somewhat differently. Those in Scotland and Wales produce slightly more equal educational outcomes at 15 than those in England

and Northern Ireland, according to the OECD Programme for International student Assessment (PISA).

The 2009 PISA study of literacy skills amongst 15 years olds shows that educational outcomes in the UK are more unequal than in most of the OECD countries where tests were conducted (Green and Janmaat, 2011).

The gap between the mean scores of UK students in the 90th and 10th percentiles was 246 points – the equivalent of six years of schooling on the average across OECD countries. PISA 2009 showed that the variance in scores in the UK have only reduced marginally since the 2000 survey. Amongst the 34 countries tested, the UK had the 11th highest total variance in scores.

The UK is also notable for degree to which the average performance within a school is influenced by the social characteristics of its intake. Across all OECD countries, on average, 57 per cent of the performance difference between schools can be attributed to the social character of the intake. In the UK (and in Luxembourg, New Zealand and the USA) the social intake accounts for over 70 per cent of performance difference between schools.

Skills distribution and social cohesion

Variation in performance among school students is one of the factors which, over time, determines the overall distribution of skills within the adult population. We found strong links between social cohesion and the distribution of adult skills.

The more unequal the skills distribution among adults, the higher the rates of violent crime and civic unrest, and the lower the levels of social trust and civil liberties. For several of the indicators, these correlations also hold over time, suggesting that the relationships may be causal. It seems likely that wide educational disparities generate cultural gaps and competition anxieties which undermine social bonds and trust.

Our research suggests that it is not so much the average level of education in a country which matters most for social cohesion, but rather how the skills acquired are spread around.

Education systems and civic competences

Civic competences are an important component of social cohesion. These refer to the knowledge, skills and values that people need to participate effectively in a liberal democratic society. We examined the links between education system characteristics and the levels and distributions of civic competences across countries.

When compared with comprehensive systems, selective education systems have:

- higher levels of social segregation across classrooms
- greater disparities in civic knowledge and skills and
- larger peer effects on civic knowledge and skills (meaning that the latter are strongly affected by the social backgrounds and achievement levels of other students in the class).

Implications for policy

We urge policymakers in the UK to take account of the potentially negative impact that educational inequality can have on social cohesion.

Social cohesion in the UK has always depended on high levels of civic participation and a widespread belief in the availability of individual opportunities and rewards based on merit. In the current period of austerity, where opportunities for young people are substantially reduced, there is a serious danger that these shared beliefs will be eroded, thus weakening social bonds. In such circumstances it is particularly important that the education system is seen to offer opportunities for all students.

Reading 5.3

The spiral curriculum

Jerome Bruner

Bruner's classic text, *The Process of Education* (1960), is premised on the idea that students are active learners who construct their own knowledge and understanding. Challenging the constraining effects of those advocating subject-based and developmental progression, he argued that all knowledge can 'be taught in some intellectually honest form to any child at any stage of development' (p. 33). It is then revisited, successively, at further levels of difficulty. Bruner draws particular attention to the place of narrative in learning and in 'making sense' through life.

If there is value in these ideas, they have significant implications for progression in curriculum planning.

Edited from: Bruner, J. S. (2006) *In Search of Pedagogy Volume II: The Selected Works of Jerome S. Bruner.* New York: Routledge, 145–6.

A very long time ago I proposed something which was called a spiral curriculum (1960). The idea was that when teaching or learning a subject, you start with an intuitive account that is well within the reach of the student, then circle back later in a more powerful, more generative, more structured way to understand it more deeply with however many recyclings the learner needs in order to master the topic and turn it into an instrument of the mind, a way of thinking. It was a notion that grew out of a more fundamental view of epistemology, about how minds get to know. I stated this view almost in the form of a philosophical proverb: Any subject could be taught to any child at any age in some form that was honest. Another way of saying the same thing is that readiness is not only born but made. You make readiness.

The general proposition rests on the still deeper truth that a domain of knowledge can be constructed simply or complexly, abstractly or concretely. The kid who understands the intuitive role of the lever and can apply it to the playground see-saw is getting within reach of knowing the meaning of quadratic functions. He now has a grasp of one instantiation of an idea that makes teaching him about quadratics a cinch. I'm saying this because we have done it. Give me a balance beam with hooks placed at equal distances along it, some weights that you can hang on the hooks of the balance beam to make it balance, and I will show you. A ten-year-old I was working with once said to me: 'This gadget knows all about arithmetic'. That gave me pause, and I tried to convince him that it was he who knew arithmetic, not the balance beam. He listened politely, but I don't think I succeeded; maybe that will come later along the curriculum spiral. Anyway, he had learned a meaning of expressions like $x2 + 5x + 6$ and why they balance – mean the same – as ones like $(x +2)(x + 3)$.

The research of the last three decades on the growth of reasoning in children has in the main confirmed the rightness of the notion of the spiral curriculum in spite of the fact that we now know about something called domain specificity. It is not true now, nor was it ever true, that learning Latin improves your reasoning. Subject matters have to be demonstrably within reach of each other to improve each other. There isn't infinite transfer. On the other hand, there is probably more than we know, and we can build up a kind of general confidence that problems are solvable. That has a huge transfer effect. The kid says, 'Now how would we do that?' using a kind of royal 'we'. A good intuitive, practical grasp of the domain at one stage of developmental leads to better, earlier, and deeper thinking in the next stage when the child meets new problems. We do not wait for readiness to happen. We foster it by making sure they are good at some intuitive domain before we start off on the next one.

However, it's interesting that we don't always do it. It is appalling how poorly history, for example, is taught at most schools and at most universities. Teachers needs to give students an idea that there are models for how events happened historically, even if we give them a sort of Toynbeyan model, to the effect that there is challenge and response, or the kind of Paul Kennedy model of what happens to wealthy nations. The particular model doesn't matter, just so it is clear and coherent so that kids can say, 'Pretty smart, but it doesn't work'. We need models that can be given some basic sense even though they are rejected later. One way to do it is by placing emphasis upon what is story-like about the model. For what we grasp better than anything else are stories, and it is easy for children (or adults) to take them apart, retell them, and analyse what's wrong with them.

The most natural and earliest way in which we organize our experience and our knowledge is by use of narrative. It may be that the beginnings, the transitions, the full grasps of ideas in a spiral curriculum depend upon embodying those ideas initially into a story of narrative form in order to carry the kid across any area where he is not quite grasping the abstraction. The story form is the first one grasped by kids, and is the one with which they all seem most comfortable.

Reading 5.4

The ragged-trousered philanthropist

Jill Jameson, Yvonne Hillier and Derek Betts

In this reading Jameson, Hillier and Betts draw attention to the important role part-time teachers play in educating students in the FAVE sector. The discussion notes the rise in numbers of part-time teachers in recent years. It explores how these part-time staff have been deployed in FAVE settings and the opportunities they have been given to participate in professional development activities. The research found that part-time staff were performing an invaluable service, but most felt underpaid, under-supported and under-resourced. When you reflect on this reading, consider the following question: What practical steps could employers take to better support part-time teachers to develop their practice in teaching, learning and assessment, while also opening up opportunities for part-time teachers to participate in professional communities of practice?

Jameson, J., Hillier, Y. and Betts, D. (2004) *The Ragged-trousered Philanthropy of LSC Part-time Staff*. Presented at the British Educational Research Association Conference, UMIST, Manchester, 16–18 September.

The learning and skills sector is the largest educational sector in the UK, a significant employer of large numbers of part-time staff housed in many different kinds of Post-16 institutions, from FE colleges to Adult and Community Learning providers. Current ambitions to improve learning and teaching in the sector are intrinsically linked to the work of part-time staff, but as yet only patchy attention has been paid to the ways in which part-time staff are recruited, deployed, developed and supported. Although some Learning and Skills Council (LSC)-funded institutions appear to employ part-time staff effectively, good quality is by no means assured uniformly. Worrying indicators of an increasing casualisation of staffing in the sector have, in addition, been noted by Further Education National Training Organisation (FENTO), raising concerns about the replacement of full-time staff by part-timers. In such a situation, significant responsibilities may be allocated to part-time staff who lack adequate development and support. This paper reports on the results of a 2003–4 investigative research study by a project team from the London and South East Learning and Skills Research Network (LSE LSRN). The research project examined the role of part-time staff in a number of major participating institutions in London and the South East. The aims of the research were to identify and explore current policy and practice in the deployment and development of part-time staff, making recommendations for differentiated models of good practice for employing part-timers in terms of the quality of learning and teaching in the LSC sector from the perspective of the needs of learners, and the types of institution involved. Using data collected from 710 questionnaire responses from LSC institutions in London and the South East, institutional profiles provided by project team members and interviews with questionnaire respondents, this paper provides a detailed analysis of the rich data emerging from part-time staff and their employing institutions. One of the findings was that the sector could be described as being *'raggedy'* –there is in some cases a notable lack of resources to support part-time staff who are sometimes insufficiently trained, equipped and developed. And yet, a strong finding emerged, also, of a deeply philanthropic motivation in part-timers' work: such staff often carry out significantly more responsibilities and activities than they are recognised and paid for. In most cases part-time staff enjoy their work. Large numbers in participating institutions of this research project remain in the sector for many years, working to an advanced age. The overwhelming commitment of part-time staff to students is worthy of both praise and appreciation. However, to ensure such good will is neither exploited nor relied on in ways detrimental to quality learning outcomes, it is necessary to make sure that appropriate models of good practice are followed in the deployment and development of part-timers. This paper concludes, therefore, by proposing a model of good practice for the deployment, development, support and professional accreditation of part-time staff in the sector, providing recommendations for the introduction of this model into LSC-funded institutions.

During 2002–3, the Learning and Skills Research Network (LSRN) for London and the South East (LSE), hosted by the Learning and Skills Development Agency (LSDA), invited ideas for regional research projects from Post-16 education and training network members. A number of responses were received, from which was developed the research project focusing on the deployment and development of LSC part-time staff in terms of the impact of these aspects of the employment of part-timers in the achievement of quality outcomes in learning for students in a number of selected case study institutions in London and the South East. The key focus for the work was on teaching staff, rather than on administrative or other support staff.

The project focus, framed at the outset of the research, was on: *'The development and deployment of part-time staff in the learning and skills sector'*. The aims of the research were to identify current practice in the professional development of part-time staff in the LSC sector, to examine policies for the deployment and development of teaching staff, to explore how staff were deployed and how they participated in professional development from the perspective of full-time, part-time and managerial staff, and to examine the impact of this development on the quality of teaching and learning from the point of view of the learner. As the project progressed through its data collection and analysis stages, it became clear that the last aim – the examination of learners' views on the effectiveness of part-time staff – was too ambitious for the collection of primary data sources within the scope of the project, in view of the substantial nature of the time, resources and work involved in meeting the first three main aims. It was therefore decided that the first three aims would provide a realistic main focus for the research. From this, inferences could be drawn in relation to the last aim, which could then form the subject of a follow-up research project. The project was allocated LSDA research funds by the LSE LSRN for a small amount of paid time for project team participants to be spent during a period of roughly one year.

Project team members devised a questionnaire for part-time LSC staff that was distributed in the summer of 2003. In September, 2003, it became clear that the rich data collected in the 710 questionnaires returned by London and South East part-timers required and deserved more substantial levels of investment in time and resources for research analysis and reflective consideration than the project had funding for. The project had unexpectedly tapped into a wealth of findings indicating there was scope for considerable further work in the analysis of the important role played by part-timers in LSC institutions. It began to emerge that the subject of 'part-timeness' continued to be an area of key national concern and interest, highlighted in significance by increasing concerns raised about the relative fragmentation of the workforce in further and adult education, and its increasing size and influence on performance since FE institutions' incorporation 1993.

The project team used a collaborative case study research methodology, in which the analysis of themes emerging in relation to the 'cases' were triangulated across three levels of inquiry – (1) the national (macro) 'case' level for part-time staff, in terms of overall historical and current national theorising, data collection and debate in terms of the role of part-time staff within the LSC sector; (2) the institutional (meso) level of 'cases', based on the analysis of the way in which individual case study institutions were employing and developing part-time staff; (3) the individual (micro) level, as part-time staff each provided within themselves unique individual specialist 'cases' for investigation and further development. The research took a case study approach (Bassey, 1999, Yin, 1994), based on Yin's concept of multiple-case study design using replication logic (Yin, 1994: 44–52). The 'cases' analysed by the project team comprised matched pairs of institutions from further education (FE) and adult and community learning (ACL) within the two regions of London and the South East.

Principles of cooperative inquiry established by Reason and Heron (1995) and Heron (1996) provided a framework for the establishment of an inquiry methodology in which all members of the project team were valued for their role in shaping the project's aims, methodology and processes. A consciously 'critical intersubjectivity', as encouraged by Reason and Heron, was adopted, in which participants were regarded as co-researchers and co-subjects within an ongoing collaborative partnership of equals. Within this, the project coordinators acted as facilitators, respectively taking various roles as chair, guide and/or note-takers within democratically established project team meetings.

One of the emerging findings was that LSC sectoral employment of part-timers could be described as being *'raggedy'*: the expectations of staff tended to be *'fuzzy'*. This seemed to be an area in which institutions were in general having some difficulty in achieving compliance with best employment and staff development practices.

Yet respondents seemed to have, despite this *'raggedness'* in conditions of employment, an overwhelming long-standing commitment to the learners they taught. In fact, the data seemed to suggest that part-time staff support to learners was often freely given and sometimes marked by what seemed to be a *'philanthropic'* professional approach to additional unpaid duties. Despite some of the barriers part-time staff encountered in their attempts to provide a quality learning experience, there appeared to be a notable ongoing professional commitment to students' well-being and achievement. It seemed that sometimes part-time staff were going out of their way, sometimes at their own expense, to cater effectively for the needs of their learners, even in difficult circumstances in which they had minimal resources and little support.

The research found overall that part-time staff in further education and adult colleges are performing an invaluable service, but most feel underpaid, under-supported and under-resourced. Part-time staff experience relatively low rates of pay, inadequate office space and facilities, and limited access to staff development and training. However, the project also found that part-time staff routinely demonstrate high levels of enthusiasm, profession-alism and commitment to their job, and that there are many rewards gained in their work through contact with learners. Emerging themes from the interview transcripts highlighted the *'energy, excitement, goodwill and commitment'* shown by part-timers towards their jobs, the fact that teachers saw themselves as *'a good, but underused resource'*, that their *'aspirations tend to be modest – a desk, key, locker, etc.'* and that part-timers did not see any disadvantage for learners in the fact of their own part-timeness, considering themselves to be *'professional'* in taking care to *'protect the learners from their own problems'* as part-timers, and ensuring that they did not *'undermine the value of the insti-tution'*. Institutional loyalty and high-minded dedication to the work of supporting learners in their teaching was a feature of the questionnaire responses and interviews.

Relationships
How are we getting on together?

6

The readings in this group emphasize the role of good relationships in classrooms, workshops, studios, workplaces and the other FAVE contexts in which teachers work. The main focus here is upon minimizing behavioural difficulties and providing positive conditions for learning. Underlying processes are analysed and suggestions offered to enable the development of good relationships between teachers and students, and between students.

The first reading (6.1) supports the view that the emotional climate and demonstrations of empathy by teachers in classrooms, workshops, studios, workplaces and other FAVE contexts is crucial to student learning. Gipps and MacGilchrist (6.2) focus on teacher expectations and their consequences and evidence of their impact, both positive and negative, are reviewed. Bennett (6.3) focuses on the qualities of teachers and identifies five virtues, which will undoubtedly resonate with the experiences of teachers across the FAVE sector.

The parallel chapter in *Reflective Teaching in Further, Adult and Vocational Education* addresses similar issues and provides further practical advice and guidance. There are specific sections on developing good interpersonal relationships in FAVE contexts and supporting positive conditions for advancing learning. The professional skills of teachers are discussed. Finally the chapter focuses on enhancing the learning climate, supporting self-esteem and developing the inclusive classroom.

On *reflectiveteaching.co.uk* there are additional ideas on the issues raised in this chapter and 'Notes for Further Reading'. Within the section on 'Deepening Expertise' you will find that relationships are at the heart of its organizing conceptual framework.

Reading 6.1

Rites of passage
Bridget Cooper and Mike Baynham

This extract is edited from a study of a number of skilled trades courses in FE. The most significant and recurring theme in the discourses of the vocational teachers interviewed in this study was the empathy that they felt for their students. The following brief discussion of different aspects of empathy offers insights into some of the more subtle aspects of teaching and learning in FAVE contexts.

Edited from: Cooper, B. and Baynham, M. (2005) 'Rites of passage: Embedding meaningful language, literacy and numeracy skills in skilled trades courses through significant and transforming relationships'. National Research and Development Centre for Adult Literacy and Numeracy. London: NRDC.

Emotions

Significantly, all the staff in this study considered emotional issues and staff empathy to be central to teaching and learning relationships, which were associated with personal, one-to-one conversations, concerning pasts and futures. Pete, the vocational tutor, is an experienced and skilled professional who used to run his own business.

Pete: But I can still remember that (negative school experience) and I can empathise with these lads – they've gone through school and come out with nothing and I [they] see [this particular trade] as a chance?

Janet: Having one to one time is vital – the most important thing is to have empathy with the students – it doesn't matter how well you know the subject matter if you can't relate to the students.

Jean (a highly experienced Language, Literacy and Numeracy tutor and middle manager): Empathy – not just the skills level – I want to know what motivates a student – what their anxieties are – where they'd like to go to – where if they can choose it where they see themselves going to – because I want to know what's going on with them – what's happening in their head because if you don't know that you can't know what's interfering with what's happening on paper.

Careful observation of students meant tutors saw the hidden feelings which affected learning and revealed whether real learning was happening or whether students were just going through the motions.

Janet: I watch their body language – observe them constantly – are they just following a pattern in their work or are they understanding? I'm watching everything they do.

They used physical body language to reassure and communicate.

Harry: Positive feedback and lots of back tapping – lots of males – lots of body language sometimes they need a little cuddle – you know putting an arm round them as they go up the corridor for their break.

Personal, more equal and individual treatment

Teaching and interaction was individualised for each student.

Janet: It changes with every student – even the way you greet them – I greet Dean in a different way – some like formality, some don't.

Everyone interviewed echoed this idea and stressed the importance of individual relationships, the closeness, the personal knowledge, the positive interactions, the mutuality of human respect involved in the teaching and learning process both with colleagues and students.

Harry: I think the main thing I've always found if you take an interest in them they will give you much, much more back – I knew more about the students than I knew about my own kids – I knew what they did on Friday, Sat, Sun, I knew what they were doing in midweek and I saw more of them. When you consider – when was the last time a parent saw 30 hours (of their children)? – and very, very close – very close – classroom workshop – working – pat on the back – they love it – pat on the back – bit of body language – "You've made a great job".

Relationships

Good relationships are highly significant, building trust and gradually exposing problems which can then be addressed.

In Janet's words they are: The most important part – you can't make somebody learn – they've got to want to learn – and to work with me – they've got to trust me – lots of the barriers to learning can come from personal aspects rather than educational ones – need to open up and trust me and that what I'm telling them is right – it doesn't start off as personal but in one to one all home life troubles come out eventually – the major reason why they're not learning.

This personal understanding allows ongoing formative assessment and adaptive scaffolding, encompassing both emotional and academic issues.

Gary: It's being interested in them as people – [] but in here but it helps with your teaching because if you know they've got issues at home – it can explain bad behaviour – it can explain why they're not doing homework – it can explain why their work dips or falls or rises – and I can allow a bit – you cannot be as ruthless with them – it's just a better teaching approach if you know them personally – you know what to expect from them.

Personal interests are encouraged and discussed in lessons too, again to value students and give confidence.

The two behind me begin talking about pool. "How do you play pool?" says one student to John, who Janet has to help a lot. He is clearly knowledgeable about the game and Janet and the other boy listen respectfully to his reply. He is animated and confident about it – Janet doesn't interrupt and bring him back to task because this is something where he feels he has credibility, if not in other areas. The ensuing conversation around numeracy similarly aims to develop confidence: "This one's a bit tricky," she says as they start, in a very positive way. "Well done!" – he gets it fairly easily, "That usually gets everybody (fooled) but not you!" – grins.

There are many opportunities for students to take the initiative, ask questions and take control of learning. They are given time to think and come up with their own solutions and have their knowledge valued. Their personal interests and experience are valued and tutors and students were aware of how this helped build positive feelings about self in relation to others as described by Watson and Ashton (1995) and Clark (1996).

A more positive adult atmosphere – rites and responsibilities of passage

This emotional and academic closeness creates a different atmosphere in college, which is preferred to school and is helped by the smaller groups and better student-tutor ratios. Having two or more adults, with often less than 15 students, contributed to a less confrontational atmosphere and improved learning.

Harry: We're certainly happy with it (having Language Literacy and Numeracy (LLN) tutors in classes) – the good thing about it is they're probably supporting the students who would be disruptive because they wouldn't be able to keep up with the class and therefore it's making for a more stable environment for all the students [] we'll get better achievements, we'll be able to watch the more disruptive students and help them – help them along the way, not just keep the beady eye on them – let's help this person along the way.

The tutor/student relationship transforms from one of unequal surveillance to more equal dialogue and support and turns disruptive students into progressing students. Having some opportunities for one-to-one time releases students from oppressive peer pressure and transforms behaviour and attitudes to learning.

Janet: You've got an hour 1–1 – release (them) from peer pressure and give personal attention. (they) can be nervous in a group – one to one – adorable!

Pete concurred: "Cos a lot of them like to work on their own in a quiet environment or they like to come into the workshop with a group that they don't know, so they can carry on working at their own pace with no peer pressure."

Students also preferred the equal, friendly, relaxed and realistic treatment and rapid support provided in smaller groups with good teacher/student ratios, which appear to be less stressful for tutors and students.

John: A lot better cos you don't get treated as a child you get treated as an adult.

Steven: They call you first names and just talk to you about stuff sometimes – they say "What did you do … – we even ask," What did you do? … we talk about women … they've just got more personality … sometimes they're funny a bit (they joke) yes – I mean at school you'd get some of them (that were funny) but not a lot – cos at school they're under stress.

Steven: It's good – because if somebody puts their hand up and says, "I need your help" – there's always a tutor free – so if Pete is busy, Janet can, just like, help.

Reading 6.2

Teacher expectations and pupil achievement

Caroline Gipps and Barbara MacGilchrist

In this review, Gipps and MacGilchrist summarize key evidence on the significance of teachers' maintaining high expectations and pupil performance. There seems to be little doubt that this is a crucial factor in effective teaching, as children's self-confidence flourishes from the affirmation and encouragement of their teachers. Again, as in the previous readings, teacher and pupil behaviour are seen to be inextricably linked. Interestingly, however, research studies of classroom practice often document relatively low levels of explicit encouragement, praise and communication of expectations.

Can you support the performance of your students by explicitly conveying your confidence in them? How do you think they will respond?

Although this paper is set in the schools sector, it is not difficult to see important parallels between teacher expectations and student achievement in the FAVE sector.

Edited from: Gipps, C. and MacGilchrist, B. (1999) 'Primary School Learners'. In Mortimore, P. (ed.) *Understanding Pedagogy and its Impact on Learning.* London: Paul Chapman: 52–5.

One of the hallmarks of effective teachers is their belief that all children can achieve. This belief manifests itself in a variety of ways in the classroom, the most common being through the high expectations teachers set for the children they are teaching. When drawing attention to some of the knowledge and skills teachers need to have in order to bring about effective learning, Mortimore (1993) identified the essential need for teachers to have psychological and sociological knowledge: 'Psychological knowledge so that they can understand how young minds operate and how young people cope with different cultural patterns and family traditions. Sociological knowledge of the way factors such as race, gender, class or religion operate to help or hinder successful teaching' (1999, p. 296).

The research literature that has focused on the relationship between disadvantage and achievement and the extent to which schools can enhance the achievement of pupils whatever their background provides important sociological knowledge for teachers. Two common themes emerge from the literature. The first is that socioeconomic inequality is a powerful determinant of differences in cognitive and educational attainment (Mortimore and Mortimore, 1986). Longitudinal studies support this finding (Douglas, 1964, Davie et al., 1972). Social class, along with ethnic background, gender and disability, has been found to have a substantial influence on the life chances of young people. The other common theme is that schools can and do make a difference, but that some schools are much more effective than others at counteracting the potentially damaging effects of disadvantage (Edmunds, 1979; Rutter et al., 1979; Reynolds, 1982; Mortimore et al., 1988; Smith and Tomlinson, 1989; Sammons et al., 1995).

There have been numerous studies to identify the characteristics of highly successful schools (Sammons et al., 1995). Whilst researchers are rightly cautious about identifying causal relationships, the review of the effectiveness literature by Sammons et al. (1995) has revealed a set of common features that can be found in effective schools. The majority of these concern the quality and nature of teaching and learning in classrooms along with the overall learning ethos of the school. Some draw attention in particular to the relationship between teachers' beliefs and attitudes and pupils' progress and achievement.

The idea of a self-fulfilling prophecy was first introduced by Merton (1968), and the well-known study by Rosenthal and Jacobson (1968) demonstrated how this concept can operate in the classroom. They showed that it was possible to influence teachers' expectations of certain pupils even though the information they had been given about those pupils was untrue. In their review of the literature Brophy and Good (1974) and Pilling and Pringle (1978) identify the power of teacher expectation in relation to pupils' learning.

In two studies of primary age pupils (Mortimore et al., 1988; Tizard et al., 1988), the importance of teacher expectations emerged. Tizard and colleagues focused on children aged four to seven in 33 inner London infant schools. The purpose of the research was to examine factors in the home and in the school that appeared to affect attainment and progress during the infant school years. Particular attention was paid to the different levels of attainment of boys and girls, and of white British children and black British children of AfroCaribbean origin. The team found that there was a link between disadvantage and pupil progress and attainment. The literacy and numeracy knowledge and skills that children had acquired before they started school were found to be a strong predictor of attainment at age seven.

The study was able to identify those school factors that appear to exert a greater influence on progress than home background. The two most significant factors were the range of literacy and numeracy taught to the children and teachers' expectations. Whilst each of these factors was independently associated with progress, the team found that the school and class within it that the child attended proved to be an overriding factor in terms of the amount of progress made. A relationship was found between teacher expectations and the range of curriculum activities provided for children, especially in the areas of literacy and numeracy. The team reported that, of the school based measures we looked at, we found that teachers' expectations of children's curriculum coverage showed the strongest and most consistent association with school progress' (op cit.: 139). Where teachers had low expectations of children they provided a narrower curriculum offering.

The Junior School Project (Mortimore et al., 1988) was a longitudinal study of a cohort of seven year old pupils in fifty London schools. The project drew together different aspects of disadvantage. Using sophisticated research techniques the team was able to account for what were called pupil and school 'givens'; for example, they were able to take account of pupil factors such as home language, family circumstances, age and sex, and school factors such as size and the stability of staffing. This enabled the team to focus on those factors over which the school had control, such as teaching methods, record keeping and curriculum leadership. They were able to examine which of these factors appear to have a positive impact on pupils' progress and achievement.

The research revealed significant differences in children's educational outcomes during the Junior years. Age, social class, sex and race were each found to have an impact on cognitive achievement levels at age seven and eleven. For example, at age seven those children whose parents worked in non-manual jobs were nearly ten months further ahead in reading than pupils from unskilled manual homes. By the end of the third year the gap had widened. It was also found that with non-cognitive outcomes, such as behaviour and self-concept, there were differences according to age, social class, sex and race. Overall, however, it was found that it was the social class dimension that accounted for the main differences between groups of pupils.

It was the focus on progress that the pupils made over the four years of the study that demonstrated that some schools (and the teachers within them) were far more effective than others. With reading, for example, the average child in the most effective school increased his or her score on a ten point reading test by 25 points more than the average child attending the least effective school. The team found that schools which did better on one measure of academic progress tended to do better on others, and that effective schools tended to be effective for all pupils regardless of social class, ethnic group, sex or age.

High teacher expectations were a common characteristic of these schools. The team looked at ways in which expectations were transmitted in the classroom. They found, for example, that teachers had lower expectations of pupils from socioeconomically disadvantaged backgrounds. Denbo's (1988) analysis of the research literature over a twenty year period supports the importance of teacher expectation. Denbo found that many studies demonstrated that both low and high teacher expectation greatly affected student performance. It has been demonstrated that if appropriate teaching styles and teaching expectations are used (OFSTED, 1993a) then pupils can become positive about learning and improve their levels of achievement.

If the learner is seen as an active partner in the learning process, then his/her motivational and emotional state becomes more relevant. One of the school outcomes studied by Mortimore et al. was the attitude of students towards themselves as learners. The team designed a measure of self-concept which revealed clear school differences. Some schools produced pupils who felt positive about themselves as learners regardless of their actual ability. Others produced pupils who were negative about themselves even though, according to their progress, they were performing well. Kuykendall (1989) argues that low teacher expectations have been shown to reduce the motivation of students to learn, and that 'perhaps the most damaging consequence of low teacher expectations is the erosion of academic self image in students' (p. 18). Mortimore (1993) supports this view: 'for a pupil who is regularly taught by a teacher with low expectations, the experience can be demoralizing and too often leads to serious underachievement' (p. 295). Not unrelated to this, he draws attention to the need for teachers to provide good role models for pupils.

It is interesting that these findings mirror, in many respects, some of the studies about the brain and learning referred to earlier. Drawing on the work of LeDoux (1996), Goleman (1996) argues that emotions play a key role in cognitive development. He takes the view that emotional intelligence, as he calls it, is a vital capacity for learning. It involves, for example, motivation, the ability to persist and stay on task, control of impulse, regulation of mood and the capacity for keeping distress from swamping the ability to think. Not unrelatedly, Smith (1998) comments that many learners in the classroom avoid taking risks and prefer to stay in 'the comfort zone'. He reminds us that young learners will happily 'copy out in rough, copy it out in neat, draw a coloured border around it, highlight the key words in primary colour, draw you a picture' but that this 'rote, repetitive comfort zone activity is not where real learning takes place' (p. 43). He describes how studies of the brain indicate that 'the optimal conditions for learning include a positive, personal leaning attitude where challenge is high and anxiety and self-doubt is low' (p. 41). In her review of the literature on effective primary teaching, Gipps (1992) identified some important factors that mark out effective primary teaching. Amongst these is 'the importance of a good positive atmosphere in the classroom with plenty of encouragement and praise, high levels of expectations of all children and high levels of work related talk and discussion' (p. 19). She came to the conclusion that, over and above what theories inform us about good teaching, theorists tell us that children are capable of more than we expect.

So, it seems clear that teachers do have beliefs about how children learn and that they need a teaching strategy able to negotiate a path among the rocks and hard places of context, content, child and learning. This resonates with the complexity of real classrooms. Furthermore, those teachers who see children as thinkers, and therefore capable of achieving more and more, are the ones who can enable children to view themselves as able to learn. This is a virtuous circle which needs to be encouraged.

Reading 6.3

Virtues of great teachers: Justice, courage, patience, wisdom and compassion

Tom Bennett

> In this reading an experienced secondary practitioner speaks plainly about the characteristics of 'great teachers'. Tough-minded talk is underpinned by more tender-minded commitments, and this combination gives food for thought about the personal characteristics which contribute to the establishment of classroom authority and enactment of the teacher role.
>
> Although this study is set in the secondary school sector, the classic virtues of the mind, the body and of character are relevant to the practice of teaching in any sector.
>
> How do you stand in relation to the five 'virtues' which Bennett identifies?
>
> *Edited from:* Bennett, T. (2012) *Teacher: Mastering the Art and Craft of Teaching*. London: Continuum, 71–121.

To Aristotle, there were many virtues – of the mind (like intelligence, knowledge and memory), of the body (such as dexterity and strength), and of character (such as courage, forbearance and temperance). It's virtues of character that concern us here – and I identify five below.

Justice

Justice is a vital ingredient in the repertoire of a teacher. Children are HYPERsensitive (original emphasis) to justice – particularly when they inhabit the lighter side of the scales. Funnily enough, kids rarely cry foul when the wheel of fortune lands them on the jackpot.

If you were trying to alienate and annoy children – if you were, for some kamikaze reason, in the mood to see exactly how quickly you could piss the kids off to the point where they refuse to even breathe if you ask them, then simply do this; be arbitrary, be unfair. Treat some as favourites for no discernible reason, and others as enemies with equally random justification. Watch how quickly they start to hate you with a vigour that can actually be weighed by a set of kitchen scales. It won't take long, I promise.

Your ability to provide justice is intrinsically tied in with your role as an adult. Remember that for most children, adults are still seen as the masters of the universe, the law-givers and the magistrates of all that is good and reasonable. Adults are supposed to be fair.

It is an act of appalling betrayal for an adult to be unfair to a child, precisely because it is an attribute so valued by society that we need to encourage it as much as possible. Sure, we can never remedy the intrinsic unfairness of the world, but that's the point – we create communities for mutual benefit, not merely egoism. And if you want children to grow up with a sense of fairness, they have to be treated fairly themselves.

Courage

Now we turn to courage, the virtue of appropriate bravery. Bravery concerned Aristotle very much; he regarded it as being pivotal in a person's character. With this virtue, possessed in correct proportions, all other moral actions were possible. In teaching, as in life, courage is the quality that precedes all others. You can be a tyrant and teach (although I wouldn't advise it), but you cannot be a mouse. The question for any classroom practitioner is; do you have the willpower to say to another human being, I know what is best for you?

Courage is the root and the soil of authority. I have never seen a job where it is so tested, so frequently, as those which involve dealing with the public. And dealing with the children of the public is just as demanding, if not more so.

Classroom life is primarily a battle of wills, make no mistake. You may have very agreeable classes, but you are unlikely to have a class so blissfully helpful that you won't have to bend them to your will at some point. And it is more than likely that you will have to do it a lot.

Patience

Patience, far from being the mousy virtue of the librarian, is closely linked to courage. It describes fortitude under pressure, and the ability to bear intolerable loads with tolerance and calm.

The role of the teacher demands patience because students, being human, don't always show linear progress in their learning. This is because understanding doesn't follow the straight line of graph paper: small mental breakthroughs happen in fits and starts; eureka moments occur in the unlikeliest of environments; effort varies from child to child and from day to day, so that children who have been working at straight Ds all year can suddenly put in a fit of effort towards their exams and leap up to a B.

It also takes a new teacher a long, long time to build up relationships with their class – maybe a year, maybe more or less, depending on the demographic, the rigour of the school, the teacher, and a million other factors. How often have I heard a teacher wail at me, 'I tried the things you advised; detentions, praise, clear boundaries, and they're still acting up.' The teacher is usually talking to me after a few weeks of these methods, oblivious to the fact that such strategies can take months and months and months of time. But they have been trained to expect results that happen as swiftly as sodium dropped into water, buzzes and bubbles. The human character is far less prescribed than that.

Wisdom

Wisdom is far more apparent in demonstration than by definition. Aristotle makes a distinction between theoretical and practical wisdom. Theoretical is the one we could identify with knowledge: to know a lot. Practical wisdom is when we see it put into practice. It is thus far closer to comprehension and understanding than it is to mere memorization. But skills are non-existent without content: to be wise about something is both to know a great deal about it, and to be able to put that knowledge to sound effect. Wisdom is a rational process of evaluating and identifying processes that reach from aims towards successful outcomes. It requires speculation, imagination and creative thinking, and application through practice.

Wisdom in the classroom allows us to understand the bigger picture of what is going on. For example, in my experience, broadly speaking, noisy classes learn less than ones that can be quiet on a regular basis; I base this axiom on the simple truth that being quiet allows one to listen and to think, and to write and to work without distraction. But this is not always the case: some activities require noise; some thrive because of it, like debates or hot-seating. Wisdom is the ability to remember that a noisy class might not be the worst thing in the world; to take a step back and ask oneself, what is the aim of the task I have set these students? And if the answer isn't impeded by the noise they produce, then wisdom asks, is the noise so bad after all? In this context, wisdom is a way of seeing the forest and not focusing on the bark of the trees.

This ability to discern the bigger picture also applies to teacher/student relationships. There is a tension that exists between general rules for everyone to follow and exceptions to those rules depending on circumstances. For example, every decent classroom will have general rules about conduct and behaviour, at least for reference when they are broken. But equally every teacher will be aware of times when exceptions could – or in fact should – be made. The teacher needs to have the wisdom to realize when the greater ends of education are served by enforcing rules and when they are not.

Compassion

The idea that compassion is an important virtue in teaching is simultaneously both obvious and controversial. In the first instance, it is a profession where the wellbeing of others is part of the intrinsic aim of the role. You are there to better the education of the children in your charge, and that is automatically directed towards others. What could be more compassionate than that? Well, for a start teachers haven't always been associated with the engines of delight and charm that we now know them to be; in fact it would be fair to say that until the second half of the twentieth-century, many people's experiences of formal education would have been characterized equally with punishment and discomfort as with cuddles. Indeed, some would say that in order to be a teacher, an adult, an authority and a professional, it is best if one doesn't suffer too much compassion, and that one should treat students with a dispassionate regard for nothing other than their academic wellbeing.

But this is a false dichotomy, for the emotional and intellectual aspects of compassion will always exist together. The key question for teachers is this: how do you balance them?

Compassion is important because, whilst learning can be enormous fun, it can also be enormously dry. Those who say that all learning and all lessons must engage or entertain are, to be honest, a bit simple. I regard them as well-meaning but essentially quite stupid.

The teacher's job is to direct the children through education; to teach them the best that we have learned so far, to enable them to exceed us, to exceed even themselves. But it isn't always enjoyable. And it is perfectly normal for a child at times to resist the delights of the classroom. In other words, sometimes some children won't enjoy doing as they're told. I do hope this isn't a shock. But as teachers, our job, our duty is to consider the long-term interests of the child even if they themselves do not perceive the benefit.

Engagement
How are we managing behaviour?

7

The readings in this chapter are concerned with the particular issue of managing behaviour. The key message here is that although it is important to develop a range of engaging strategies (including those which are assertive), in principle good behaviour is best achieved by engaging students constructively and with respect for them as unique human beings.

Doyle (7.1) analyses the complexity of classrooms and the challenges of teacher decision-making. Cowley (7.2) offers ten practical strategies which she suggests should make a difference in achieving good behaviour. Chaplain (7.3) rehearses the ways in which rules, routines and rituals can be used to establish authority and maintain a positive learning environment. Duckworth (7.4) illustrates how the behaviour of adult Basic Skills learners can prove to be a challenge in the classroom. This set of readings offers a wealth of practical ideas for managing behaviour.

The parallel chapter in *Reflective Teaching in Further, Adult and Vocational Education* has sections on understanding classroom behaviour, establishing authority, engaging students, managing challenging behaviour and dealing with difficult episodes and incidents. It concludes with 'Key Readings' suggestions and signals additional sources of support.

Supplementary materials are also available on *reflectiveteaching.co.uk*. These include 'Reflective Activities', 'Notes for Further Reading', a compendium and links to further sources.

Reading: 7.1

Learning the classroom environment

Walter Doyle

This reading from Doyle highlights some of the reasons why classroom teaching is so difficult to do well, and gives some useful pointers to making it easier. In his view, classroom environments are highly complex and events often unfold simultaneously in ways which cannot be foreseen. Doyle believes that teachers develop strategies and skills for reducing some of this complexity, and identifies five ways in which this is done.

Does your classroom sometimes feel complex in the ways which Doyle describes? How helpful are the skills which he suggests?

Edited from: Doyle, W. (1977) 'Learning the classroom environment: An ecological analysis', *Journal of Teacher Education,* XXVIII (6), 51–4.

Deliberation about the nature of teaching skills has generally centred on the teacher's ability to manage subject matter – to explain content, formulate questions, and react to student answers. Naturalistic studies of classrooms suggest, however, that knowing how to manage subject matter sequences represents only a small part of the skill necessary to be a teacher.

Salient features of classrooms

The most salient features of the classroom for the student teachers in my study were multidimensionality, simultaneity and unpredictability. The following brief discussion of these categories will clarify the nature of environmental demands in classrooms.

Classrooms were multidimensional in the sense that they served a variety of purposes and contained a variety of events and processes, not all of which were necessarily related or even compatible. In classrooms, student teachers confronted groups with a wide range of interests and abilities as well as a diversity of goals and patterns of behaviour. In addition, they faced a multiplicity of tasks that included such matters as processing subject matter information, judging student abilities, managing classroom groups, coping with emotional responses to events and behaviours, and establishing procedures for routine and special assignment, distribution of resources and supplies, record keeping, etc. These tasks also interacted in the sense that ways of dealing with one dimension (e.g. distributing resources and supplies) had consequences for other dimensions (e.g. managing classroom groups) and in the sense that procedures at one point established a precedent that restricted options at a later time It was not uncommon to find student teachers initially over-whelmed to some degree by the sheer quantity of activities, many of which were seen to interfere with their primary interest in managing subject matter.

In addition to the quantity of dimensions in classrooms, many events occurred simultaneously. In a discussion, for instance, teachers needed to attend to the pace of the interaction, the sequence of student responses, fairness in selecting students to answer, the quality of individual answers and their relevance to the purposes of the discussion, and the logic and accuracy of content while at the same time monitoring a wide range of work involvement levels and anticipating interruptions. While giving assistance to individual students, teachers also had to remember to scan the rest of the class for signs of possible misbehaviour or to acknowledge other students who were requesting assistance. Examples such as these can be easily multiplied for nearly any set of classroom activities.

The simultaneous occurrence of multiple events, together with the continuous possibility of internal and external interruptions, contributed to an unpredictability in the sequence of classroom events, especially for student teachers who had not yet learned to anticipate consequences. Student teachers often found it difficult to predict student reactions to a set of materials or to judge how much time it would take to complete an activity. They were also frequently frustrated by changes in the normal schedule, breakdowns in equipment, and interruptions. The fact that classrooms can go in many different directions at any given point in time often complicated the task of enacting lesson plans in intended ways.

Strategies and skills for reducing complexity

Analysis of induction sequences indicated that all teachers developed strategies that could be interpreted as attempts to reduce the complexity of the classroom environment. There appeared to be considerable variations, however, in the success of different strategies.

In cases labelled 'unsuccessful', student teachers appeared to attempt to reduce classroom complexity by ignoring the multiplicity and simultaneity of the environment. In many instances, this method of reducing complexity involved (a) localizing attention to one region of the classroom; and (b) being engrossed in one activity at a time.

Successful strategies tended to be more congruent with the multiplicity and simultaneity of the environment. A preliminary attempt to codify these skills produced the following categories:

Chunking, or the ability to group discrete events into large units;

Differentiation, or the ability to discriminate among units in terms of their immediate and long-term significance;

Overlap, or the ability to handle two or more events at once;

Timing, or the ability to monitor and control the duration of events; and

Rapid judgement, or the ability to interpret events with a minimum of delay.

Discussions with cooperating teachers during the three-year course of the present research suggested that these categories represent a part of the tacit knowledge experienced teachers have about the way classrooms work.

The first two skills, chunking and differentiation, suggest that student teachers undergo a concept formation process during which they learn to classify and interpret classroom events and processes in ways that are relevant to the demands created by multi-dimensionality, simultaneity, and unpredictability. In describing pupils, for instance, successful student teachers tended to classify individuals in terms of their potential for disruption, skills in classroom tasks, inclinations to participate in lesson activities, etc. They seemed to know that the movement of some students around the room to secure supplied or sharpen pencils could be ignored whereas the movement of other students required careful monitoring. Similarly, successful teachers learned to judge content in terms of how students would react to it and how difficult it would be to implement in the classroom, in contrast to those who retained purely academic criteria for content adequacy. In sum, successful student teachers transformed the complexity of the environment into a conceptual system that enabled them to interpret discrete events and anticipate the direction and flow of classroom activity. In addition they learned to make rapid judgments about the meaning and consequences of events and to act decisively.

The skills of overlap and timing supplement the interpretive strategies of chunking, differentiation, and rapid judgment in ways that enable successful student teachers to regulate classroom demands to some degree. The need for overlap was a continuing condition in classrooms. Successful teachers were able to divide attention between several simultaneous dimensions of classroom activity structures. They were also easily distracted by changes in sound or movement in the classroom. Hence they were in a position to react to developing circumstances as necessary. During the course of the observations, timing also emerged as an especially salient skill for managing classroom demands, one that operated on several levels. It was apparent, for example, that timing was related to the effectiveness of directives to individual students (e.g. 'Stop talking and get back to work!'). Successful managers tended to pause and continue to gaze at the target student for a brief period after issuing such a directive. The target student typically returned to work immediately after receiving the directive, but looked up again in one or two seconds. If the teacher was still monitoring the student, there was a greater likelihood that the directive would be followed. Unsuccessful managers, on the other hand, tended to issue directives and continue on as if compliance had been achieved. Over time, this latter pattern seemed to result in directives being ignored and, therefore, reappeared more frequently with less effect.

Reading 7.2

Ten strategies for managing behaviour

Sue Cowley

Sue Cowley's books, despite their provocative titles, contain a great deal of grounded and educationally effective advice on classroom practice. In this illustrative reading, as she explains: 'Controlling a large group of people is difficult in any situation, but when some of your students have no wish to be in school, let alone in your lesson, life can become very difficult indeed. The ten strategies described below are relatively easy to apply, and should cost you little in the way of stress.'

Might some of these strategies work for you?

Edited from: Cowley, S. (2010) *Getting the Buggers to Behave.* London: Continuum, 39–53.

1. Learn to 'read and respond'

You can hype up a class, and equally you can calm it down. Sometimes you'll catch yourself getting the students overexcited, and you'll automatically take measures to bring down the excitement levels. This effect is particularly vivid with young children: even the way your voice sounds is enough to get some classes hyped up. You can also have exactly the same effect on individual students, particularly when you are dealing with their behaviour.

The ability to 'read and respond' to a class or an individual, by adapting what you do instantly, is a subtle skill to learn. It comes more easily with experience, and also as you get to know your class and the people within it. To 'read and respond', you need to: make on-the-spot judgements during the lesson; base these judgements both on how students are responding to the activities that you're doing, and also on how your approaches to behaviour are working; adapt or even throw away a lesson activity if it's not working; change your behaviour management techniques if necessary; be particularly flexible on days when there are already high levels of tension in the class or with particular individuals.

2. Wait for silence

Waiting for silence is one of the most important techniques a teacher can use to encourage and enhance learning. When I say 'wait for silence', I don't mean get your students silent and then talk at them endlessly. What I mean is when you need to talk to the whole class you should not address the students until they are completely silent and fully focused on you (or on whoever is speaking). This applies at the start of the day or lesson, for instance when taking the register, and also at any time when you wish to talk to the class (whatever age the students are). When you get silent attention you send a clear message: the learning is important and you will not allow it to be jeopardized.

In your quest to get silence, it is better to use non-verbal, rather than verbal, techniques.

These create less stress for you and add less noise to your classroom. They also give a sense of control and confidence.

Talk about your expectation of silent attention in your first lesson with a class. Get them thinking about why this boundary is so important. Model the behaviour you're after – listen really carefully to your students when they are talking, and try never to talk over a class.

3. Make use of cues

A lot of teacher stress is caused by fairly low-level misbehaviour. The idea behind the use of cues is to get the students doing the behaviour you do want, rather than letting them behave incorrectly first, and then having to tell them off. You can use cues for any behaviour that is repeated regularly, and they can be verbal or non-verbal. Cues often change over time, becoming a form of shorthand understood by all.

Take, for example, 'answering questions'. Start any whole-class question with the phrase: 'Put your hand up if you can tell me …'. By specifying the behaviour you want (hands up), you anticipate and overcome the incorrect response (calling out). This can gradually be abbreviated to 'Hands up' or just a slight raise of your hand.

4. Give them 'the choice'

We cannot actually force our students to behave – we can only make it seem like the best of all possible options. Ideally, we want them to take responsibility for their own actions, and for the consequences of those actions. This is important in creating a positive and effective environment for learning. It is also vital in setting people up for their lives beyond education, when the choices they make about behaviour become potentially that much more crucial.

This is where the technique of 'the choice' comes in. There are essentially two choices: either the students do as you ask, or they accept the consequences of a refusal to comply. You want to get on with teaching and learning – if their behaviour makes that impossible, you utilize the rules of the organization to impose a consequence. This is only fair on the majority who do want to learn. If we make the choices and consequences simple and clear enough, this can prevent misbehaviour occurring or escalating. It also encourages students to consider and change their negative behaviours, to avoid unwelcome consequences in the future.

'The choice' helps you depersonalize a range of tricky situations, because it puts responsibility in the hands of the student. It is up to her to decide how she wishes to behave, and which consequences she is willing to receive. Your role is that of 'police officer' – applying the code of conduct of the place where you work. When using 'the choice': state the behaviour you require; make clear the positive benefits of doing as you ask; make clear the consequences of refusing to comply; give the student a short time to consider her decision. If she decides not to comply, apply the consequences. Aim to sound disappointed, rather than vengeful when doing this.

5. Be reasonable, but don't reason with them

So long as you are reasonable with your students, and you don't have unrealistic expectations about how they will work or behave, then there is no need to actually reason with

them over what you do ask them to do. Here are some examples of how this might work with different age groups:

Early years: It's perfectly reasonable to insist they don't paint on the walls. So long as you don't get cross about the odd splash on the floor.

Primary: It's perfectly reasonable to have silence to explain an activity. So long as you don't take 15 minutes to explain it.

Secondary: It's perfectly reasonable to ask students to write in silence. So long as you don't expect them to write for hours at a time.

The 'being reasonable' part of the equation is tricky to manage – you need to make difficult decisions about the right balance to strike. Set high standards, and expect the very best, but be realistic as well. If you are too authoritarian with your demands, then confrontations and difficulties will arise. Similarly, if you're too relaxed, students will take advantage.

6. Use statements, not questions, and assume compliance

Learn to use statements about what you want in relation to behaviour. This is much more helpful than questioning student actions – you state what they should be doing, rather than complaining about what they are not. It also gives the impression of someone who knows what she wants, and who has confidence that the children will comply.

Here are a few examples of questions, and how they might be rephrased as statements:

'Why aren't you doing the work?' becomes 'I want you to get on with the activity now, so you can leave on time.'

'Why are you being so silly?' becomes 'I want you to sit properly on your chair and focus on the learning, thanks.'

'Why aren't you listening?' becomes 'Everyone looking this way and listening in silence, thanks.'

When you're making these positive statements about what you want, you can also use a technique called 'assumed compliance'. All that is meant by this term is that you say 'thanks' (you assume they'll do it) rather than 'please' (you're hoping they will). If you use these two techniques simultaneously, it gives the added benefit of making you sound like a teacher who is very positive, certain and confident about getting what she wants.

7. Use repetition

Much of the time, when we say something, we expect it to be heard and understood the first time around. This is not necessarily a sensible expectation to have, and it can lead to unnecessary misunderstandings and confrontations. Classrooms and other teaching spaces can be noisy and confusing places for our students: there might be many different reasons why they do not respond immediately to your directions. Here are some of the times when you might usefully use repetition with your students: to get their attention before you give an instruction; to ensure they are listening if you need to warn them about a potential sanction; because they might not hear your instructions the first time you give them; to clarify any possible misunderstandings and make your wishes perfectly clear; to reinforce your instructions and make it clear that they must be followed.

8. Set targets and time limits

Learning always works best when you've got clear objectives – a specific target at which to aim. Targets can help you harness our natural sense of competition: perhaps against others, but more importantly against our own previous best. Having a clear amount to achieve, within a set time frame, helps create a sense of urgency and pace to the work. It gives a clear structure – something definite towards which the students can work. Targets also help your less able children feel a sense of achievement. When the teacher asks the class to work in groups to find five ideas in 3 minutes, even the least able should be able to contribute to this task. You might use a whole range of different targets: a target for how many words or answers the students must complete; a time for completing the activity; a target for improving behaviour, such as staying in seats. When setting targets, use the following tips to help you get it right: make sure your targets suit the students; keep targets short and specific for maximum impact; add visual prompts to aid understanding; use your voice, or even some music, to create a sense of pace and urgency; use language to enhance your students' motivation levels: words such as 'competition', 'prize' and 'challenge'; make sure any rewards offered for completion of targets are ones that really appeal to the group or the individual.

9. Use humour

Humour is incredibly powerful in the classroom. Teachers who make their students laugh, and who can laugh with them when appropriate, inevitably form good relationships with their classes. Of course there are times when you can't see the funny side. On a Monday morning/Friday afternoon, when you're tired, hungover, getting a cold or are just plain cranky, you might not feel in the mood for a stand-up comedy routine. But if you can take a fun approach to the job, and make the work and the lessons seem like light relief, this will definitely help you to manage behaviour.

Alongside its beneficial effects on your students, humour: offers a respite from the tension that can build up in a poorly behaved class; makes your work fun for yourself and your students; helps you stay relaxed and rational; helps you avoid defensiveness.

Use humour to dissipate the threat of low-level personal insults: be clear that you refuse to take this kind of stuff seriously and your students will soon give up on doing this. With older students, you can turn an insult on its head by agreeing with what the student has said. So, if a student says, 'Your hair looks really stupid like that, Miss', you might answer (deadpan), 'Yes, I know, I'm planning to sue my hairdresser'. Learn to laugh at yourself when you make a mistake, for instance tripping over or saying something daft. Students love a teacher who is willing to be self-deprecating. It's a good way of undermining the image of teacher as authoritarian figure, and it shows that you don't take yourself too seriously.

10. Put yourself in their shoes

When you're dealing with persistent misbehaviour, it is easy to lose your sense of perspective. You may begin to feel that students are deliberately being awkward, and even that they have a personal vendetta against you. In turn, this leads to overreactions to what is actually relatively minor misbehaviour.

Develop the ability to step outside yourself, and to view what happens from your students' perspective. Become a reflective teacher, constantly engaged in a process of self-analysis. This in turn will feed into every aspect of your practice.

When an activity doesn't seem to be working, or the students start misbehaving, put yourself in their shoes to try to work out why: is there too much listening and not enough doing? Is the concept too hard for the class to grasp? Do the students find this particular topic area boring? Is this work too easy for the group?

Sometimes you can't do much about the situation – they have to get through a particularly tough bit of learning. But at least if you put yourself in their shoes, you can understand why they might fidget. Similarly, you can analyse your own teaching by using this approach. If your students often become confrontational with you when you try to discipline them, step back and view the way that you deal with behaviour from the outside. Are you saying or doing something to exacerbate the situation? Are there external factors at work?

Reading 7.3

Rules, routines and rituals in behaviour management

Roland Chaplain

> This reading combines the knowledge of a social psychologist with the expertise of a classroom practitioner. While facing the need for the teacher to 'be in charge', Chaplain shows how careful use of rules, routines and rituals can contribute enormously to creating a positive environment for learning. He draws attention to the nesting of classroom behaviour policies within those of the school.
>
> Although this reading is written in a school context, it is easy to see how the rules, routines and rituals advocated by Chaplain could be adopted to FAVE contexts.
>
> Is there any scope for the further development of rules, routines or rituals to help in achieving your classroom goals?
>
> *Edited from:* Chaplain, R. (2003) *Teaching Without Disruption in the Primary School.* New York: Routledge, 140–55; also in *Teaching Without Disruption in the Secondary School.* New York: Routledge.

In the classroom, the teacher should be in charge.

Rules

Intelligently constructed rules can help establish teacher control and facilitate learning, provided that their meaning is clear, they are supported by the relevant rewards and sanctions, and the teacher behaves assertively. The main function of classroom rules is to set limits to pupils' behaviour and to make them aware of the conditions required for success. They operate in a preventative or feed forward way to establish and maintain order and momentum. This does not mean pupils are not treated warmly or that humour, developing relationships and mutual respect are also not important. Indeed, a principal objective of having rules is to create a safe and warm environment through making clear what the teacher values as important to ensure pupils' success and to develop positive working relationships.

Rules operate at both the classroom and whole-school levels, the latter representing the core behavioural expectations for the school to provide consistency and predictability for both staff and pupils.

Classroom rules should focus on making a classroom safe, keeping pupils on legitimate tasks and promoting appropriate social behaviour.

Rules to avoid the dangers of running in class, messing about in science lessons, or not checking gym equipment before it's used, are clearly necessary and need little, if any, qualification. In addition to physical safety, rules provide psychological safety at both cognitive and emotional levels. Disruption in class interferes with the learning process in various ways; cognitively by disturbing concentration and attention and emotionally by making people feel anxious or worried.

A teacher's behaviour towards a class will support pupils' needs, changing its emphasis from early encounters to later in the school year. Early stages focus on defining expectations and boundaries and involve relatively high levels of direction, whereas in later stages, pupils are given differentiated levels of responsibility and diversity in learning experiences, informed by performance feedback. In such ways, in addition to signalling the rights and responsibilities of pupils, rules help to create the conditions for learning (Rudduck et al., 1996).

To have a set of rules to cover all possible situations would result in a rather long unmemorable and unmanageable list, so the number of rules should be kept to a minimum. I recommend a maximum of five simply worded and easy to remember rules. Hargreaves et al. (1975) recommended five types of rules which relate to: movement; talking; time; teacher-pupil relationships; and pupil-pupil relationships. There are clear overlaps between the different types.

Five basic principles to consider when deciding how to develop rules are:

1 keep 'em positive. The wording of a rule can make or break it. Rules should reflect what you value and want to encourage in your classroom.

2 keep 'em brief. Rules should include only key concerns. Make sure they are kept brief and snappy as this makes them easier to remember.

3 keep 'em realistic. Set rules which reflect expectations that are appropriate and achievable by you or the class.

4 keep 'em focused. The overall objective for having rules is self-regulation. Rules should concentrate on key issues, including being aware of personal safety and the safety of others; consideration of others; cooperation; honesty; friendliness; as well as attending to legitimate classroom activity and maintaining appropriate nose levels for specific contexts.

5 keep 'em. If the rule is worth having in the first place, then it needs to be regularly reinforced. If you find it is not working or has lost its relevance, then either modify it or drop it. Do not make rules ineffective by applying them one minute and letting them slide the next.

Rules supported by rewards and sanctions, which demonstrate clear cause and effect relationships, remove ambiguity for staff and pupils. Sanctions should be predictable and hierarchical. 'Fuzzy' sanctions or threats which are not carried through are a waste of time. Being clear about what sanctions are available in school and which are appropriate for particular types of misdemeanour, how they are organised and who has the authority to issue and carry them through, helps to remove ambiguity and allows both teacher and class to focus on the task in hand – that is, teaching and learning.

Routines

Routines are used to manage everyday social behaviour around school and in class, as well as supporting teaching and learning. They are often organised around a particular time (such as the start of a lesson, for example), a place (classroom) or context (group work). Their object is to add meaning to rules and to translate their spirit into action. If being polite is an important rule, then the routines established for greeting pupils and staff when they arrive in school or class, how equipment is shared and empowering people to have their thoughts and feelings heard should reflect this. If not disturbing other pupils while working is a rule, then a routine for checking or marking pupils' work, distributing materials and moving around the classroom should ensure that disruption to pupils is minimalised. Well thought-out and communicated routines facilitate the smooth running of lessons, keeping pupils on-task and maintaining the efficient and well-ordered operation of your classroom.

Some routines operate at the school level (lunchtime, assemblies), others at the classroom level (getting work out, changing activities). There are a great many routines roughly similar to all schools, whilst others vary significantly between schools to reflect different cultures and contexts, as well as the values and beliefs of those responsible for running the schools. Common routines include those used to control movement around the school, entering classrooms, getting work out, issuing materials, asking questions, putting things away and so on.

Particular teachers and subjects require different routines. Non-teaching activities such as getting pupils ready to learn, distributing materials and marking work, whilst necessary, can take up substantial amounts of teaching time, but well thought-out routines can streamline these activities, increasing the time available for learning.

Efficient routines thus provide teachers with more time to teach, and pupils with more time to learn. Spending time planning and reviewing routines beforehand pays dividends, since it provides pupils with a sense of organisation and order. Experienced teachers spend considerable time in their early encounters with pupils teaching them routines. This is not to suggest that routines are only important in early encounters; spending time establishing and practising routines results in them becoming automatic and triggered by simple ritualised behaviours – clapping hands, a stare, or folding arms, for example.

Rituals

Rituals also offer a very powerful form of demonstrating authority to all members of the school community. They give shape to, and facilitate, the smooth running of the school day. A ritual, such as assembly, requires participants to behave in a formalised way and includes particular actions, words and movements. It involves a series of routines occurring in a particular sequence. How pupils enter assembly often reflects how they are expected to enter other formal areas, such as classrooms. There may be modifications to give the assembly more status, such as playing music when people enter. The rules about who is expected, or permitted, to speak, and in what order, is usually fairly easily understood. These routines and procedures are usually learnt at first by instruction and prompting, and later by internalising the various routines involved.

Rituals also provide a sense of community and social identity, incorporating feelings of belonging and security which can be emotionally uplifting and within which personal development can take place. Assemblies are events which promote the social identity of the school and are used as a vehicle for reminding pupils of what is valued – for example, giving prizes for positive behaviour or publicly admonishing unacceptable behaviour. Similar processes operate in the classroom, but with less formality.

In the classroom, a rule (respecting others, for example) will be supported with routines (in this example, pupils raising their hands before asking questions) and is often triggered by a teacher's ritual of moving to a particular place or through the use of a gesture (such as a raised finger to forewarn an individual eager to shout out an answer). Other rituals include standing or sitting in particular places in the classroom and clapping hands or folding arms in order to elicit particular behaviour such as gaining attention.

Reading 7.4

Violence in the learning trajectories of Basic Skills learners and the implications of this in shaping the curriculum

Vicky Duckworth

In this extract Duckworth draws upon her experience of living and working with learners from disadvantaged backgrounds, and argues that the notion of neo-liberalism and its implication that an individual is free to determine their own pathway is limited by the impact of structural and historical inequalities: gender, race and class, and other markers of identity that shape the learners' educational journeys. One way in which this happens is that learners from disadvantaged backgrounds are not considered to have the right attributes to progress. The following reading focuses on issues from the study which asks 'why' and 'how' structures of inequality and domination are reproduced across the public and private domains of the learners' lives.

Edited from: Duckworth, V. (2013) *Learning Trajectories, Violence and Empowerment Amongst Adult Basic Skills Learners.* Monograph: Educational Research. Routledge: London.

Overview

On exploring the learning journeys of sixteen of my former adult Basic Skills learners, from the first arrival at college there was a strong feeling that, mirroring their experiences at school, they would be judged by teachers and peers as 'no hopers'. There was also a link between what they considered their 'poor' literacy skills and viewing themselves as childlike because of that. This is hardly surprising when in all aspects of society including entering learning, Basic Skills learners are labelled as lacking and in many case put to the bottommost of the list when it comes to the hierarchy of employment and courses offered in college. Further to this, the dominant discourse that runs through Adult Education (like that of compulsory education) is often constructed on a deficit model which positions the learners as lacking in relation to what are widely deemed as the norms of literacy.

This learner marginality relates to the dynamics of symbolic violence (Bourdieu, 1991). The concept of symbolic violence offers a structure to explore how education is part of symbolic process of cultural and social reproduction (Bourdieu and Passeron, 1977), put simply rather than eliminating social inequality which education advocates, it cements it more into society. For example, schools and colleges appear to be neutral, but the cultural capital a middle class learner brings from home (literacy practices, books, music lesson, visits to theatre etc) to achieve success in gaining qualifications can be seen as 'natural' rather than the result of them transferring this 'inherited' cultural capital into the academic success of 'qualifications' and cultural capital. This lack of recognition is how symbolic violence maintains its effect. However, it is important to note that symbolic violence is as real and harmful as any other form of violence.

As such it is important to be aware that learners' histories and biographies in the private (for example, home and family) and public (for example, education and work) domains of their life can impact on their learning environments. Teachers' awareness and sensitivity to the issues, including the physical and symbolic violence learners bring into the classroom and the development of approaches for dealing with them effectively is important if the barriers are to be addressed. This may entail therapeutic interventions for those who are most vulnerable such as those with mental health issues and/or physical disabilities. Indeed, literacy education has been shown to enhance confidence, contribute to social and political participation and lead to benefits in the public and private domains of learners' lives.

So what can be done?

The participatory action research facilitated the development and delivery of a critical curriculum. It allowed me to address the conflict for basic skills tutors between enacting the dominant ideologies of individualism and exploring the structural inequalities which have impacted on the learners' lives, so they can challenge these inequalities. To explore these structural inequalities, it required that I had not only a theoretical framework to explore and explain them, but also an alternative pedagogical approach.

So what?

I suggest that a way to challenge an instrumental curriculum is to move towards a *caring, critical, co-construction model* (CCCM) based on a social approach (Duckworth, 2014). Social approaches to literacy are sometimes grouped together under the remit of the New Literacy Studies (Barton, 1994; Barton and Hamilton, 1998; Gee, 1996; Street, 1984). Within this complex view of the nature of literacy we can highlight that literacy has many purposes for the learner. It challenges the dominance of the autonomous model, and recognises how literacy practices vary from one cultural and historical context to another. For example, in the private domain of home and public domain of formal education, literacy practices, identities and discourse are produced by power and ideology so that literacy is shaped differently in different contexts. This focus can support tutors to shift from a narrow competency based approach, which separates the literacies from their context and instead harness the everyday practices learners bring into the classroom. Providing a curriculum which is culturally relevant, learner driven and socially empowering (Freire, 1993; Barton et al., 2004, Duckworth, 2013, 14) can offer the opportunity to challenge symbolic violence and promote dialogic communication between the teacher and the learners to actively involve them in their own education and co-creation of the curriculum whereby their needs, motivations and interests are the driving factors (see McNamara, 2007; Duckworth, 2008; Johnson et al., 2010; Thomas et al., 2012).

Within my classroom the learners' lives, dreams and experiences were embedded into the curriculum using their narratives and poetry etc. This allowed the sharing of obstacles and solutions to overcome them. In this capacity the narratives are themselves a real capital which can be pulled on by others to inspire and offer strategies to move forward. This also acknowledged and valued their experiences, challenging and replacing the negative labels, where they blamed themselves for being 'thick' and 'stupid' because they struggled in literacies with the development of new, shared knowledge where they were able to see the inequalities and violence in their lives this had stemmed from and challenge it.

Joanne's story

When Joanne, a single mum with three children, arrived at college, she struggled to read and write. Having worked as a machinist in a factory, the breakup of her relationship had been the catalyst to her returning to education. Initially she sat at the back of the class, lacking confidence and avoiding eye contact. However, after Joanne joined the research group, we began to spend more time together. This allowed me the opportunity to speak to Joanne in detail about the barriers she had faced and her hopes and aspirations for the future. Initially, she described why she had come to college:

> *I want to be able to fill in forms on me own and be more confident in me spelling.*

As Joanne's confidence increased in both herself and her writing skills, there was a simultaneous shift in aspirations. We spoke of the pathways she could take following Level Two. This was the first time she had planned for the future. She began to make choices that she previously thought were deemed as not for people from her background. She began to speak about a career rather than a job, describing how:

> *"I want to be a good role model for my children, getting a career can give us all a better future" she said, with a determination and optimism.*

Joanne was breaking down the barriers that had held her back for so long and was now on her way – successfully completing a level two course in Literacy and Numeracy; she progressed onto an Access to Nursing Course then to University to pass her diploma and is now a qualified staff nurse working in the north of England. The transformation of her aspiration and her life impacted on her children's progression and the transformation in the dynamics of the family. She no longer felt childlike but empowered to support her children. Their grades improved and Joanne felt much more confident and valued in her role as a mother (McNamara, 2008).

And now what?

Adult education needs to dis-entangle itself from neoliberal fusion to create space for contextualised and emancipatory learning. However, the potential for resistance and counter hegemonic practice remains a challenge to teachers. Teachers need to be aware of how their beliefs and practices may be inclined by perceptions of learners' ability tied to class, gender and ethnicity and to challenge the reproductive tendencies these perceptions involve. Teachers can use diversity positively to enhance the learning experience of individuals and the group, rather than seeking to normalise and elide difference (Duckworth, 2014). Adult education, including informal and formal education; literacy, language and numeracy can offer learners a better chance of acquiring the tools needed to run their own lives; empowering them and their local and wider community. And it is by working together as practitioners, policy makers, researchers and learners that we can build a better society for all, and not just the privileged few, based on justice, equality and hope for the future.

Spaces
How are we creating environments for learning?

The readings in this chapter are intended to help with understanding class-rooms as learning environments. Bransford et al. (8.1) summarize much accumulated knowledge when they advise that learning environments should focus upon learners' knowledge, assessment and community. Edwards (8.2) introduces the concept of affordance to highlight the potential uses to which resources can be put and illustrates this in relation to the affordances of ICT. Kress (8.3) illustrates the importance of an ecological analysis in reviewing the impact of the 'digital revolution' upon schools. This discussion can quite easily be extended to experiences in FAVE contexts. In the contemporary world we now experience multimodal forms of communication and design which afford radically new learning experiences and challenge traditional curricula and teaching methods. Biesta and James (8.4) focus upon the ways in which learning cultures in FAVE contexts might be transformed and how, through such transformations, learning might be improved.

The parallel chapter in *Reflective Teaching in Further, Adult and Vocational Education* addresses similar issues and suggests activities to increase the effec-tiveness of classroom organization. The first section discusses learning environ-ments formal and informal and in a variety of FAVE contexts. We then focus on the use of space, resources and time. Section 3 of this chapter is concerned with the use of technology for learning. Finally in Section 4 the emphasis is upon the management of students and other learning support assistants.

The emphasis throughout is on achieving coherence between learning aims and the way in which the learning is organized and then working towards consistency between the various organizational elements. The chapter concludes with suggestions of 'Key Readings'. In addition, *reflectiveteaching. co.uk* also offers many further ideas and activities.

Reading 8.1

Designs for learning environments
John Bransford, Ann Brown and Rodney Cocking

This is a second reading from a classic US review of contemporary knowledge on learning (see also **Reading 4.1**). In this case, the focus is on the design of learning environments. The four characteristics identified, with central foci on learners, knowledge, assessment and community, have been much cited.

What implications, in your view, does this analysis of effective learning environments have for practice?

Edited from: Bransford, J. D., Brown, A. L. and Cocking, R. R. (1999) *How People Learn: Brain, Mind, Experience and School.* Washington, DC: National Academy Press, xvi–xix.

Theoretical physics does not prescribe the design of a bridge, but surely it constrains the design of successful ones. Similarly learning theory provides no simple recipe for designing effective learning environments, but it constrains the design of effective ones. New research raises important questions about the design of learning environments – questions that suggest the value of rethinking what is taught, how it is taught, and how it is assessed.

A fundamental tenet of modern learning theory is that different kinds of learning goals require different approaches to instruction; new goals for education require changes in opportunities to learn. The design of learning environments is linked to issues that are especially important in the processes of learning, transfer and competent performance. These processes, in turn, are affected by the degree to which learning environments are student centred, assessment centred, and community centred.

We propose four key characteristics of effective learning environments:

Learner-centred environments
Effective instruction begins with what learners bring to the setting: this includes cultural practices and beliefs, as well as knowledge of academic content. A focus on the degree to which environments are learner centred is consistent with the evidence showing that learners use their current knowledge to construct new knowledge and that what they know and believe at the moment affects how they interpret new information. Sometimes learners' current knowledge supports new learning; sometimes it hampers learning.

People may have acquired knowledge yet fail to activate it in a particular setting. Learner-centred environments attempt to help students make connections between their previous knowledge and their current academic tasks. Parents are especially good at helping their children make connections. Teachers have a harder time because they do not share the life experiences of all their students, so they have to become familiar with each student's special interests and strengths.

Knowledge-centred environments

The ability to think and solve problems requires knowledge that is accessible and applied appropriately. An emphasis on knowledge-centred instruction raises a number of questions, such as the degree to which instruction focuses on ways to help students use their current knowledge and skills. New knowledge about early learning suggests that young students are capable of grasping more complex concepts than was believed previously. However, these concepts must be presented in ways that are developmentally appropriate by linking learning to their current understanding. A knowledge centred perspective on learning environments highlights the importance of thinking about designs for curricula. To what extent do they help students learn with understanding versus promote the acquisition of disconnected sets of facts and skills? Curricula that are a "mile wide and an inch deep" run the risk of developing disconnected rather than connected knowledge.

Assessment to support learning

Issues of assessment also represent an important perspective for viewing the design of learning environments. Feedback is fundamental to learning, but feedback opportunities are often scarce in classrooms. Students may receive grades on tests and essays, but these are summative assessments that occur at the end of projects. What are needed are formative assessments, which provide students with opportunities to revise and improve the quality of their thinking and understanding. Assessments must reflect the learning goals that define various environments. If the goal is to enhance understanding and applicability of knowledge, it is not sufficient to provide assessments that focus primarily on memory for facts and formulas.

Community-centred environments

The fourth, important perspective on learning environments is the degree to which they promote a sense of community. Students, teachers, and other interested participants share norms that value learning and high standards. Norms such as these increase people's opportunities and motivation to interact, receive feedback, and learn. The importance of connected communities becomes clear when one examines the relatively small amount of time spent in school compared to other settings. Activities in homes, community centres, and after-school clubs can have important effects on students' academic achievement.

New technologies

A number of the features of new technologies are also consistent with the principles of a new science of learning.

Key conclusions:

- Because many new technologies are interactive, it is now easier to create environments in which students can learn by doing, receive feedback, and continually refine their understanding and build new knowledge.

- Technologies can help people visualise difficult-to-understand concepts, such as differentiating heat from temperature. Students are able to work with visualisation and modelling software similar to the tools used in nonschool environments to increase their conceptual understanding and the likelihood of transfer from school to nonschool settings.

- New technologies provide access to a vast array of information, including digital libraries, real world data for analysis, and connections to other people who provide information, feedback, and inspiration, all of which can enhance the learning of teachers and administrators as well as students

There are many ways that technology can be used to help create such environments, both for teachers and for the students whom they teach. However, many issues arise in considering how to educate teachers to use new technologies effectively. What do they need to know about learning processes? About the technology? What kinds of training are most effective for helping teachers use high-quality instructional programs? What if the software and teacher-support tools, developed with full understanding of principles of learning, have not yet become the norm?

Reading 8.2

Environment, affordance and new technology
Anthony Edwards

The concept of 'affordance' is a powerful idea in relation to classroom provision and practice. It refers to the potential uses of something (perhaps maths equipment, art materials or a new software program), and to the activities which such potential uses make possible. The term invites teachers to consider the environment of their classrooms and the available resources, and to reflect creatively on possibilities and constraints for teaching and learning activities. Affordance is often used in discussion of software, and the reading describes a taxonomy of ICT affordances.

What are the main affordances of your working environment, and what others might be developed?

Edited from: Edwards, A. (2012) *New Technology and Education*. London: Continuum, 86–8.

The theory of affordances was first developed by the American psychologist James Gibson (1904–79) as a result of work he did with pilots during the Second World War on the depth of perception. He argued that there are features of the environment 'that afford (i.e. enable) perception and action in that environment'.

> *They are not constructed by the person. They exist independently in the environment, and are discovered rather that constructed by the actor. Thus, a rigid surface stretching to the horizon under our feet affords locomotion; an object of a certain size affords grasping and so on.* (Boyle et al., 2004: 296)

Affordances, therefore, are the perceived 'and actual properties of a thing, primarily those functional properties that determine just how a thing could possibly be used' (Salmon, 1993: 51).

Wertsch (1998) applied Gibson's theory to digital technologies. He regarded the computer as a tool that amplified opportunities to combine physical with symbolic forms of action. This interchange often reflects complex thought processes that are dependent on both the learning environment and the capability for action of the learner.

Teachers appear to go through a number of developmental stages when employing technology in the classroom. They begin by regarding the computer in particular as either a substitute for pencil and paper, or as a machine tutor. Some move towards viewing it as a support for cognitive activity, which learners could not undertake without it (Somekh, 1994).

The rate at which teachers move through these stages is not only dependant on pedagogy, the local context and the subject discipline in which they are working, but also on their own ICT competence. Research indicates that once they have acquired an appropriate level of proficiency, they adopt an integrated, enhanced or complimentary approach to utilizing technology (Laurillard, 2008). An integrated approach involves carefully reviewing the curriculum and only employing ICTs when they can contribute to specific aims and objectives. An enhanced approach is one in which the technology is used to enrich the learning experience in the classroom. A complimentary approach is one in which the technology is used to support aspects of pupils' work, such as helping to bridge the gap between school and home. Competence by itself is not sufficient to guarantee that teachers, regardless of pedagogy, use ICTs effectively in the classroom. They must also understand the potential the technology has to affect teaching and learning. This is its 'affordance' – that which the tool makes possible.

A taxonomy of affordances

Conole et al. (2004) have developed a taxonomy of ICT affordances. The taxonomy seeks to establish the possibilities for action that ICTs offer not only to the teacher but to the learner, as well. They are categorized as accessibility, change, collaboration, diversity, multimodality, nonlinearity and reflection, and are explained below.

Accessibility A vast amount of information is now readily available to teachers and learners from many sources, including shared networks and websites. For the teacher, the challenge is helping learners to know how to use what is available. For the learner, the challenge is not searching but selecting.

Change Rapid change to the information available can be made as a result of new technologies. News about political unrest or freak weather can be transmitted around the world in an instant, regardless of the proximity of the recipient to the event. While this provides unprecedented opportunities to remain au courant, the information can be subject to inaccuracies, lacking in authority and posted with little reflection. For the educator, the challenge is to help learners to make informed decisions despite this immediacy.

Collaboration Digital technologies have the potential to link people together through new forms of online communication, including chat rooms, forums and mailing lists. This can foster discourse but also lead users to engage with each other on a superficial level, and for them to lack a clear identity. For the educator, the challenge is to ensure that learners have the appropriate communication and literacy skills.

Diversity ICTs can expose learners to things beyond their immediate environment and can draw on the experiences of others, including subject experts who are necessarily close by or teachers. Computer simulations also offer the user the opportunity to model complex behaviours and systems that would not be available otherwise. For the teacher, it raises questions about how well those in their care are taught to distinguish what 'is real and what is rendered real via the technology' (Conole et al., 2004: 117).

Multimodality A combination of touch, vision and voice can be used to access some technologies. By employing voice-activated software, users can issue commands at the same time as writing, reading or sending a message. This not only enables multitasking, but it makes it more possible for learning to take different forms. Learners can easily hear, figuratively feel (through simulation), read and see material in whatever combination is appropriate to their needs.

Nonlinearity Some technologies such as the World Wide Web allow those using search engines to approach their task in any number of different ways. Web pages, unlike the rooms in a house, can be entered or exited from any point, not just by the equivalent of the front or back door. This equates to a system in which output is not directly related to input and from an educational perspective is an important facility. It allows learning to be based on experimentation and trial and error rather than as a series of graded steps with none of the shortcuts that the behaviourists are so fond of. ICT affordances may not only reside in a computer but also in software packages, websites and multimedia, or connected peripheral devices.

Reflection Technologies which allow for discourse to occur over an extended period time (asynchronous) and can make use of archived material (such as forums) without the need for immediate responses have the potential to nurture reflection and present 'new opportunities for knowledge claims to be considered and subject to the critical gaze of much wider and more diverse communities of practice' (Conole et al., 2004: 118). For the educator, the challenge is how to make sure the learners take the time to reflect properly.

Reading 8.3

The profound shift of digital literacies
Gunther Kress

> The range of technological experience, and digital sophistication, of many children and young people is now very considerable – and often leaves schools and teachers behind. Kress discusses how new textual learning spaces and modes of communication are being created by screen-based technologies, and considers how children are developing skills and capabilities to exploit these. The challenges for schools, both today and in the future, are profound.
>
> Although this reading is set in the schools context, the issues it raises regarding digital literacies make it easy to see its relevance to FAVE contexts.
>
> How is your school adapting to contemporary developments in communication technology and popular culture?
>
> *Edited from:* Kress, G. (2010) 'The Profound Shift of Digital Literacies', in Gillen, J. and Barton, D. (eds) *Digital Literacies. TLRP – Technology Enhanced Learning*. London: Institute of Education, 2–3.

My interest is meaning-making in communication. Communication is a social activity, and as such it is embedded in the wider social environment. That environment is marked by great instability, so that communication is becoming ever more problematic. Digital literacies are in a deep and profound sense new literacies, not merely the traditional concept of literacy – reading and writing – carried on in new media.

I wish to draw attention to the radically changing forms and functions of texts, which go beyond traditional conceptions of what literacy is and has been. I consider productive aspects to be at least as significant as receptive – text-making as important as text-receiving – though I also suggest that distinction is increasingly challenged in the environment of digital technologies.

In the current period writing is being affected by four factors:

1 Texts are becoming intensely multimodal, that is, image is ever-increasingly appearing with writing, and, in many domains of communication, displacing writing where it had previously been dominant.

2 Screens (of the digital media) are replacing the page and the book as the dominant media.

3 Social structures and social relations are undergoing fundamental changes, as far as writing is concerned, predominantly in changes of structures of authority, and in the effects of changing gender formations.

4 Constellations of mode and medium are being transformed. The medium of the book
and the mode of writing had formed a centuries-long symbiotic constellation; this is
being displaced by a new constellation of medium of the screen and mode of image.
The consequences of this shift are profound.

The effect of these four together amount to a revolution in the world of communication.

Multimodality

Contemporary texts are becoming ever more multimodal, that is, they combine writing and
image (on screen or page); writing, image, moving image, music and speech (on a DVD,
on a website); or gesture, speech, image, spatial position (in face to face (f2f) interaction).
This requires that we think newly about reading and writing, but also that we think about
the meaning- contribution of all other modes that appear in texts. We can no longer treat
image as merely decorative, or even just as 'illustration': images are now being used to
make meaning just as much – though in different ways – as is writing.

The increased use of images is not making texts simpler, as is often claimed. Multimodal
texts demand new ways of reading: the meaning of each mode present in the text has to
be understood separately, and its meaning conjoined with all others that are present, and
brought into a single coherent reading. The demands on writing have both changed and
multiplied. Socially, there is now recognition of much greater cultural and social diversity
and an expectation that this diversity is acknowledged. Writing now has to be considered
in relation to audience, and in relation to the other modes which may be present in the
textual ensemble, and their communicational functions. Writing is becoming part of a
larger and encompassing design effort in the making of texts.

Design

The new environments are encouraging a new disposition towards making texts and
towards reading texts. Readers, as indeed writers and designers, will now need to treat all
features of the graphically presented text as meaningful. Where before their training had
disposed them to attend to language in a much more abstract way – to grammar, words,
syntax – now they need to attend to all features of a text. In other words their disposition
has changed from a linguistic to a semiotic one.

Both the making of text and the reading of text demands much more attention to all
possible means of making meaning. Design requires the apt use of all resources (modes,
genres, syntax, font, layout, etc.) to content and to audience. So, the facility offered by
digital media shifts notions of making texts from 'using the available resource of writing
in relation to my purposes and according to convention' to 'using apt resources for that
which I wish to represent in order to implement the design that I have, given my understanding of the relevant characteristics of the social environment in which I am producing
this text.'

It is relatively straightforward to see design in text-making; however design is also at work in text 'reception'. Where more traditional texts such as books have strict order at various levels, and given entry-points, multimodal texts, with their organisation on visual principles, and their multiple entry-points offer and even expect the reader to construct the order of reading for her/himself. In effect, reading the multimodal text makes readers into the designers of the texts they read.

Reading with digital media makes reading into an activity in which in many or most instances it is possible to change the text that I am reading as I read it. This changes the status of author and of text radically. In reading I can become author in a way which before had been possible only 'inwardly' (and in theory).

Implications

The use of screens and the implications of that use for pedagogies as well as for forms of writing, need to be fully understood. Screens encourage profoundly different approaches to reading than did the traditional page. The phenomenon of hyper-textuality chimes with larger social moves away from hierarchical and towards more lateral structures. A user of the screen who has several windows open at the same time – attending to chat, surfing the internet, listening to sound-as-music, is engaged in forms of 'attention' management entirely unlike the withdrawing, reflective modes of reading traditional written text, a mode still encouraged and rewarded in schools. The task will be to attend to both dispositions, bringing out, in ways plausible and relevant to young text-makers, the continuing value of each.

Those who have grown up in a world where the screen and its potentials have already become naturalised, are taking as natural all the potentials of the screen, including its social potentials and consequences – in terms of action, agency, modes to be used, modes which are focal, forms of production and reading.

If the school remains obliged to adhere to the characteristics of the former semiotic and social world, there will be an increasingly vast gap of practice, understanding, and disposition to knowledge.

Reading 8.4

Improving learning cultures in further education: Understanding how students learn

Gert Biesta and David James

In this reading James and Biesta advance an approach to educational improvement which aims to capture the complex interaction between the many factors, dimensions and influences that shape the learning experiences of students studying in further education contexts. Their approach is informed by a cultural understanding of learning. From this perspective *learning cultures* are taken to be the social practices through which people learn. According to James and Biesta, learning cultures exist through interaction and communication and are produced and (re)produced by individuals just as much as individuals are (re)produced by cultures.

Based upon detailed ethnographic research in 17 learning sites in further education and illustrated by case studies, James and Biesta invite us to consider:

- what do learning cultures in FE look like and how do they transform over time?
- how do learning cultures transform people?
- how can people (tutors, managers, policymakers, but also students) transform learning cultures for the better?

On the basis of the above James and Biesta offer practical guidance for researchers, policymakers and practitioners for implementing change for the better.

Edited from: James, D. and Biesta, G. (eds) (2007) *Improving Learning Cultures in Further Education.* Abingdon: Routledge.

In this reading we have tried to give an answer to the question how teaching and learning in Further Education might be improved. Our answer is deceptively simple: change the culture! But transforming a learning culture is more easily said than done. This is because learning cultures are complex and multifaceted entities.

Although it is not easy to change a learning culture, the overall conclusion of our research is that because learning cultures are partly constructed by people, there is scope for some significant change through which improvements can be brought about. We focus on the ways in which learning cultures might be transformed and on how, through such transformations, learning might be improved. We begin with the description of four characteristics of learning cultures in Further Education that, despite the many differences, were relatively common across most sites in our research. We then present six research-supported broader principles for improving learning in Further Education. Next we discuss four possible 'drivers' for improvement, that is, four constituents of learning cultures which in our view and based on the findings of our research, are crucial for the transformation of learning cultures and the improvement of learning.

The learning culture of Further Education

(1) *The central significance of the tutor in learning*
Despite the fact that the role and position of tutors has significantly changed over the past decades, and despite the fact that much teaching in Further Education is far less teacher-led than it has been in the past, our research confirmed the central significance of the tutor in a wide range of different forms and practices of learning. However, there was considerable variation in tutor position. Some tutors were more independent than others and had more room for manoeuvre. Some were teaching in course that they had started themselves – others had to 'deliver' courses of which they actually disapproved.

(2) *Status and qualification hierarchies*
The Further Education sector (excluding sixth form colleges) has always dealt with students, young and old, looking for a second chance in education. Often these are people for whom schooling has been problematic. These are often working class students and/or students from minority backgrounds. Further Education has developed a welcoming ethos and a set of practices to work with such students. However, this has contributed to its relatively low status compared with schools and Higher Education, and this status permits forms of funding and managerialism that are more extreme than in other education sectors. The status issue impacts on different courses and sites in different ways, often risking detriment for those on lower status routes within the Further Education portfolio. This is more than the distinction between academic and vocational. There are significant hierarchies within and between vocational qualifications which affect recruitment, progression and student and tutor identity.

(3) *Inadequate funding and a rigid audit regime*
Learning in Further Education is pressured and destabilised by a combination of inadequate and unstable funding and a rigid audit regime, focused on retention, achievement and inspection standards. This leads to a situation in which tutors spend much of their time striving to protect the existing learning culture from external damage – such as dramatic reductions in class contact time, imposed register systems that do not fit with patterns of attendance and learning, and tensions between inclusion and high achievement rates. Dealing with this entails extensive underground working, with many tutors routinely engaged in working well beyond their job descriptions, simply to keep classes afloat. Our evidence suggests that these pressures increased during the period of the research, with increasingly detrimental effects. Rather than improving learning, such managerial approaches threatened its quality, and tutors were running out of the energy and morale needed to resist them.

(4) *External 'agenda setting'*
Pressures to improve teaching and learning in Further Education are primarily externally driven and generally by concerns other than the nature of teaching and learning. Over the last 50 years, there have been repeated calls for the improvement of teaching and learning in Further Education to solve perceived social and moral problems among youth; the inadequacy of Vocational Education and Training for employers; insufficient skill levels

to ensure the nation's global competitiveness; and the need for a cost-effective Further Education service. Beneath these different calls for improvement, lies a basic problem: the demand that the sector provides effective responses to some of the country's major social, employment and economic needs, but with ever-decreasing resources.

Improving learning: Six research-supported principles

1. Improving learning entails more than increasing its effectiveness. It is important to supplement judgements about learning effectiveness with judgments about the value of learning, and to make issues of effectiveness subordinate to issues of value.

2. There are many different positive learning processes and outcomes, beyond the achievement of a qualification. Different groups and different individuals may appropriately value different things, and operate legitimately with different conceptions of good learning. There is a need to support a diversity of positive learning experiences, as well as recognising that some learning can also be harmful.

3. Improving the effectiveness of learning entails modifying learning cultures, for example by increasing functional synergies and reducing dysfunctional tensions.

4. In enhancing learning cultures, 'what works' is often localised and context specific. Attempts to impose rigid standard procedures are often negative rather than positive in effect.

5. Because of 4, improving learning in FE entails creating maximum space for localised initiative, creativity and professional judgement, and creating more synergistic cultures to support and reward such initiatives.

6. The improvement of learning requires a reflectively critical understanding at all levels of intervention: government, college, tutor and, where possible, student.

Drivers for improvement

(1) *Student interests.* What students in FE want and need is very varied, between and within particular courses. Their FE experience is not simply about passing qualifications and getting a good job – though these were goals for many. Students want to enjoy their learning, and to be able to balance their studies with other personal priorities, be that economic survival, supporting a family, doing an existing job, or sustaining a vibrant lifestyle. To operationalise this force for improvement requires the acknowledgment that sometimes students legitimately want things that policy does not support. It is also necessary to challenge student assumptions and expectations as part of the educative process.

(2) *Tutors' professionalism.* We found dedicated staff, determined to do an excellent job, often in difficult conditions. If this reservoir of tutor experience, altruism and professionalism were recognised and supported, major improvements in learning would follow. This would entail creating more space for tutor autonomy and collaboration, encouraging, rewarding, sustaining and supporting creativity, imagination and innovation, and providing better tutor learning opportunities, including challenging expectations and assumptions. Tutors need more expansive learning environments at work, including opportunities to step outside the working context and engage with critical thinking – for example through engagement in research or other HE-linked courses and activities.

(3) *Pedagogy.* Our data supports the view of teaching as an art rather than a technical craft. Though there are some common features of good pedagogy that can be applied almost anywhere, the nature of that application differs significantly between different sites and their learning cultures. Often the good pedagogy we observed did not completely fit the criteria set out for national standards and inspection, and what worked well for one tutor in one site might not have worked for a different tutor, or in a different site. A greater understanding of and support for excellent pedagogy that is particular to a tutor's personal approach and professional judgement and that is sensitive to the nature of the particular learning culture, should be combined with staff development that encourages critical friendship and sharing of expertise (see also Fielding, 1999).

(4) *Taking a Cultural View of Learning.* Though student interests, tutor professionalism and pedagogy all strongly influence learning, they need to be considered together with the other factors listed earlier in relation to learning cultures as a whole. Recognising and acting upon this would open up the biggest improvements in learning of all. Our analysis suggests that sites where many of the cultural influences are broadly synergistic are likely to produce more effective learning.

If it is granted that these four drivers are crucial in attempts to improve learning cultures in FE, then it follows that such attempts should be guided by the following four aims:

1 Maximising student agency
2 Maximising tutor professionalism
3 Improving pedagogy
4 Enhancing synergies between aspects of a learning culture.

part three

Teaching for learning

Curriculum
What is to be taught and learned?

9

A curriculum reflects the values and understanding of those who design and construct it. The readings in this chapter together with the parallel text *Reflective Teaching in Further, Adult and Vocational Education* are intended to support a new era in curriculum planning, where teachers in the FAVE sector may return to the more active roles in curriculum planning and development they once held. With reference to examples from the field of Adult Language Literacy and Numeracy (ALLN), Hamilton and Hillier (9.1) illustrate how the development of a national curriculum led to ideological dilemmas and pedagogic tensions in practice. Key issues about knowledge are then introduced. Young (9.2) argues that a concern with knowledge should not be seen to be old-fashioned but as a means of gaining access to powerful ways of thinking. Unwin (9.3) focuses upon key issues in curriculum design in the field of vocational education and draws attention to the intrinsic value of practical learning and the importance of relevance

The parallel chapter in *Reflective Teaching in Further, Adult and Vocational Education* begins with a discussion of principles of curriculum provision in the FAVE sector, drawing attention to the importance of aims, values, knowledge and development. It then goes on to discuss different forms in which the curriculum is designed and experienced as well as the ways in which curriculum development is constrained. Other key elements of curriculum design are then reviewed, including how knowledge, concepts, skills and attitudes make up a balanced curriculum. The chapter then describes the structure and content of national curricula in the FAVE sector. Finally, the chapter concludes with a section on subject knowledge and teacher expertise.

There is also a selection of 'Key Readings' in relation to each of the topics covered on *reflectiveteaching.co.uk*. Additional ideas on the issues raised in this chapter are offered in the section on 'Deepening Expertise'.

Reading 9.1

Curriculum and method in a student-centred field
Mary Hamilton and Yvonne Hillier

This reading investigates the idea of a 'student-centred curriculum'. It presents a range of examples that illustrate how the meaning of a 'student-centred curriculum' has changed over time and how this meaning has been shaped by a range of factors in the context of adult literacy, numeracy and English for Speakers of Other Languages (ESOL) teaching over the last 40 years. Reflecting on these examples raises three interesting questions: first, what has the term 'student-centred curriculum' meant at different moments in the past? Second, what factors played a role in shaping these different accounts of a 'student-centred curriculum'? Finally, when compared with our current practice, what do these examples reveal about the strengths and challenges of our own definition and delivery of an inclusive curriculum for all of our learners?

Edited from: Hamilton, M. and Hillier, Y. (2006) *Changing Faces of Adult Literacy, Numeracy and Language.* (Trentham Books – Gillian Klein now based with IOE publications), Chapter 8: Curriculum.

Curriculum and method in a student-centred field

There's trends when I look back at it. There was all this individualised learning and then there was group learning and then there was open learning in basic skills, then there was family learning and now there's work-placed learning. That seems to be the latest bit of the evolution I feel, new students, new ways of working. (RP, ALLN Tutor, Manchester)

People entering the field of teaching in Adult Literacy, Language and Numeracy (ALLN) in 1970 brought with them a range of methods and ideologies from other fields. More than any other theme in our research, being student-centred underpins the rationale of ALLN practice (Hillier, 1998). This chapter traces the development of student-centred provision and its underpinning theoretical roots. The current term for student-centred is learner-centred, and we have used these terms interchangeably.

Part One: Definitions, challenges and development

Definitions

Any new field needs to establish what it does by defining its boundaries, specifying what it stands for and what methodologies can be employed to bring about its stated aims. This does not necessarily happen in a logical or chronological way. In ALLN, a major challenge was to find a methodology that worked with people who had not succeeded in education as children. The most obvious aspect of ALLN is that the learners are all adults who are assumed to make autonomous choices about their learning. The principle of treating people as adult learners is something that underlines the whole of post-compulsory pedagogy, along with debates over how to characterise the differences between how adults and children learn (Hillier, 2002, Fawbert, 2003, Armitage et al., 1999).

Practitioner definitions of being student-centred

Being student-centred, or learner-centred can mean different things to different people. The practitioners we interviewed specified particular activities or approaches, when they talked about student ownership of the curriculum. When practitioners discuss learners, they acknowledge their wide experience of life by the time they choose to improve their basic skills. They often come forward for help as a result of a major life change such as death of a partner, having children, being offered promotion at work, all of which involve them in having to use their language, literacy or numeracy in different ways. Learners are referred by a number of agencies involved in public services such as housing, employment and health and not all learners were necessarily committed to giving up time to attend classes and, for learners in prisons, issues of voluntarism are considerably more complex.

A brief history of student-centred curriculum and method in ALLN

Origins in one-to-one

Nearly all literacy provision was initially through pairings of a learner with a tutor, usually a volunteer. The benefit of this approach is working solely to the individual needs of learners on their own terms and, given a history of previous failure, many adults were making good progress with individual attention from a volunteer tutor, having spent their childhood hiding in the back of classrooms, or even truanting to avoid the difficulty of coping in large classes (Herrington, 1994).

Group work

One-to-one tuition was succeeded by group work, partly as funding became available to pay for tutors and to provide appropriate accommodation. Tutors, often with volunteer support, would work with small groups of learners where a low student staff ratio was promoted. A typical session for a group tutor working in a student-centred way would begin with perhaps a spelling exercise that could lead on to writing at different levels to meet the mixed abilities of people in the group. There might follow individual work, and then further group work, particularly for learners arriving later in the session. This mixture of group activities and individual work enabled volunteers to help out with individual learners, whilst fostering group cohesion.

Group work has its challenges, particularly for managing 'roll on, roll off' type of provision, where students attend irregularly, and join throughout a term. In some cases, institutional provision did not necessarily fit a student-centred approach, particularly in FE, where people had to enrol in September and, if they missed this, they had to wait a further year to join a course. However, flexibility of provision was a central characteristic of the student-centred approach, particularly during the 1980s. People would not necessarily come forward to improve their basic skills but would do so if they were learning a skill which they perceived to be of more direct use, such as cookery, or vocational subjects. Indeed, one of the key tensions in the field has been how to express basic skills in the curriculum and through promotion, and whether to teach people 'by stealth'.

In the 1990s there was massive disruption institutionally to ALLN, particularly through the influence of funding. The wider influences of technology and accreditation changed the nature of the curriculum and methodology in ALLN. However, regardless of *where* learners met, they generally were taught in smaller groups than in more mainstream provision, and were increasingly encouraged to learn through individual programmes agreed with their tutors. The influence of meeting learner needs which typified ALLN had now permeated the rationale for teaching across post-compulsory education.

English for Speakers of Other Languages (ESOL) practitioners have argued that their provision is distinctly different from literacy. Learner needs are diverse, and the idea that these can be met within small group teaching is contested. For ESOL tutors, the management of groups involved not only issues around different levels of ability and experience, but other cultural issues that needed to be addressed to be truly student-centred.

Being student-centred had become an almost unchallengeable approach by 2000, even though everyday practice in the classroom varied widely. Wherever learners participated in improving basic skills, they would be encouraged to do so through focusing on *their* needs, at times to suit them, in places that were convenient for them, and with practitioners who had access to an increasing range of materials and approaches which claimed to enhance the learner-centred rationale. This dogma was used to sell the idea of improving basic skills to employers, public service brokers and to the general public and is now enshrined in the field through the use of individual learning plans (ILPs), despite an increasingly standardised top-down service.

Part Two

Theoretical roots

How did the student-centred approach become such a 'mantra' in ALLN? One answer is that the field, being nascent, was susceptible to influences from other linked professional practices, which were drawn upon but also partially rejected in helping to solve this comparatively new phenomenon. Below we examine the key influences on the field.

Primary schooling

Practitioners were recruited from a number of backgrounds, particularly primary, remedial and special education. The teaching methods, critiqued as well as utilised within the early days of the field, were derived from other areas of education.

Whole language and language experience approaches in schools were being promoted by educationalists and writers such as Britten (1975), Rosen (1973), Searle (1971, 1982) and Kohl (1976). ESOL teachers were being introduced to communicative language theories and the idea of a range of repertoires for linguistic expression. There were demands for plain English and to admit a range of expressions of popular culture into the classroom. Numeracy teaching was influenced by the Cockroft report (1982).

Special and remedial schooling

Teachers in special and remedial education had developed practices that dealt with literacy, numeracy and, later, language. Dyslexia became recognised and for adults, diagnosis of being dyslexic helped account for their lack of progress as children.

English language teaching

The influx of Commonwealth families into the UK from the 1950s onwards required a new approach to teaching English. The communicative approach to English (see Carter, 1997) was influential in the UK, whereas the multi-literacies genre was more important in Australia (see Hamilton, in Fieldhouse, 1996). Disputes about how to deal with language variety began as a result and continues to rage today.

The curriculum

Initially there was no prescribed curriculum and tutors chose what to do with their learners, with huge variations in programmes. Centres ran dedicated short courses, for example, a ten week spelling course. Other programmes led to Access courses, and combined basic skills with a range of disciplines. A fundamental debate in teaching literacy and language has centred on how much standard English should be taught whilst respecting language variety. ESOL tutors argued that grammar was a fundamental aspect of their work. Learners wanted to know about grammar and how to speak 'properly', whereas tutors were doing their best to respect the learners own dialects and spoken language, a reverse of the accepted situation where tutors try to correct their learners' language. Family learning provision deals with grammar and issues of voice and register, simply because the parents want to know what their children are being taught. It links to work on critical language awareness (Ivanic, 1998; Carter, 1997) and the need to recognise language variety and focuses on technique and structure, even by those who had previously eschewed this approach.

The primary method used in the early days of literacy work, especially for beginner readers, was the language experience approach. People were asked to talk about an aspect of their life, for example, their family, and the tutor would write a sentence in the learner's own words which would then be worked on for reading, spelling and grammar purposes, depending on the person's level of literacy at the time. As spelling and grammar followed this approach, it was seen to be a 'meta' approach which subsumed the more technical aspects.

Materials and methods

Whatever method was used in basic skills teaching, appropriate materials were required. A fortunate consequence of the dearth of appropriate materials arose from the BBC campaign which produced a tutor handbook and a student workbook.

We are struck by how the same skills and resourcefulness that practitioners were forced to employ in materials production continued to be used with each new wave of technology. We have lots of examples of innovations and of home made, individualised and adapted materials. Tutors now carry laptops around with them, rather than plastic bags full of books, nomadic as always *'trundling those damn machines about'* (AB, ALLN Tutor, Manchester).

Today, the word 'curriculum' invariably has prescriptive connotations, meeting Awarding Body (AB) standards, or national requirements. From our analysis of the past three decades we can see that, over the first ten years, there was little accreditation and little explicit coherence or curriculum. It would be inaccurate to argue that accreditation created a curriculum, but it did help define it.

> Good teaching is good teaching, and if you are teaching something well you almost unwittingly will be teaching to the core curriculum. Almost unwittingly you will be working towards accreditation. (AW, ALLN tutor, Norfolk)

Student writing

Students were encouraged to write about themselves, to publish their work and, in some cases, to use their writing as a platform to challenge cuts in funding and provision, and wider policy issues of the day that affected them, such as unemployment (see Chapter 4). The curriculum content and activities of the student writing movement affected social relations in the learning situation. It changed how the teachers' role was perceived, now acting as mediator and scribe rather than expert (see Mace, 2002). It opened up new possibilities for the students' role in management and decision-making surrounding the teaching, learning and editing process.

Part Three

Tensions and debates

The tensions in the field continue to influence how people define and practice a student-centred curriculum. Such practices extend beyond the field of ALLN to the post-compulsory sector generally (Armitage et al., 1999; Fawbert, 2003; Hillier, 2005).

A student-centred field is not simple or homogenous, and its ethos does not reflect the underlying tensions that have served to maintain the dynamic growth and dialogues found within the field today. Early on, disagreements over whether people should be taught on a one-to-one basis or in groups, served to lay the foundations of different provision replicated across the country.

The current shape of ALLN owes much to the deeply held belief that student-centredness is an ideologically appropriate approach to adopt. This ideology at times conflicts with the major influences on the field such as accreditation, widening participation, ensuring adults are able to function in society and particularly in the workplace, and globalised factors including accountability and surveillance. Even student writing, which might seem comparatively non-controversial, proved to be the reverse. It has been criticised for not providing the best way to help people improve their basic skills and in terms of political control exercised over students.

Reading 9.2

Powerful knowledge

Michael Young

The role of subject knowledge in curriculum is surprisingly controversial – and debate sometimes becomes politicized. Michael Young helpfully distinguishes between 'knowledge of the powerful' (which might be deemed elitist) and 'powerful knowledge' (which is expected to provide opportunities for all). He argues that powerful knowledge is increasingly specialized and distinct from everyday experience – so schools must accept responsibility, in pupils' best interests, for teaching subject matter which is not familiar to students. This argument makes an interesting contrast with the position of the Plowden Report. Although this reading refers to forms of knowledge in the schools sector, it is not difficult to see how the same issues are relevant to the FAVE sector.

Do you see subject knowledge in the curriculum as a constraint on learning or a source of opportunities?

Commissioned for this volume: Young, M. (2013) *Powerful Knowledge in Education.* London: University of London, Institute of Education.

What knowledge?

In using the very general word 'knowledge' I find it useful to distinguish between two ideas 'knowledge of the powerful' and 'powerful knowledge'. 'Knowledge of the powerful' refers to who defines 'what counts as knowledge' and has access to it. Historically and even today when we look at the distribution of access to university, it is those with more power in society who have access to certain kinds of knowledge. It is this that I refer to as 'knowledge of the powerful'. It is understandable that many sociological critiques of school knowledge have equated school knowledge and the curriculum with 'knowledge of the powerful'. It was, after all the upper classes in the early nineteenth century who gave up their private tutors and sent their children to the Public Schools to acquire powerful knowledge (as well, of course, to acquire powerful friends). However, the fact that some knowledge is 'knowledge of the powerful', or high-status knowledge as I once expressed it (Young, 1971; 1998), tells us nothing about the knowledge itself. We therefore need another concept in conceptualising the curriculum that I want to refer to as 'powerful knowledge'. This refers not to whose has most access to the knowledge or who gives it legitimacy, although both are important issues; it refers to what the knowledge can do – for example, whether it provides reliable explanations or new ways of thinking about the world. This was what the Chartists were calling for with their slogan 'really useful knowledge'. It is also, if not always consciously, what parents hope for in making sacrifices to keep their children at school; that they will acquire powerful knowledge that is not available to them at home.

Powerful knowledge in modern societies in the sense that I have used the term is, increasingly, specialist knowledge. It follows therefore that schools need teachers with that specialist knowledge. Furthermore, if the goal for schools is to 'transmit powerful knowledge', it follows that teacher–pupil relations will have certain distinctive features that arise from that goal. For example:

- they will be different from relations between peers and will inevitably be hierarchical;
- they will not be based, as some recent government policies imply, on learner choice, because in most cases, learners will lack the prior knowledge to make such choices.

This does not mean that schools should not take the knowledge that pupils bring to school seriously or that pedagogic authority does not need to be challenged. It does mean that some form of authority relations are intrinsic to pedagogy and to schools. The questions of pedagogic authority and responsibility raise important issues, especially for teacher educators, which are beyond the scope of this reading. The next section turns to the issue of knowledge differentiation.

Knowledge differentiation and school knowledge

The key issues about knowledge, for both teachers and educational researchers, are not primarily the philosophical questions such as 'what is knowledge?' or 'how do we know at all?' The educational issues about knowledge concern how school knowledge is and should be different from non-school knowledge and the basis on which this differentiation is made. Although the philosophical issues are involved, school/non-school knowledge differences raise primarily sociological and pedagogic questions.

Schooling is about providing access to the specialised knowledge that is embodied in different domains. The key curriculum questions will be concerned with:

- the differences between different forms of specialist knowledge and the relations between them;
- how this specialist knowledge differs from the knowledge people acquire in everyday life;
- how specialist and everyday knowledge relate to each other; and
- how specialist knowledge is pedagogised.

In other words, how it is paced, selected and sequenced for different groups of learners. Differentiation, therefore, in the sense I am using it here, refers to:

- the differences between school and everyday knowledge;
- the differences between and relations between knowledge domains;
- the differences between specialist knowledge (e.g. physics or history) and pedagogised knowledge (school physics or school history for different groups of learners).

Underlying these differences is a more basic difference between two types of knowledge. One is the context-dependent knowledge that is developed in the course of solving specific problems in everyday life. It can be practical – like knowing how to repair a mechanical or electrical fault or how to find a route on a map. It can also be procedural, like a handbook or set of regulations for health and safety. Context-dependent knowledge tells the individual how to do specific things. It does not explain or generalise; it deals with particulars. The second type of knowledge is context-independent or theoretical knowledge. This is knowledge that is developed to provide generalisations and makes claims to universality; it provides a basis for making judgments and is usually, but not solely, associated with the sciences. It is context-independent knowledge that is at least potentially acquired in school, and is what I referred to earlier as powerful knowledge.

Inevitably schools are not always successful in enabling pupils to acquire powerful knowledge. It is also true that schools are more successful with some pupils than others. The success of pupils is highly dependent on the culture that they bring to school. Elite cultures that are less constrained by the material exigencies of life, are, not surprisingly, far more congruent with acquiring context-independent knowledge than disadvantaged and subordinate cultures. This means that if schools are to play a major role in promoting social equality, they have to take the knowledge base of the curriculum very seriously – even when this appears to go against the immediate demands of pupils (and sometimes their parents). They have to ask the question 'is this curriculum a means by which pupils can acquire powerful knowledge?' For children from disadvantaged homes, active participation in school may be the only opportunity that they have to acquire powerful knowledge and be able to move, intellectually at least, beyond their local and the particular circumstances. It does them no service to construct a curriculum around their experience on the grounds that it needs to be validated, and as a result leave them there.

Conceptualising school knowledge

The most sustained and original attempt to conceptualise school knowledge is that developed by the English sociologist Basil Bernstein (Bernstein, 1971; 2000). His distinctive insight was to emphasise the key role of knowledge boundaries, both as a condition for the acquisition of knowledge and as embodying the power relations that are necessarily involved in pedagogy. Bernstein begins by conceptualising boundaries in terms of two dimensions.

First he distinguished between the classification of knowledge – or the degree of insulation between knowledge domains – and the framing of knowledge – the degree of insulation between school knowledge or the curriculum and the everyday knowledge that pupils bring to school.

Second, he proposed that classification of knowledge can be strong – when domains are highly insulated from each other (as in the case of physics and history) – or weak – when there are low levels of insulation between domains (as in humanities or science curricula). Likewise, framing can be strong – when school and non-school knowledge are insulated from each other, or weak, when the boundaries between school and non-school knowledge are blurred (as in the case of many programmes in adult education and some curricula designed for less able pupils).

In his later work Bernstein (2000) moves from a focus on relations between domains to the structure of the domains themselves by introducing a distinction between vertical and horizontal knowledge structures. This distinction refers to the way that different domains of knowledge embody different ideas of how knowledge progresses. Whereas in vertical knowledge structures (typically the natural sciences) knowledge progresses towards higher levels of abstraction (for example, from Newton's laws of gravity to Einstein's theory of relativity), in horizontal (or as Bernstein expresses it, segmental) knowledge structures like the social sciences and humanities, knowledge progresses by developing new languages which pose new problems. Examples are innovations in literary theory or approaches to the relationship between mind and brain.

Bernstein's primary interest was in developing a language for thinking about different curriculum possibilities and their implications. His second crucial argument was to make the link between knowledge structures, boundaries and learner identities. His hypothesis was that strong boundaries between knowledge domains and between school and non-school knowledge play a critical role in supporting learner identities and therefore are a condition for learners to progress.

Conclusions

I have argued that, whatever their specific theoretical priorities, their policy concerns or their practical educational problems, educational researchers, policy makers and teachers must address the question 'what are schools for?' This means asking how and why schools have emerged historically, at different times and in very different societies, as distinctive institutions with the specific purpose of enabling pupils to acquire knowledge not available to them at home or in their everyday life. It follows, I have argued, that the key concept for the sociology of education (and for educators more generally) is knowledge differentiation.

The concept of knowledge differentiation implies that much knowledge that it is important for pupils to acquire will be non-local and counter to their experience. Hence pedagogy will always involve an element of what the French sociologist Pierre Bourdieu refers to, over-evocatively and I think misleadingly, as symbolic violence. The curriculum has to take account of the everyday local knowledge that pupils bring to school, but such knowledge can never be a basis for the curriculum. The structure of local knowledge is designed to relate to the particular; it cannot provide the basis for any generalisable principles. To provide access to such principles is a major reason why all countries have schools.

The concept of knowledge differentiation sets a threefold agenda for schools and teachers, for educational policy makers and for educational researchers.

First, each group (separately and together) must explore the relationship between the purpose of schools to create the conditions for learners to acquire powerful knowledge and both their internal structures – such as subject divisions – and their external structures

– such as the boundaries between schools and professional and academic 'knowledge producing communities' and between schools and the everyday knowledge of local communities.

Second, if schools are to help learners to acquire powerful knowledge, local, national and international groups of specialist teachers will need to be involved with university-based and other specialists in the ongoing selection, sequencing and inter-relating of knowledge in different domains. Schools therefore will need the autonomy to develop this professional knowledge; it is the basis of their authority as teachers and the trust that society places in them as professionals. This trust may at times be abused; however, any form of accountability must support that trust rather than try to be a substitute for it.

Third, educational researchers need to address the tension in the essentially conservative role of schools as institutions with responsibility for knowledge transmission in society – especially as this aspect of their role is highlighted in a world increasingly driven by the instabilities of the market. However, 'conservative' has two very different meanings in relation to schools. It can mean preserving the stable conditions for acquiring 'powerful knowledge' and resisting the political or economic pressures for flexibility. A good example is how curricular continuity and coherence can be undermined by modularisation and the breaking up of the curriculum into so-called 'bite-sized chunks'. The 'conservatism' of educational institutions can also mean giving priority to the preservation of particular privileges and interests, such as those of students of a particular social class or of teachers as a professional group. Radicals and some sociologists of education have in the past tended to focus on this form of conservatism in schools and assume that if schools are to improve they have to become more like the non-school world – or more specifically the market. This takes us back to the tension between differentiation and de-differentiation of institutions that I referred to earlier.

In summary, I have made three related arguments.

The first is that although answers to the question 'what are schools for?' will inevitably express tensions and conflicts of interests within the wider society, nevertheless educational policy makers, practising teachers and educational researchers need to address the distinctive purposes of schools. (Reading 1.1)

My second argument has been that there is a link between the emancipatory hopes associated with the expansion of schooling and the opportunity that schools provide for learners to acquire 'powerful knowledge' that they rarely have access to at home.

Third, I introduce the concept of knowledge differentiation as a principled way of distinguishing between school and non-school knowledge. Contemporary forms of accountability are tending to weaken the boundaries between school and non-school knowledge on the grounds that they inhibit a more accessible and more economically relevant curriculum. I have drawn on Basil Bernstein's analysis to suggest that to follow this path may be to deny the conditions for acquiring powerful knowledge to the very pupils who are already disadvantaged by their social circumstances. Resolving this tension between political demands and educational realities is, I would argue, one of the major educational questions of our time.

Reading 9.3

Vocational education matters

Lorna Unwin

> Despite the high-quality provision in many parts of Europe, vocational education has rarely been taken seriously in the UK. In this reading, Unwin highlights the intrinsic value of practical learning in all forms, and the contribution which it can make to personal well-being and social cohesion as well as to economic productivity. In schools, early work and later learning, practical learning and vocational education deserves to be taken very seriously.
>
> In what ways does practical activity enhance your own learning?
>
> *Edited from:* Unwin, L. (2009) *Sensuality, Sustainability and Social Justice: Vocational Education in Changing Times.* Professorial Inaugural Lecture, Institute of Education, University of London, 4 February.

Over the past 150 years or so, many commentators have been concerned to expose the serious deficiencies in provision for vocational education and training (for contemporary critiques and reviews of the historical commentary, see, Unwin, 2004; Warhurst et al., 2004; Wolf, 2002; Keep and Mayhew, 1999; Green, 1990; Bailey, 1990). These critiques have drawn attention to: the separation of vocational education from general education; the failure to establish dedicated vocational institutions; the lack of investment in the development of vocational teachers; the acceptance by successive governments that only employers should determine the content and form of vocational qualifications; and the lack of labour market regulation.

But let's step back from the critiques of government policy and consider the meaning and purpose of vocational education in contemporary society.

One of the few academics to devote time and energy to the study of vocational education was the American philosopher, John Dewey. He placed the concept of the 'vocational' in the wider context of viewing one's life as a whole. Dewey (1915) argued that vocational education helps people consider what kind of lives they want to lead and to identify the type of skills and knowledge they might require to achieve their goals. He added that vocational education was more than preparation for an occupation, rather it was a means to develop an understanding of the historical and social meanings of that occupation, paid or unpaid. As such, participation in vocational education is an important means for all individuals to connect their interests and abilities with the world around them.

Three stages of vocational education can be identified. First, there is vocational preparation prior to entering the labour market. Provision at this stage faces particular challenges in relation to the creation of satisfactory simulated work environments, access to up-to- date equipment, and the vocational expertise of teachers. Second, apprenticeship, where it exists, is an age-old model of learning (still used in occupations as diverse as medicine and hairdressing) that conceives vocational preparation as a combination of work experience, job-specific training and vocational education. Done well, apprenticeship creates a space within which the development of occupational expertise and induction into an occupational community will also involve wider conversations about the aesthetic and moral dimensions of working life. Finally, further vocational development relates to the stage beyond apprenticeship when the work itself becomes the source of learning. All workers need to improve their expertise and extend their knowledge to some degree, and they and their employers need to regularly reappraise the relationship between the worker's capability and the changing requirements of the workplace (Fuller and Unwin, 2004).

All three phases demand a sophisticated understanding of the importance of what Richard Sennett (2008: 9) terms 'craftsmanship'. He writes:

Craftsmanship may suggest a way of life that waned with the advent of industrial society – but this is misleading. Craftsmanship names an enduring, basic human impulse, the desire to do a job well for its own sake.

In his book, Sennett calls for a 'vigorous cultural materialism' in order to bring together concern for culture and the objects and activities of everyday life. Crucially, this relates to the process of making and mending. It is, he suggests, through making things that people can learn about themselves.

Further, Sennett argues that three basic abilities form the foundation of craftsmanship:

- the ability to localise (making a matter concrete);
- to question (reflecting on its qualities);
- and to open up (expanding its sense).

Sennett states that, to deploy these capabilities, 'the brain needs to process in parallel visual, aural, tactile, and language-symbol information' (p. 277).

Certainly, practical activity motivates a great many people to learn. It also tends to be a much more social and collective process and, hence, is an excellent vehicle for building the inter-personal skills that are important in the workplace.

Such arguments go way beyond the view that 'practical learning' is simply a panacea for the need to engage young people who are not amenable to traditional subject-centred general education.

Indeed, these points challenge the reductionist conception of competence that still underpins the design of the vocational qualifications.

Vocational education done well will inspire young people, and will motivate older workers to up-skill and re-skill. It is different to academic education and demands a more sophisticated pedagogy as it requires learning to switch across environments – from classroom to workplace to workshop – it demands that teachers really are expert and up-to- date and that equipment is appropriate and of the highest quality – above all, it is expensive.

Vocational education is central to social justice and social cohesion and to the renewal of the economy. We need a new approach that situates the development of vocational expertise within a social partnership that allows employers, vocational educators and institutions, local government, and trade unions to create programmes for all grades of workers.

Planning

How are we implementing the curriculum?

10

The readings in this chapter address key issues in curriculum planning and implementation. We begin with an analysis offered by an inspector from the Office for Standards in Education (Ofsted), the government inspection organization responsible for the external evaluation of education in England, regarding factors which constitute outstanding teaching in the FAVE classrooms she observed (10.1). David Berliner's classic paper (10.2) offers ideas for describing and analysing the use of time – thus enabling or constraining opportunities to learn. Haynes (10.3) provides a fresh account of progression and differentiation drawing upon his own experience. Hattie (10.4) extends his work on the effectiveness of particular teaching strategies. Interestingly he offers the notion of 'mind frames' to conceptualize 'visible learning' as a way of structuring expert knowledge.

The parallel chapter in *Reflective Teaching in Further, Adult and Vocational Education* moves through successive levels of curriculum planning. It begins with a discussion of short-, medium- and long-term planning, before moving on to focus on the structuring of programmes of study and schemes of work. Characteristics of the curriculum such as breadth, balance, progression and relevance are interwoven into the discussion.

As usual, the chapter concludes with suggestions for 'Key Readings' in relation to each of the topics covered. Additional ideas and regularly updated materials can also be found on *reflectiveteaching.co.uk*.

Reading 10.1

Outstanding teaching – the reality
Harriet Harper

This reading is an extract from a book which focuses on an analysis of 20 lessons observed by Her Majesty's Inspectors (HMI). These were lessons that an experienced HMI, who specialized in the lifelong learning sector, remembered as being outstanding not just in terms of the grade but also in the literal sense – they 'stood out' from others because they were *so* good. Don't continue reading, though, if you're expecting this article to provide 'top tips' for a grade 1 lesson or yet another checklist. Teaching is much too complex for that.

How could you investigate your own practice in respect of the findings from Harper below?

Edited from: Harper, H. (2013) *Outstanding Teaching in Lifelong Learning.* London: Open University Press/McGraw-Hill Education.

The purpose of the research was not to provide a definitive definition of outstanding (that is probably impossible as it depends on who is trying to define it and why and as such it is usually highly contentious and political). Rather, it was to look at these real lessons in detail and to pin down what – if anything – they had in common and the extent to which the practice observed aligns to any particular pedagogical approach.

Interestingly, reflecting the diversity of the lifelong learning sector itself, the lessons had little in common in terms of setting, subject and level, type of student or resource or even gender or experience of teacher. The sample included twenty different subjects, four of which were A- or AS-levels, twelve were vocational, one was teacher education and the other three were adult and community learning courses. Thirteen of the lessons took place in general further education colleges, two in sixth-form colleges, three in community centres, one in a work-based learning provider and another in a young offenders' institution.

There was no magic formula or one-size-fits-all template. Every lesson was different and contingent on the professional judgement of the teacher in that particular setting, at that time and with that particular group of students. As experienced practitioners know, what works well in one context may not in another and so the transfer of 'good practice', assuming one can agree on the identification of it, is much more difficult than it initially appears to be. For that reason, it's not helpful to use the term 'best practice' as this implies there is one single transferable teaching method that can be applied to all lessons.

The research provided evidence to debunk many of the myths about observation, excellence and inspection that abound within the sector. For example, it really is not necessary – or indeed educationally desirable – to start every lesson by mechanistically reading out learning outcomes. Neither is it *essential* to use technology, present the perfect lesson plan, put on a performance or routinely change activities to be judged outstanding,

What the twenty lessons *did* have in common was the fact that the teachers were all very highly skilled practitioners. The common features in the lessons were the factors that teachers had responsibility for and could control. While they could not choose the setting or the students, they did what teachers always do – regardless of the latest fad, government initiative, inspection framework or technological advance – plan, teach and assess. So, what did these twenty teachers do to make their lessons so good?

They had clearly put considerable thought into the planning stage, although this did not necessarily present itself in the form of meticulous or lengthy lesson plans. Learning outcomes appeared to be authentic and were written in plain English, not arbitrarily plucked out of a syllabus or text book, and they were closely aligned to the context and chosen teaching and assessment methods.

You may be surprised to learn that several of the lessons were what some observers might consider to be old-fashioned in terms of their format and structure. For example, one A-level lesson was very much 'chalk and talk'. An access to social work lesson revolved solely around discussion and in another lesson, media studies students did not move away from their computers for 90 minutes. In each case, though, as in the other seventeen lessons, the teachers' approaches worked extremely well.

In terms of common pedagogical characteristics, the teaching methods used in the twenty lessons were mostly based on problem-solving and/or authentic tasks, discovery rather than telling, structured discussions and independent learning. Across the twenty lessons, teachers spent much more time listening and observing, than they did talking. Not one of the 330 or so students escaped involvement in meaningful activity.

Of course, this emphasis on active or experiential learning is not at all uncommon in the lifelong learning sector and does not in itself constitute an outstanding or even satisfactory lesson. It is certainly not the case that *any* activity is better than a didactic approach to teaching. Those of you who routinely observe lessons will be all too familiar with 'busy' lessons and students who appear to be 'engaged' when in fact they are learning very little and also – at the other extreme – with didactic lectures which, if done extremely well, can be highly stimulating and successful.

Throughout the lessons teachers gave plenty of feedback to help students to make sense of what they were learning and what they needed to do to make further progress. These teachers carefully planned the use of context-specific assessment methods, including problem-solving tasks relating to everyday life, written exercises, observation, role play, discussion, presentations and peer marking. Unsurprisingly, question and answer featured in all the lessons. Too often, this most popular assessment tool is used poorly but in these lessons, the teachers demonstrated considerable expertise in the way in which they asked questions. They did so not just to check levels of understanding, but also to elicit information and views and – as importantly – to encourage thinking and discovery.

The very well designed assessment tasks provided students with opportunities to demonstrate the impact of their understanding. For example, learners were able to explain in their own words how the human eye works, discuss with confidence local housing policies, lay bricks competently, use mathematical equations to solve real problems, explain to their peers how to look after a gerbil and successfully change a carburettor.

In terms of personality and style, the teachers were not particularly flamboyant, emotional or extrovert but they were passionate and enthusiastic about both their subject and their teaching. They appeared to want genuinely to be in the lesson in order to share that passion and to help their students to learn, enjoy learning and achieve well. It was evident to the learners, as well as to the observers, that these dual professionals – including a chef, classicist, social worker, hairdresser and physicist – were experts in their subjects as well as in the associated pedagogy. Because of this, they were able to structure very skilfully the unfolding of various concepts and/or practical skills in ways that students found meaningful, challenging and achievable.

So far, a picture has been presented of twenty well planned lessons, based mostly on active learning, taught by enthusiastic teachers. Most likely, that would not have been enough to make them stand out. Another factor contributing to the success of these lessons was that the teachers demanded high standards and learners adapted to the requirements made of them. The lessons were clearly not just about getting through the syllabus, passing an assignment, preparing for an examination or even impressing the observer. The lessons were designed and managed to focus unashamedly on the genuine development of students' knowledge and skills.

It was certainly not the case that these teachers had students who were 'easy' to teach. In fact, some groups were what many would consider to be particularly difficult. Students' high level of motivation was, to a large extent, a product of the way in which they were taught and the skilfully subtle manner in which these teachers managed their lessons.

Classroom (or in other cases, laboratory, workshop or workplace) management was superb and included all the classic techniques used by really good teachers, many of which might go unnoticed to an inexperienced eye. Teachers proactively and unobtrusively prevented any kind of disruptive behaviour or lulls in momentum. They got lessons off to a very brisk start and kept the activities sufficiently challenging, interesting and purposeful.

These lessons are a reminder that there need not be a clash between a focus on high standards and the lifelong learning sector's well-deserved reputation for being inclusive. The fact that the students worked to a high standard and remained motivated was no accident. Inclusive practice is much more than simply being nice to learners and creating a pleasant environment, important though that is. These teachers had created a highly supportive and inclusive atmosphere combined with a serious approach to learning. They made their lessons both enjoyable and rewarding for all students, regardless of their background, circumstances or prior attainment.

The teachers of these outstanding lessons demonstrated not just their excellent 'observable' teaching skills but also the knowledge, values and beliefs that had shaped their practice.

Reading 10.2

Instructional time – and where it goes
David Berliner

The use of time in the classroom is a fundamental consideration when providing opportunity for students to learn. This reading introduces some ways to think about the use of time in the classroom, and offers some different ways to classify such time. Opportunity to learn is quite closely correlated with outcomes, and yet contemporary empirical studies still record very large amounts of time in schools in which curricular learning is not taking place. Somehow, time 'evaporates'.

What could you do to increase the proportion of time which your pupils actually spend on curricular learning?

Edited from: Berliner, D. (1990) 'What's all the Fuss about Instructional Time?', in M. Ben-Peretz and R. Bromme (eds) *The Nature of Time in Schools.* New York: Teacher College Press, 3–35.

- Allocated time, usually defined as the time that the state, district, school, or teacher provides the student for instruction. For example a school may require that reading and language arts be taught 90 minutes every day in the second grade. Allocated time is the time block set aside for that instruction– 90 minutes a day, or 7 .5 hours a week or 300 hours a school year. Sometimes this is called scheduled time, to distinguish it from the time actually allocated by teachers. This can prove an important distinction when the concept of allocated time is used to create a variable for a research study. When that is the case it has been found that measures of allocated time derived from any source other than direct observation of teachers invariably overestimate the actual time provided in schools for instruction in a curriculum area. In the original 'model of school learning,' the article that began contemporary research on instructional time, allocated time was called 'opportunity to learn.'

- Engaged time, usually defined as the time that students appear to be paying attention to materials or presentations that have instructional goals. When the concept of engagement is used to create the variable of student engaged time the variable is usually measured by classroom observers or coded from videotapes of students in learning situations. Students' self-reports of engagement have also been used as a variable. Engaged time is always a subset of allocated time. A synonym for engaged time is 'attention.'

- Time-on-task, usually defined as engaged time on particular learning tasks. The concept is not synonymous with engaged time, but is often used as if it were. The term time-on-task has a more restricted and more complex meaning than does the term engaged time. It makes clear that engagement is not all that is desired of students in educational environments. Engagement in particular kinds of tasks is what is wanted. Thus, engagement may be recorded when a student is deeply involved in mathematics or a comic book during a time period allocated to science. Time-on-task, however, would not be recorded because the task in which students were to be attentive was science. Time-on-task should be thought of as a conjunctive concept, not nearly as simple a concept as engagement. This distinction, though often lost, makes clearer that time is, in a sense, a psychologically empty vessel. Time must be filled with activities that are desirable. Time-on-task as a variable in empirical research is usually measured in the same ways as engagement, though when the distinction noted above is kept in mind, the curriculum, instructional activities, or tasks in which the student engages are also recorded.

- Academic learning time, usually defined as that part of allocated time in a subject- matter area (physical education, science, or mathematics, for example) in which a student is engaged successfully in the activities or with the materials to which he or she is exposed, and in which those activities and materials are related to educational outcomes that are valued. This is a complex concept related to or made up of a number of other concepts, such as allocated time (the upper limit of ALT); time-on-task (engagement in tasks that are related to outcome measures, or, stated differently, time spent in curriculum that is aligned with the evaluation instruments that are in use); and success rate (the percent of engaged time that a student is experiencing a high, rather than low, success experience in class). Academic learning time is often and inappropriately used as a synonym for engagement, time-on-task, or some other time-based concept. Its meaning, however, is considerably more complex than that, as will be elaborated on below.

- Transition time, usually defined as the non-instructional time before and after some instructional activity. The occurrence of transition time would be recorded within a block of allocated time when a teacher takes roll or gives back homework at the beginning of an instructional activity; and it would be recorded when books are put away or jackets and lunches are brought out at the end of an instructional activity. The concept describes the inevitable decrease in time allocated for instruction that ordinarily accompanies mass education.

- Waiting time, usually defined as the time that a student must wait to receive some instructional help. The time spent waiting to receive new assignments from the teacher, on a line to have the teacher check work, or waiting for the teacher's attention after raising one's hand in class are examples of waiting time. This member of the family of instructional time concepts is concerned with instructional management and is not to be confused with wait-time the time between the end of a question asked by the teacher and beginning of a response by a student. The latter member of the family of instructional time concepts is concerned with instruction and cognition, rather than classroom management.

- Aptitude, usually defined as the amount of time that a student needs, under optimal instructional conditions to reach some criterion of learning. High aptitude for learning something is determined by fast learning; low aptitude is reflected in slow learning. This time-based definition of aptitude is unusual and will be elaborated on below. A definition of this type serves to point out how some members of the instructional time family do not, at first glance, seem to be family members.

- Perseverance, usually defined as the amount of time a student is willing to spend on learning a task or unit of instruction. This is measured as engagement, or the time-on-task that the student willingly puts into learning. Perseverance is another of the instructional time concepts that do not at first appear to belong to the family. Although this concept is traditionally thought to be a motivational concept, when operationalized in a certain way, it becomes a variable that is measured in time, and thus becomes an instructional time concept as well.

- Pace, usually defined as the amount of content covered during some time period. For example, the number of vocabulary words covered by Christmas, or the number of mastery units covered in a semester will differ from classroom to classroom. In educational systems where standardized tests are used as outcomes, and where those tests sample items from a broad curriculum, students whose teacher exposes them to the most content ordinarily have a better chance of answering the test questions. As the pace of instruction increases, however, depth of coverage usually decreases.

Reading 10.3

Progression and differentiation

Anthony Haynes

This reading offers insights on the significance of progression and differentiation for curriculum planning and classroom practice. It concludes with a refreshing acknowledgement of the challenge of achieving differentiation in classrooms and a realistic appreciation of the potential for improvement as skills and expertise develop with experience.

Acknowledging its difficulty, do you envisage providing progression and differentiation as a positive professional challenge?

Edited from: Haynes, A. (2010) *The Complete Guide to Lesson Planning and Preparation.* London: Continuum, 135–47.

The planning and preparation stage of teaching could be thought of in terms of a building. First we put in place the four cornerstones – our understanding of:

- Educational aims
- The needs of stakeholders, especially pupils
- The context in which we are teaching
- The cognitive structure of what we teach.

These cornerstones both delimit and support what we do. Next we construct the first storey – the curriculum. This provides the basis on which we can add the second storey, medium term planning and the third – short-term planning, including three rooms of particular importance: time, space and language.

Now we need to put a roof on the building. This entails putting two concepts into place: (a) progression and (b) differentiation. I figure these in terms of the building's roof because they are over-arching concepts. They apply throughout and across the curriculum, in every class at every stage.

To understand these two concepts, it may help now to switch metaphors. Think, for a moment, of teaching as an activity that has two dimensions.

- There is what we might call the vertical axis, namely time. Progression in education is a vertical concept: that is, it is concerned with the order in which we do things and the question of when we do them.
- Differentiation, on the other hand, is a horizontal concept. It is concerned with differences, at any particular stage in the curriculum – differences between pupils, differences in the provision we make for them and, crucially, the relationship between these two set of differences.

Progression

In order to decide how to sequence the curriculum, we need to examine it from the point of view of the learner. The question that matters is not, 'What do we want teach when?' but rather, 'What would make sense to the learners and help them to learn?' How can we help them to move on from one thing to another, both onwards and upwards, building as they do so on previous learning?

To do this, we need to look both forwards and backwards in the curriculum. For a moment, let's take the example of English teaching in secondary schools. Suppose we want pupils in one year group to be able to compare characters from two different stories. This poses two challenges: they have not only to understand each of the characters, but also to organize their ideas within a comparative structure (e.g. they may need to learn how to employ phrases such as 'The main similarity' or 'In contrast'). In this case it may well help if at a previous stage in the curriculum the pupils have had some experience of comparative study based on simpler material – a couple of short articles, for example. Thus we might plan backwards, as it were, by deciding to include such an exercise in the scheme of work for the preceding term. And we can plan forwards too. If, to continue our example, pupils complete a comparative study of two characters from different stories now, what could they move on to later? Perhaps a comparative study of the stories as a whole, including more characters or other aspects such as plot? Perhaps a comparative study of two longer texts?

As always, it helps to integrate our thinking here with our model of the curriculum. That is, it helps to think through the potential continuities not only in terms of subject matter (perhaps the most obvious type), but also in terms of cognitive structure and modes of learning.

Differentiation

Differentiation is the process of adapting educational activity to suit the diverse needs and characteristics of the learners. The aim of course, is to optimize the learning of each pupil. That aim is very easy to state, but difficult to achieve in practice.

Essentially, there are three ways of proceeding.

First, one may differentiate by outcome. The teacher may set the same task for all pupils, who might then produce very different outcomes. That isn't necessarily a bad thing. For example, in art each pupil may be asked to produce a collage from a certain selection of materials. The results may differ wildly. Well, differences in personal style are one of the things that make art fun. The results may differ in level of achievement too (some may be more inventive, composed, etc. than others). That too is not necessarily a problem. It is useful for assessment purposes (this is, after all, how examinations commonly work). And it may be useful developmentally too: the question would be how much the task had done to help each pupil's collage-making abilities develop.

But although differentiation by outcome isn't necessarily a problem, it can be. If some pupils are set a task that is beyond them and they simply flail and fail, that is no good to anyone. The pupils don't develop and they become dispirited. It isn't even very useful for the purposes of assessment. (After all, if you were to set a degree-level Mathematics paper to the population at large, most people would score zero – which would reveal nothing.) To rely willy-nilly on differentiation by outcome is less than professional.

The second way to differentiate is by task. That is, one sets different tasks to different pupils based on one's baseline assessment of them. This method clearly has one advantage: it can help the teacher to ensure that each pupil is working in what psychologists (Vygotsky, 1978) call the Zone of Proximal Development (ZPD). 'ZPD' refers to that area of learning that takes pupils beyond what they already know, but within achievable limits.

There are, however, disadvantages to differentiating by task. The main problem is that the success of the method depends on the matching of task to pupil, which in turn depends on the accuracy of the teacher's judgement and the baseline assessment on which it is based. If the selection is poor, the classroom will be full of bored or dispirited pupils.

A third way to differentiate is by support. That is, one can vary the level and means of support that pupils receive. For example, a teacher might set a task such as practising their tennis serves. Some pupils might be able to do that unaided (or by aiding each other). They might know what a good serve is supposed to be like and which parts of their own serves they need to work on. Others might have little or no idea what to do. They would need to receive some additional support, at least to get them underway.

Here educators sometimes use the analogy of scaffolding. Asking pupils to complete a task can be like asking them to climb an object, a tree, say. Some might be able to climb without any scaffolding. Some might need scaffolding to support them throughout. Others might need some at first but then find they can do without.

These, then – differentiation by outcome, by task and by support – are three main ways to differentiate. In most contexts the teacher will probably need to use each of the three at some point.

Let me finish with some reflections on my own experience. Differentiation is an issue that has concerned me a great deal: the more I've thought about teaching, the more it has figured – and the more aware I've become of how my own practice has fallen short. But I have also realized that, in this area at least, perfectionism probably isn't a helpful frame of mind. I suggest that even if you could decide what a perfectly differentiated lesson for your class might be, you probably couldn't provide it. If, like me, you find that perfection is beyond you, my suggestion is rather that you aim for proficiency. I've found in any case that often the first few steps in differentiation can carry you quite a long way – not least because when pupils sense you making those steps they are more likely to try to meet you half way.

When I began teaching I certainly approached lesson planning in terms of 'one size fits all.' I then gradually moved into a second phase, where typically I would start by designing a 'one size fits all' lesson and then work out ways of differentiating for particular pupils or groups. Now, I tend to use a more flexible approach. I first ask myself, 'What are we trying to do here?' and then try to think of a range of ways of getting there. I like this kind of creative approach, but I don't think I could have worked like that when starting out. In teaching, it seems to me, one can't do everything at once.

Reading 10.4

Mind frames for visible learning
John Hattie

Hattie picks up on his meta-analysis of the effect-sizes of teaching strategies, and proposes that adopting 'mind frames' for visible teaching and learning will make a significant difference to student learning. Rather like TLRP's principles, this is a way of structuring knowledge for expert interpretation of rapidly changing classroom circumstances. Fragmentary research findings make more practical sense when placed within theoretically robust frameworks of professional understanding.

As your expertise develops, can you see the shape of an emerging framework of understanding? It will need to be your own.

Edited from: Hattie, J. (2012) *Visible Learning for Teachers: Maximizing Impact on Learning.* Abingdon: Routledge, 1–20.

What are the attributes of schooling that truly make the difference to student learning? The 'visible' aspect refers first to making student learning visible to teachers, ensuring clear identification of the attributes that make a visible difference to student learning, and all in the school visibly knowing the impact that they have on the learning in the school (of the student, teacher, and school leaders). The 'visible' aspect also refers to making teaching visible to the student, such that they learn to become their own teachers, which is the core attribute of lifelong learning or self-regulation, and of the love of learning that we so want students to value. The 'learning' aspect refers to how we go about knowing and understanding, and then doing something about student learning. A common theme is the need to retain learning at the forefront and to consider teaching primarily in terms of its impact on student learning.

Figure 10.4.1 sums up the high-level principles which I propose:

Visible teaching and learning occurs when learning is the explicit and transparent goal, when it is appropriately challenging, and when the teacher and the student both (in their various ways) seek to ascertain whether and to what degree the challenging goal is attained. Visible teaching and learning occurs when there is deliberate practice aimed at attaining mastery of the goal, when there is feedback given and sought, and when there are active, passionate, and engaging people (teacher, students, peers) participating in the act of learning. It is teachers seeing learning through the eyes of students, and students seeing teaching as the key to their ongoing learning. The remarkable feature of the evidence is that the greatest effect on student learning occurs when teachers become learners of their own teaching, and when students become their own teachers. When students become their own teachers, they exhibit the self-regulatory attributes that seem most desirable for learners (self-monitoring, self-evaluation, self-assessment, self-teaching).

Figure 10.4.1
Know thy impact:
mind frames for
visible learning

I see learning through the eyes of my students

Mind frames

- I am an evaluator/
  activator
- I am a change
  agent
- I am a seeker
  of feedback
- I use dialogue
  more than
  monologue
- I enjoy challenge
- I have high
  expectations for all
- I welcome error
- I am passionate
  about and promote
  the language
  of learning

**A cooperative
and critical
partner**

- I use learning
  intentions and
  success criteria
- I am for surface
  and deep outcomes
- I consider prior
  achievement and
  attitudes
- I set high
  expectation targets
- I feed the gap in
  student learning

**An adaptive
learning expert**

- I create trusting
  environments
- I know the power
  of peers
- I use multiple
  strategies
- I know when and
  how to
  differentiate
- I foster deliberate
  practice and
  concentration
- I know I can
  develop confidence
  to succeed

**A reciever
of feedback**

- I know how to use
  the three feedback
  questions
- I know how to use
  the three feedback
  levels
- I give and receive
  feedback
- I monitor and
  interpret my
  learning/teaching

I help students to become their own teachers

A key premise is that the teacher's view of his or her role is critical. It is the specific mind frames that teachers have about their role – and most critically a mind frame within which they ask themselves about the effect they are having on student learning. Fundamentally, the most powerful way of thinking about a teacher's role is for teachers to see themselves as evaluators of their effects on students. Teachers need to use evidence- based methods to inform, change, and sustain these evaluation beliefs about their effect. These beliefs relate to claims about what each student can do as a consequence of the teacher's actions, and how every resource (especially peers) can be used to play a part in moving students from what they can do now to where the teacher considers they should be– and to do so in the most efficient, as well as effective, manner. It matters what teachers do – but what matters most is having an appropriate mind frame relating to the impact of what they do. An appropriate mind frame combined with appropriate actions work together to achieve a positive learning effect.

As I argued in *Visible Learning* (Hattie 2009, Reading 4.3), when teachers see learning occurring or not occurring, they intervene in calculated and meaningful ways to alter the direction of learning to attain various shared, specific, and challenging goals. In particular, they provide students with multiple opportunities and alternatives for developing learning strategies based on the surface and deep levels of learning some context or domain matter, leading to students building conceptual understanding of this learning, which the students and teachers then use in future learning. Learners can be so different, making it difficult for a teacher to achieve such teaching acts: students can be in different learning places at various times, using a multiplicity of unique learning strategies, meeting different and appropriately challenging goals. Learning is a very personal journey for the teacher and the student, although there are remarkable commonalities in this journey for many teachers and students. It requires much skill for teachers to demonstrate to all of their students that they can see the students' 'perspective, communicating it back to them so that they have valuable feedback to self-assess, feel safe, and learn to understand others and the content with the same interest and concern' (Cornelius-White, 2007: 23).

The act of teaching requires deliberate interventions to ensure that there is cognitive change in the student; thus the key ingredients are being aware of the learning intentions, knowing when a student is successful in attaining those intentions, having sufficient understanding of the student's prior understanding as he or she comes to the task, and knowing enough about the content to provide meaningful and challenging experiences so that there is some sort of progressive development. It involves a teacher who knows a range of learning strategies with which to supply the student when they seem not to understand, who can provide direction and redirection in terms of the content being understood and thus maximize the power of feedback, and show the skill to 'get out the way' when learning is progressing towards the success criteria.

Of course, it helps it these learning intentions and success criteria are shared with, committed to, and understood by the learner – because in the right caring and idea-rich environment, the learner can then experiment (be right and wrong) with the content and the thinking about the content, and make connections across ideas. A safe environment for the learner (and for the teacher) is an environment in which error is welcomed and fostered – because we learn so much from errors and from the feedback that then accrues from going in the wrong direction or not going sufficiently fluently in the right direction. In the same way teachers themselves need to be in a safe environment to learn about the success or otherwise of their teaching from others.

To create such an environment, to command a range of learning strategies, and to be cognitively aware of the pedagogical means that enable the student to learn requires dedicated, passionate people. Such teachers need to be aware of which of their teaching strategies are working or not, need to be prepared to understand and adapt to the learner(s) and their situation, contexts, and prior learning, and need to share the experience of learning in this manner in an open, forthright, and enjoyable way with their students and their colleagues.

It is teachers with certain mind frames that make the difference. Powerful, passionate, accomplished teacher are those who:

- focus on students' cognitive engagement with the content of what it is that is being taught;
- focus on developing a way of thinking and reasoning that emphasizes problem-solving and teaching strategies relating to the content that they wish students to learn;
- focus on imparting new knowledge and understanding, and then monitor how students gain fluency and appreciation in the new knowledge;

- focus on providing feedback in an appropriate and timely manner to help students to attain the worthwhile goals of the lesson;
- seek feedback about their effects on the progress and proficiency of all of their students
- have deep understanding about how we learn; and
- focus on seeing learning through the eyes of their students, appreciating their fits and starts in learning, and their often non-linear progressions to the goals, supporting their deliberate practice, providing feedback about their errors and misdirections, and caring that the students get to the goals and that the students share the teacher's passion for the material being learnt.

This focus is sustained, unrelenting, and needs to be shared by all in a school.

Reading 10.5

A clear line of sight to work
Frank McLaughlin

This extract draws attention to how curriculum planning has become preoccupied with the requirements of qualification specifications, diverting attention from enduring pedagogical issues in vocational education, the needs of employers and the demands of technological developments. A four-part framework is offered as a corrective.

Edited from: Frank McLaughlin (2013) *It's about work... Excellent adult vocational teaching and learning.* London: Learning and Skills Improvement Service.

We need to put curriculum development and programme design back at the heart of vocational teaching and learning. Over the last 30 years, the emphasis has shifted from curriculum development to qualifications design, which has wrongly been equated with programme design. Together with a funding regime based on qualifications, this has exacerbated a focus on 'assessment as learning' and qualifications.

The Commission is very clear that qualifications play an important role in the English system, for employers, individuals and society more generally. But we need to turn the current way of doing things on its head and return qualifications to being the kite-mark of a learning programme, rather than the definition of a curriculum.

The process of curriculum development and design should be at the centre of the **two-way street** so that colleges, training providers and employers are directly involved, shaping programmes that reflect the up-to-date needs of occupations and workplaces, and which are based on a broader, more aspirational concept of competence...

For learners, employers and providers, this approach is more likely to ensure provision that demonstrates our four characteristics of excellent adult vocational teaching and learning:

1 a **clear line of sight to work** on all vocational programmes;

2 'dual professional' teachers and trainers who combine occupational and pedagogical expertise, and are trusted and given the time to develop partnerships and curricula with employers;

3 access to industry-standard facilities and resources reflecting the ways in which technology is transforming work;

4 clear escalators to higher level vocational learning, developing and combining deep knowledge and skills.

Pedagogy
How can we develop effective strategies?

This chapter begins with an invitation from Bruner (11.1) to consider the notion of 'folk pedagogies' and their grip upon educational practice. The idea of folk pedagogies captures all those intuitive, unexamined, theories of learning that are widespread. Simon (11.2) provides an historical explanation of why the role of pedagogy is not fully understood in societies today in terms of core beliefs. He argues that, if abilities are regarded as being fixed then teaching is not of great consequence. However if we believe that everyone has potential, then good pedagogic practice is essential to provide educational opportunities for both children and adults. Reading 11.3 offers an overview of the final report of the Commission for Adult and Vocational Teaching and Learning (CAVTL, 2013). The report highlights key issues in the curriculum design and pedagogic practice in vocational education in England (11.3). Alexander's discussion of the pedagogic repertoire (11.4) is structured in terms of the organization of interaction and then in relation to 'teaching talk' and 'learning talk'. Perrot (11.5) provides a detailed analysis of the pedagogic power of questioning skills including the 'development of an overall questioning strategy. We see how various forms of communication form the essence of pedagogic repertoire. Alexander then applies this to contrast 'dialogic' and 'transmissive' teaching'. Finally, Bathmaker (11.6) explores what the term 'vocational' has variously come to mean in the context of general vocational education in England.

The associated chapter in *Reflective Teaching in Further, Adult and Vocational Education* examines what we mean by the term pedagogy. It goes on to discuss the art, craft and science of pedagogy. Finally the chapter points to the importance of establishing a balance between knowledge and learning in order to harness the experiences and meet the needs of our students.

At the end of the chapter, suggestions for 'Key Readings' are made in relation to each of the topics covered are. These can be amplified with reference to the *reflectiveteaching.co.uk* website. The section on 'Deepening Expertise' is particularly relevant to the development of pedagogy.

Reading 11.1

Folk pedagogy

Jerome Bruner

> Bruner, from the perspective of an educational psychologist and strongly influenced by Vygotsky, is interested in how theories of the mind affect teachers' practice. He argues that teachers who theorize about learning need to take into account intuitive beliefs (which he terms 'folk pedagogy') because such beliefs may be deeply ingrained. However, teachers will also seek to change them in the light of their developing understanding of theories of mind. In this extract, he sets out why it matters that teachers understand how their perceptions of learners' minds affect how they teach. Although this reading refers to forms of knowledge in the schools sector, it is not difficult to see how the same issues are relevant to the FAVE sector.
>
> How would you characterize your 'folk pedagogies', and how do these relate to your professional understanding of teaching and learning?
>
> *Edited from:* Bruner, J. S. (1996) *The Culture of Education.* Cambridge, MA: Harvard University Press, 45–50.

Our interactions with others are deeply affected by everyday, intuitive theories about how other minds work. These theories are omnipresent but are rarely made explicit. Such lay theories are referred to by the rather condescending name of folk psychology. Folk psychologies reflect certain 'wired-in' human tendencies (like seeing people normally as operating under their own control), but they also reflect some deeply ingrained cultural beliefs about 'the mind'. Not only is folk psychology preoccupied with how the mind works here and now, it is also equipped with notions about how the child's mind learns and even what makes it grow. Just as we are steered in ordinary interaction by our folk psychology, so we are steered in the activity of helping children learn about the world by notions of folk pedagogy. Watch any mother, any teacher, even any babysitter with a child and you'll be struck by how much of what they do is steered by notions of 'what children's minds are like and how to help them learn', even though they may not be able to verbalize their pedagogical principles.

From this work on folk psychology and folk pedagogy has grown a new, perhaps even a revolutionary insight. It is this: in theorizing about the practice of education in the classroom (or any other setting, for that matter), you had better take into account the folk theories that those engaged in teaching and learning already have. For any innovations that you, as a 'proper' pedagogical theorist, may wish to introduce will have to compete with, replace, or otherwise modify the folk theories that already guide both teachers and pupils. For example, if you are convinced that the best learning occurs when the teacher helps lead the pupil to discover generalizations on her own, you are likely to run into an established cultural belief that a teacher is an authority who is supposed to tell the child what the general case is, while the child should be occupying herself with memorizing the particulars. And if you study how most classrooms are conducted, you will often find that most of the teacher's questions to pupils are about particulars that can be answered in a few words or even by 'yes' or 'no.' So your introduction of an innovation in teaching will necessarily involve changing the folk psychological and folk pedagogical theories of teachers – and, to a surprising extent, of pupils as well.

Teaching, in a word, is inevitably based on notions about the nature of the learner's mind. Beliefs and assumptions about teaching, whether in a school or in any other context, are a direct reflection of the belief and assumption the teacher holds about the learner. Of course, like most deep truths, this one is already well known. Teachers have always tried to adjust their teaching to the backgrounds, abilities, styles, and interests of the children they teach. This is important, but it is not quite what we are after. Our purpose, rather, is to explore more general ways in which learners' minds are conventionally thought about, and pedagogic practices that follow from these ways of thinking about mind. Nor will we stop there, for we also want to offer some reflections of 'consciousness raising' in this setting: what can be accomplished by getting teachers (and students) to think explicitly about their folk psychological assumptions, in order to bring them out of the shadows of tacit knowledge.

To say only that human beings understand other minds and try to teach the incompetent, is to overlook the varied ways in which teaching occurs in different cultures. The variety is stunning. We need to know much more about this diversity if we are to appreciate the relation between folk psychology and folk pedagogy in different cultural settings.

Understanding this relationship becomes particularly urgent in addressing issues of educational reform. For once we recognize that a teacher's conception of a learner shapes the instruction he or she employs, then equipping teachers (or parents) with the best available theory of the child's mind becomes crucial. And in the process of doing that, we also need to provide teachers with some insight about their own folk theories that guide their teaching.

Folk pedagogies, for example, reflect a variety of assumptions about children: they may be seen as wilful and needing correction; as innocent and to be protected from a vulgar society; as needing skills to be developed only through practice; as empty vessels to be filled with knowledge that only adults can provide; as egocentric and in need of socialization. Folk beliefs of this kind, whether expressed by laypeople or by 'experts', badly want some 'deconstructing' if their implications are to be appreciated. For whether these views are 'right' or not, their impact on teaching activities can be enormous.

A culturally oriented cognitive psychology does not dismiss folk psychology as mere superstition, something only for the anthropological connoisseur of quaint folkways. I have long argued that explaining what children do is not enough; the new agenda is to determine what they think they are doing and what their reasons are for doing it. Like new work on children's theories of mind, a cultural approach emphasizes that the child only gradually comes to appreciate that she is acting not directly on 'the world' but on beliefs she holds about that world. This crucial shift from naive realism to an understanding of the role of beliefs, occurring in the early school years, is probably never complete. But once it starts, there is often a corresponding shift in what teachers can do to help children. With the shift, for example, children can take on more responsibilities for their own learning and thinking. They can begin to 'think about their thinking' (Reading 2.4) as well as about 'the world'.

Advances in how we go about understanding children's minds are, then, a prerequisite to any improvement in pedagogy.

Reading 11.2

Why no pedagogy in England?
Brian Simon

In his classic paper, Simon explains the history of pedagogic thinking in England and the reasons why, despite early promise, it has not been as influential as elsewhere in Europe. He draws attention to assumptions about learning which became embedded within British culture and which are still in some tension today. Are abilities simply inherited? What is the 'human capacity for learning'? If one affirms the latter, argues Simon, then a science of pedagogy is essential, and should be focused on learning processes we share in common. This argument is the basis on which TLRP's principles of effective teaching and learning are based. Although this reading focuses on learning in schools, it is not difficult to see how the same issues are relevant to the FAVE sector.

Do you agree that we share fundamental processes of learning 'in common'?

Edited from: Simon, B. (1981) 'Why no Pedagogy in England?', in B. Simon and W. Taylor (eds) *Education in the Eighties: The Central Issues.* London: Batsford, 128–40.

Education, as a subject of enquiry and study, still less as a 'science', has historically had little prestige in this country, having been to all intents and purposes ignored in the most prestigious education institutions. As Matthew Arnold tirelessly pointed out over one hundred years ago, in France, Prussia and elsewhere, the problems of education for the middle class were taken really seriously. In Britain, on the other hand, everything was neglected; a laissez-faire pragmatism predominated (Arnold, 1874). This situation has, to some extent, been perpetuated. The dominant educational institutions of this country have had no concern with theory, its relation to practice, with pedagogy.

But this is only part of the picture. For whilst the public schools expressed a total disregard for pedagogy, in fact a systematic, rational approach was being developed elsewhere.

Alexander Bain's *Education as a Science* was published in 1879, reprinted six times in the 1880s, and a further ten times before 1990. Examination of student-teacher manuals indicates their indebtedness to Bain. The crucial basis for this approach lay in the theory, announced by Bain as fact, that the formation of associations of ideas in the mind was accompanied by new connections, linkages, or 'paths', in the substance of the brain. The process of education, since it consisted in the planned ordering of the child's experiences, must therefore have a necessary effect. This, of course, had been the basis of the theory of human perfectibility characteristic of the Enlightenment. The approach not only posited the educability of the normal child, it stressed the 'plasticity', as Bain put it, of brain functioning and processes. Education then, was concerned with acquired capacities and functions. It was about human change and development.

Empirical support for the theory of the formation of new connections in the brain as underlying the acquisition of new associations was available to Bain, particularly from the work of his contemporary, the neuro-psychologist Henry Maudesley. Every sense impression resulting in a 'current of molecular activity' from one part of the brain to another, Maudsely wrote, 'leaves behind it … some after-effect' or 'modification of the nerve elements concerned in its function'. This physiological process, he claimed, 'is the physical basis of memory', the 'foundation of our mental functions'.

It followed from this approach that, to order education aright in terms of the acquisition of knowledge, two things were necessary. First, to obtain a psychological (and physi-ological) understanding of the growth of human powers through infancy, childhood and youth; and second, to analyse the content of subject matter in terms of its own inner logic. Together these underlay the determination of the curriculum. But Bain was also closely concerned with motivation, discipline, teacher-pupil relationships, moral education, as well as with the mode of teaching the main curriculum areas. Seeing 'education 'specifi-cally as schooling, he covered in his book almost every relevant aspect of teaching, learning, and classroom organisation.

Of course the theories, and the practices advocated by Bain and the authors of deriv-ative teaching manuals, had their limitations as well as theoretical weaknesses. This goes without saying. But in the 1890s, the approach was serious, systematic and all-embracing. The pedagogy of this specific decade pointed the way to universal education, and was seen as such by its progenitors. What happened? Why was this embryo pedagogy not systemati-cally developed? What went wrong?

One reason was that the social and political context underwent an abrupt change. The development based on Bain's work took place within the elementary system with, at the time, a realistic prospect of organic growth. This was the backcloth, the crucial feature, of this movement as a whole. The administrative and legislative events of 1899 to 1904, almost traumatic in their effects, put a stopper on this. It abolished the School Boards, confined elementary education within precise limits, and established a new system of secondary schooling parallel to, but quite separate from, the elementary system.

This created a new situation. The social-disciplinary function of elementary education was now especially emphasised and a positive pedagogy based on scientific procedures and understanding and relevant for all was no longer seen as appropriate, or required.

However, there now emerged new local authority-controlled systems of secondary education. The more advanced local authorities, determined to extend educational provision, approached this new field with energy and developed considerable pride in the schools systems so created.

It was the establishment and rapid development of this new system of secondary schools which underlay new developments in the theory and practice of education. Thus we find, in the period 1900–14, a renewed concern to develop a relevant pedagogy and it is this that lies behind the great interest in the work of J. F. Herbart and of the Prussian educators who had developed Herbartianism into a system. Once again basing himself on associationism, Herbart set out to explain the process of human acquirements, seeing them as the result of education, of teaching and learning. His ideas were developed and their practical application modified and refined in the work of Rein at the University of Jena and other educators, and found expression in the German schools and thinking from the 1860s.

It was not until the turn of the century however, that Herbart's ideas began to make a serious impact in Britain. By the first decade of the twentieth century, most existing universities were developing and expanding their departments of education and a number of chairs in the subject now existed. These wrote books for teachers either explaining or interpreting Herbart. There was then, a brief new flowering of pedagogy – a serious concern with the theory and practice of education.

The rational foundation for pedagogical theories – for the concept of education as a science – had lain in associationist psychological theories concerning learning. These were espoused by Bain, as we have seen, and also by Herbart and his elaborators. So it was theory and practice based on these ideas which gave rise both to the positive, or optimistic, pedagogics of the 1890s relating to elementary education, and to those of the period 1900–20 relating to the new system of secondary education.

But it was just at this period that new approaches came to predominate in the field of psychology which either relegated associationism to the background, or denied its significance altogether.

The two major influences were, on the one hand, the rise of philosophic idealism, which denied the material basis of mind and decisively rejected the model of human formation; and, on the other hand, the triumph of Darwinism with its emphasis on heredity.

The demands of the system and the movement of ideas now coincided. In the field of educational theory, psychometry (or mental testing) now established its hegemony which lasted over forty years from the 1920s. The triumph of psychometry tied in with a new stress on individualism after World War I and a kind of reductionist biologism. This spelt the end of pedagogy – its actual death. If education cannot promote cognitive growth, as the psychometrists seemed to aver, its whole purpose or direction was lost.

This, I suggest, is the background to our present discontents. For a combination of social, political and ideological reasons, pedagogy – a scientific basis to the theory and practice of education – has never taken root and flourished in Britain.

For a single decade in the late nineteenth century in the field of elementary education; for a similar short period early this century in secondary education, pedagogic approaches and analyses flowered – though never in the most socially prestigious systems of the public schools and ancient Universities. Each 'system', largely self-contained, developed its own specific educational approach, each written within its narrowly defined field, and each 'appropriate' to its specific social function. In these circumstances the conditions did not exist for the development of an all-embracing, universalised, scientific theory of education relating to the practice of teaching. Nor is it an accident that, in these circumstances, fatalistic ideas preaching the limitation of human powers were in the ascendant.

Education and the technological revolution

We can no longer afford to go on in the old way, muddling through on a largely pragmatic, or historically institutionalised basis, tinkering with this and that. In spite of what must surely be temporary setbacks in the provision of educational facilities, the conditions now exist for a major breakthrough in terms of pedagogy. This statement is made on the basis of two contemporary developments, the one structural and the other theoretical. Of major importance here is the insistent tendency towards unification of the historically determined separate systems of schooling through the transition to comprehensive secondary education. This has been accomplished, in the realm of ideas or theory, by a shift in the concern of educators and psychologists from the static concepts of the child (derived from intelligence testing) towards dynamic and complex theories of child development. Both open new perspectives relating to the grounding of educational theory and practice on science (or on scientific procedures).

A revitalised pedagogy?

What then, are the requirements for a renewal of scientific approaches to the practice of teaching – for a revitalised pedagogy?

First, we can identify two essential conditions without which there can be no pedagogy having a generalised significance or application. The first is recognition of the human capacity for learning. It may seem unnecessary, even ridiculous, to single this out in this connection, but in practice this is not the case. Fundamentally, psychometric theory, as elaborated in the 1930s to 1950s, denied the capability of learning capacity, seeing each individual endowed, as it were, with an engine of a given horse-power which is fixed, unchangeable and measurable in each particular case, irrevocably setting precise and definable limits to achievement (or learning). It was not until this view had been discredited in the eyes of psychologists that serious attention could be given to the analysis and interpretation of the process of human learning.

The second condition is the recognition that, in general terms, the process of learning among human beings, is similar across the human species as a whole. As Stones (1979) puts it: 'except in pathological cases, learning capability among individuals is similar', so that, 'it is possible to envisage body of general principles of teaching' that are relevant to 'most individual pupils'. The determination, or identification, of such general principles must comprise the objectives of pedagogical study and research.

One further point must be made at the start. The term 'pedagogy' itself implies structure. It implies the elaboration or definition of specific means adapted to produce the desired effect – such-and-such learning on the part of the child. From the start of the use of the term, pedagogy has been concerned to relate the process of teaching to that of learning on the part of the child. It was this approach that characterised the work of Comenius, Pestalozzi and Herbart, and that, for instance, of Joseph Priestly and the associationist tradition generally.

Both the conditions defined above are today very widely accepted among leading psychologists directly concerned with education and with research into human cognitive development. When Bruner (1972) claimed, in a striking and well-known statement, that 'any subject can be taught to anybody at any age in some form that is both interesting and honest', he was basing himself on a positive assessment of human capacity for learning, and deliberately pointing to the need to link psychology with pedagogy. In an essay aimed at persuading American psychologists of the need to concern themselves with education

– to provide assistance in elucidating the learning process for practicing educators – he stressed his central point, 'that development psychology without a theory of pedagogy was as empty an enterprise as a theory of pedagogy that ignored the nature of growth'. 'Man is not a naked ape,' writes Bruner, 'but a culture clothed human being, hopelessly ineffective without the prosthesis provided by culture.' Education itself can be a powerful cultural influence, and educational experiences are ordered and structured to enable people more fully to realise their humanity and powers, to bring about social change – and to create a world according to their felt and recognised objectives. The major problem humanity faces it not the general development of skill and intelligence but devising a society that can use it wisely' (Bruner, 1972: 18, 131, 158).

When writing this, Bruner was clearly concerned with social change, and with the contribution that pedagogical means might make to this, as we must be in Britain in face of the dramatic social challenge that technological change now presents. And in considering the power of education, rightly ordered, to play a central part in this, it may be as well to recall that, while the simplified and certainly over-mechanistic interpretations of the associationist psychologies of the nineteenth century are no longer acceptable in the form, for instance, expressed by Alexander Bain and his predecessors, the concept of learning as a process involving the formation of new connections in the brain and higher nervous systems has in fact not only retained its force, but has been highly developed by neuro-physiologists and psychologists specifically concerned to investigate learning. Amongst these, perhaps the greatest contribution has been made by A. R. Luria in a series of works relevant to teaching, education and human development generally; but perhaps particularly in his work on the role of language in mental development, and in his theory of what he calls 'complex functional systems' underlying learning (Luria, 1962).

> It is now generally accepted that in the process of mental development there takes place a profound qualitative reorganisation of human mental activity, and that the basic characteristic of the reorganisation is that elementary, direct activity is replaced by complex functional systems, formed on the basis of the child's communication with adults in the process of learning. These functional systems are of complex construction, and are developed with the close participation of language, which as the basic means of communication with people is simultaneously one of the basic tools in the formation of human mental activity and in the regulation of behaviour. It is through these complex forms of mental activity … that new features are acquired and begin to develop according to new laws which displace many of the laws which govern the formation of elementary conditioned reflexes in animals. (1962: 4)

The work and thinking of both Luria and Bruner (as representative of their respective traditions) point in a similar direction – towards a renewed understanding both of the power of education to effect human change and especially cognitive development, and of the need for the systematisation and structuring of the child's experiences in the process of learning.

The main thrust of my argument is this: that to start from the standpoint of individual differences is to start from the wrong position. To develop effective pedagogic means involves starting from the opposite standpoint, from what children have in common as members of the human species: to establish the general principles of teaching and in the light of these, to determine what modifications of practice are necessary to meet specific individual needs. If all children are to be assisted to learn, to master increasingly complex cognitive tasks, to develop increasingly complex skills and abilities or mental operations, then this is an objective that schools must have in common; their task becomes the deliberate development of such skills and abilities in all their children. And this involves importing a definite structure into the teaching, and so into the learning experiences provided for the pupils. Individual differences only become important, in this context, if the pedagogical means elaborated are found not to be appropriate to particular children (or groups of children) because one or other aspect of their individual development or character. In this situation the requirement becomes that of modifying the pedagogical means so that they become appropriate for all: that is, of applying general principles in specific instances.

Reading 11.3

Summary report

Commission on Adult and Vocational Teaching and Learning (CAVTL)

A central strand of the UK Coalition Government's reform plan for the FAVE sector, set out in *New Challenges, New Chances*, was the establishment in 2012 of an independent Commission on Adult Vocational Teaching and Learning (CAVTL). The purpose of the Commission was to identify and promote outstanding practice in vocational education and training. This reading highlights the main findings of Commission's (2013) report and discusses how these findings might be used to support the development of pedagogic practice.

Edited from: the Commission on Adult and Vocational Teaching and Learning (CAVTL) summary report by McLaughlin (2013) and invited papers and evidence presented to CAVTL by M. Gregson and L. Nixon (2013).

Introduction

Far and away the best prize that life has to offer is the chance to work hard at work worth doing.
(Theodore Roosevelt 1858–1919)

The Commission on Adult Vocational Teaching and Learning (CAVTL) published a summary report of its findings *It's about work…Excellent adult vocational teaching and learning*, on 25th March 2013. The above quote from Theodore Roosevelt was used by the Commission to draw attention to the importance and value of doing a job in the world well and for its own sake in any field of vocational practice.

The report contributes to debates about what we do and should value and hold in high esteem in the world of work. According to CAVTL, a key priority is to ensure that the FAVE system in England produces,

'…a home-grown pipeline of skilled individuals, who can design, develop and deliver the sophisticated technology and high quality products and services which will enable the UK to compete at the highest level'.
(CAVTL, 2013: 4)

Such productive work it is argued helps build identity and self-esteem, and promotes the wellbeing of communities. The report particularly emphasises the importance of the need to have a clear line of sight to vocational practice in the workplace. A clear line of sight to work, the report claims is critical because vocational learners must be able to see why they are learning what they are learning, understand what the development of occupational expertise is all about, and experience the job in its context. The real work context of vocational education therefore is paramount and should inform the practice of vocational teaching and learning for learners, teachers and trainers. The report also points to the importance of encouraging the development of cultures and conditions for collaboration to help to deal with unexpected situations and problems that are regularly encountered in the course of any job. The key enabling factor the report points out, is to see the FAVE system, not as a separate 'sector' from the world of employers, but as two-way street where FE colleges, training providers and employers can work together in a spirit of genuine collaboration and mutual engagement. The Commission cited as examples of good practice, cases where employers did not regard themselves simply as customers of vocational teaching and learning, but were engaged at every level in helping to create and deliver excellent vocational programmes.

The Commission commended the excellent examples it found of adult vocational teaching and learning across all sectors of the economy in the UK and celebrated the considerable expertise they were able to draw upon not only in the UK but also in other countries.

The report notes that,

> 'What is clear is that the best vocational teaching and learning is a sophisticated process; it demands 'dual professionals' – teachers and trainers with occupational expertise and experience, who can combine this with excellent teaching and learning practice'.
> (CAVTL, 2013: 8).

This raises questions however about how these 'dual professionals' can and should be supported in developing the occupational and pedagogic expertise their students need and deserve.

The Role of Higher Education Institutions (HEIs) in Developing Pedagogic Practice in FAVE

The challenge then for vocational and workplace tutors is how to use pedagogic knowledge to bring all of the above aspects of vocational education together.

Vocational teachers have been trained and developed through Higher Education Institutions (HEIs) since the 1940s and many HEIs maintain a strong commitment to this provision. There are distinctive elements to what HEIs can offer initial teacher training (ITT) and continuing professional development (CPD) for vocational teachers.

With this in mind we have framed our response to the Commission's report around two important questions.

Initial Teacher Training: What does a new vocational education tutor need to know and be able to do?

The findings of the Commission indicate that new teachers of vocational education need to have,

1 The high levels of practical and theoretical knowledge and occupational and pedagogical expertise demanded of a dual professional.

2 Well-developed capacities for systematic situated practical problem solving i.e. the capacity to respond effectively to unexpected developments through collective learning in order to share and solve problems together.

3 A strong commitment to becoming a professional vocational teacher, enacting educational values in practice, with a clear sense of pride in supporting the achievements of students, apprentices, teachers and trainers.

HE Initial Teacher Training (ITT) courses support the development of high-levels of practical and theoretical knowledge and academic challenge that can extend or contest what new vocational teachers and tutors learn through experience. This challenge encourages new teachers to develop their practice by enabling them to engage systematically and critically with key ideas and research evidence form the field of vocational education. These courses also develop vocational teachers' capacities to respond effectively to unexpected developments in their teaching contexts through individual and collective reflection on practical problems and theoretical issues and by developing their capacities to systematically research their vocational education practice. In these ways vocational teachers can gain their own research-informed, deeper understandings of pedagogical and subject knowledge and learn more than just how to 'get by' or cope in the immediacy of busy and unfolding circumstances.

Continuing Professional Development: How can experienced teachers of vocational education training continue to develop?

HEIs also have a long history of providing continuing professional development (CPD) pathways for more experienced vocational teachers. They have a strong record in taking teachers who do not have traditional academic backgrounds and moving them on from their ITT programmes into BAs, MAs and Ph.Ds. in vocational education as well as in higher level study in their occupational and subject areas

The findings of the Commission indicate that teachers and trainers of vocational education need,

1 Time, encouragement and support (on and off the job) to nurture their own professional expertise.

2 Opportunities to see what cutting edge vocational teaching and learning looks like together with a chance to try out new ideas.

3 Spaces within (and beyond) their workplaces to share ideas, solve problems and learn collectively.

HEIs conduct research in vocational education and training to create new knowledge about the field, which can then inform ITT and CPD for vocational tutors. As such they are uniquely placed to support research and innovation in the vocational education sector not only because of their expertise in research in vocational educational but also because of their deep understanding of enduring and new issues in vocational education through their close connection with teachers and trainers across the sector currently engaged in programmes of ITT and CPD.

For example, the Education and Training Foundation (ETF) in collaboration with the University of Sunderland's Research Centre for Excellence in Teacher Training (SUNCETT) designed a Research Development Fellowship (RDF) programme to support practitioner research in vocational education. The ETF-SUNCETT approach to the RDF programme has developed a model for the initial and continuing professional development of vocational tutors using the principles of Joint Practice Development (JPD) (Fielding et al., 2005). This has successfully enabled significant numbers of vocational tutors from across FAVE to research and improve their pedagogic practice in meaningful, useful and sustainable ways (Gregson et. al 2014). The RDF model takes as its starting point pedagogical problems and concerns raised by vocational tutors in the contexts of their own organisations. It then provides time and spaces (on and off the job) to explore the nature of the problem more carefully, share ideas, solve problems and learn collectively. Over the past four years the RDF programme has helped hundreds of vocational tutors, learners and managers of vocational education to engage with cutting-edge research and practice in the field of vocational education and training.

The RDF programme has supported vocational tutors in trying out new ideas including innovative uses of formative assessment, the development of subject specialist vocational knowledge, creative teaching, and approaches to whole organisation improvement through CPD and has had a clear, positive and evidenced-based impact upon practice in the workplace.

It is important to note that the RDF approach to supporting the initial and continuing professional development of the pedagogic practice of vocational tutors is not a straightforward brokering transaction, which simply links the vocational teacher and the educational issues and practices in question to the relevant research literature. The ETF-SUNCETT model for the RDF provides vocational tutors with direct experience as part of a **contextualised social process** which involves challenging taken for granted world views, theories and practices and making sense of things together in different ways

We applaud CAVTL's call for the creation and development of collaborative spaces in vocational education tutors' professional development where problems and their potential 'solutions' are held tentatively and addressed incrementally and collectively.

CAVTL's eight distinctive features of vocational pedagogy

The Commission's report goes on to identify eight distinctive features of vocational pedagogy together with a number of principles of curriculum development and pedagogy. These are set out in Chapter 2 of the CAVTL report.

The following eight distinctive features are taken by CAVTL to be key elements which underpin excellent vocational teaching and learning. These are outlined below,

1 through the combination of sustained practice and the understanding of theory, occupational expertise is developed;

2 work-related attributes are central to the development of occupational expertise;

3 practical problem solving and critical reflection on experience, including learning from mistakes in real and simulated settings, are central to effective vocational teaching and learning;

4 vocational teaching and learning is most effective when it is collaborative and contextualised, taking place within communities of practice which involve different types of 'teacher' and capitalise on the experience and knowledge of all learners;

5 technology plays a key role because keeping on top of technological advances is an essential part of the occupational expertise required in any workplace;

6 excellent vocational practice requires a range of assessment and feedback methods that involve both 'teachers' and learners, and which reflect the specific assessment cultures of different occupations and sectors;

7 it often benefits from operating across more than one setting, including a real or simulated workplace, as well as the classroom and workshop, to develop the capacity to learn and apply that learning in different settings, just as at work;

8 occupational standards are dynamic, evolving to reflect advances in work practices, and that through collective learning, transformation in quality and efficiency is achieved.

(CAVTL, 2013: 9)

CAVTL's features of vocational pedagogy listed above are useful in that they offer a basis for revising and enhancing curriculum and pedagogical development in the education and training of vocational education professionals.

CAVTL's views on vocational qualifications and curriculum development

The Commission also makes it clear that the quality and relevance of vocational qualifications play an important role in the English system, for employers, individuals and society more generally. CAVTL Commissioners are critical of currently dominant practices in curriculum design and pedagogic practice in vocational education in England. They call for a radical rethink in the current way of going about curriculum design in order to return vocational qualifications to the status they once held as hallmarks of a good vocational learning brought to life through the highest levels of pedagogical expertise.

This will of course not happen overnight and we will need to proceed with care. If we are to support CAVTL in achieving its goals then it is imperative that we learn from the empirical evidence we already have available to us.

In our view and the lessons of ETF- SUNCETT model for RDF programme can offer much to those involved in the potential establishment of National Vocational Education and Training (VET) Centre recommended by the CAVTL report. CAVTL envisages that once established the National VET Centre should take responsibility for curriculum research and development of pedagogic practice in VET in England in the near future.

Reading 11.4

The need for pedagogical repertoire

Robin Alexander

> In this extract from Alexander's essays, he writes about the idea of teachers' pedagogical repertoires being paramount. Alexander argues that classroom teaching requires the judicious selection from three repertoires concerning the organization of interaction, teaching talk and learning talk. He further suggests that dialogic talk provides the best conditions for high-quality learning. Underpinning such teaching strategies, of course, are knowledge about learners, the subject to be taught and the context in which the teaching and learning take place.
>
> Is this three-dimensional analysis of pedagogic repertoire useful to you in reviewing your present practice, and ways in which you might decide to develop it?
>
> *Edited from:* Alexander, R. J. (2008) *Essays on Pedagogy.* Abingdon: Routledge, 109–13.

Here is the essence of the approach on which I have been working.

First, the idea of repertoire is paramount. The varied objectives of teaching cannot be achieved through a single approach or technique. Instead, teachers need a repertoire of approaches from which they select on the basis of fitness for purpose in relation to the learner, the subject-matter and the opportunities and constraints of context.

The idea of repertoire can be extended infinitely, down to the finest nuance of discourse. But to make it manageable, we concentrate in the first instance on three broad aspects of pedagogical interaction: organisation, teaching talk and learning talk.

Repertoire 1: Organising interaction

The *organisational* repertoire comprises five broad interactive possibilities reflecting our earlier distinction between individualism, community and collectivism, or child, group and class:

- whole class teaching in which the teacher relates to the class as a whole, and individual students relate to the teacher and to each other collectively;
- collective group work, that is group work which is led by the teacher and is therefore a scaled-down version of whole class teaching;
- collaborative group work in which the teacher sets a task on which children must work together, and then withdraws;
- one-to-one activity in which the teacher works with individual children;
- one-to-one activity in which children work in pairs.

Thus the organisational possibilities are whole class, group and individual, but group and individual interaction subdivide according to whether it is steered by the teacher or the children themselves. A competent teacher, arguably, needs to able to manage all five kinds of interaction, and select from them as appropriate.

Repertoire 2: Teaching talk

The *teaching talk* repertoire comprises the five kinds of talk we observed in use across the five countries in the international study. First, the three most frequently observed:

- *rote:* the drilling of facts, ideas and routines through constant repetition;
- *recitation:* the accumulation of knowledge and understanding through questions designed to test or stimulate recall of what has been previously encountered, or to cue students to work out the answer from clues provided in the question;
- *instruction / exposition:* telling the student what to do, and/or imparting information, and/or explaining facts, principles or procedures.

These provide the familiar and traditional bedrock of teaching by direct instruction. Less frequently, but no less universally, we find some teachers also using:

- *discussion*: the exchange of ideas with a view to sharing information and solving problems;
- *dialogue:* achieving common understanding through structured, cumulative questioning and discussion which guide and prompt, reduce choices, minimise risk and error, and expedite the 'handover' of concepts and principles.

Each of these, even rote, has its place in the teaching of a modern and variegated curriculum, but the last two – discussion and dialogue – are less frequently found than the first three. Yet discussion and dialogue are the forms of talk which are most in line with prevailing thinking on children's learning.

It's important to note that there's no necessary connection between the first and second repertoires. That is to say, whole class teaching doesn't have to be dominated by rote and recitation, and discussion isn't confined to group work. Discussion and dialogue, indeed, are available in all five organisational contexts (see Figure 11.4.1).

The possibility in Figure 11.4.1 that students can, without teacher intervention, achieve dialogue (which as defined here guides learners cumulatively towards understanding) as well as discussion (which is more exploratory in intent) may elevate some eyebrows. But this is perfectly feasible, given heterogeneous grouping and the different ways and rates in and at which children learn. Vygotsky envisaged the zone of proximal development being traversed 'under adult guidance or in collaboration with more capable peers.' (Vygotsky, 1978: 6).

Indeed, Bell and Lancaster exploited peer tuition 200 years ago in their monitorial systems, though admittedly with rote and memorisation rather than dialogue in mind.

	Rote	Recitation	Exposition	Discussion	Dialogue
Whole class teaching	✓	✓	✓	✓	✓
Collective group work (teacher led)		✓	✓	✓	✓
Collaborative group work (pupil led)				✓	✓
One-to-one (teacher led)		✓	✓	✓	✓
One-to-one (pupil pairs)				✓	✓

Figure 11.4.1
Combined repertoires for classroom teaching

The idea has been revived in more ambitious form through peer mentoring/tutoring (Hargreaves, 2005), and 'learning partners' (Williamson, 2006).

Repertoire 3: Learning talk

The third repertoire is the child's rather than the teacher's. It constitutes not how the teacher talks or organises interaction, but how the children themselves talk, and the forms of oral expression and interaction which they need to experience and eventually master. This learning talk repertoire includes the ability to:

- *narrate*
- *explain*
- *instruct*
- *ask different kinds of question*
- *receive, act and build upon answers*
- *analyse and solve problems*
- *speculate and imagine*
- *explore and evaluate ideas*
- *discuss*
- *argue, reason and justify*
- *negotiate.*

Such abilities are associated with four contingent abilities which are vital if children are to gain the full potential of talking with others:

- *listen*
- *be receptive to alternative viewpoints*
- *think about what they hear*
- *give others time to think.*

Learning talk repertoires such as this depending on how one conceives of human development on the one hand and the curriculum on the other – are often missing from discussion of classroom interaction. Because the teacher controls the talk, researchers tend to start and finish there, focusing on teacher questions, statements, instructions and evaluations and how children respond to them, rather than on the kinds of talk which children themselves need to encounter and engage in.

Principles of dialogic teaching

So far we have a view of classroom talk which requires the judicious selection from three repertoires – organisation, teaching talk and learning talk. Now we come to the heart of the matter. I submit that teaching which is dialogic rather than transmissive, and which provides the best chance for children to develop the diverse learning talk repertoire on which different kinds of thinking and understanding are predicated, meets five criteria. Such teaching is:

- *collective:* teachers and children address learning tasks together, whether as a group or as a class;
- *reciprocal:* teachers and children listen to each other, share ideas and consider alternative viewpoints;
- *supportive:* children articulate their ideas freely, without fear of embarrassment over 'wrong' answers; and they help each other to reach common understandings;
- *cumulative:* teachers and children build on their own and each other's' ideas and chain them into coherent lines of thinking and enquiry;
- *purposeful:* teachers plan and steer classroom talk with specific educational goals in view.

The genealogy of these criteria is complex. Suffice it to say that it combines (i) a positive response to what I and others have observed by way of effective classroom interaction in the UK and elsewhere; (ii) an attempt to counter the less satisfactory features of mainstream classroom interaction (which, for example, tends not to exploit the full collective potential of children working in groups and classes, is one-sided rather than reciprocal, is fragmented or circular rather than cumulative, and is often unsupportive or even intimidating to all but the most confident child); (iii) distillation of ideas from others working in this and related fields – thus, for example, the criterion of reciprocity draws on the pioneering work of Palincsar and Brown (1984) among others, while cumulation reflects not only Bakhtin (e.g. 1986) but also the entire weight of post-Enlightenment understanding of how human knowledge, collectively as well as individually, develops.

Reading 11.5

Using questions in classroom discussion

Elizabeth Perrot

This is a detailed reading on the various skills and strategies involved in the use of questions in classroom discussion. This is an essential part of any teaching repertoire. Perrot considers how to use questioning to improve both the quality of children's thinking, particularly with reference to 'higher-order thinking', and the extent of their participation. Finally, she reviews some of the most important issues in the development of an effective overall questioning strategy. Although this reading is set in schools, it is not difficult to see how the same issues are relevant to the FAVE sector.

Questioning is one of the most important techniques of teaching and taping a session when using questioning is always revealing. What does Perrot's analysis of skills offer to you?

Edited from: Perrot, E. (1982) *Effective Teaching: A Practical Guide to Improving Your Teaching.* London: Longman, 56–91.

Research studies carried out in many parts of the world have shown that the majority of teacher's questions call for specific factual answers, or lower cognitive thought. But higher cognitive questions, which cause pupils to go beyond memory and use other thought processes in forming an answer, have an important role. While both types of questions have their part to play in teaching, a heavy reliance on lower-order questioning encourages rote learning and does little to develop higher-order thinking processes.

Teaching skills associated with helping pupils to give more complete and thoughtful responses are: pausing, prompting, seeking further clarification and refocusing a pupil's response.

Teaching skills associated with increasing the amount and quality of pupils' participation are: redirecting the same question to several pupils, framing questions that call for sets of related facts, and framing questions that require the pupil to use higher cognitive thought.

Such teaching skills are a means to an end (pupils' behaviour). Therefore, you must have clearly in mind the particular end you wish to achieve. Additionally you must become a careful observer of pupils' behaviour, since their reactions can give you valuable clues about the effectiveness of your own performance.

Helping pupils to give more complete and thoughtful responses

Pausing: If the teacher's object is to sample what the class knows within a relatively short time and to elicit brief answers, 'rapid-fire' questioning is an appropriate skill. On the other hand, if the teacher's objective is to provide an atmosphere more conducive to discussion, in which pupils will have time to organize longer and more thoughtful responses, he must adopt a more appropriate questioning procedure. One skill that may be used to encourage longer and more thoughtful responses is to pause for three to five seconds after asking a question, but before calling on a pupil. The use of this skill should eventually result in longer responses because your pupils will be able to discriminate between pausing behaviour and your 'rapid-fire questioning'.

However, they will not automatically give longer answers when you first begin using pausing in your discussions. Depending upon their previous classroom experiences, relatively few pupils may respond appropriately. Some may begin to day-dream, hoping they will not be called on; others may raise their hands without first thinking. Therefore, when you first start using pausing behaviour, you should help the pupils learn what you want them to do. Immediately after the question verbal prompts can be presented, such as, 'Please think over your answer carefully', 'When I call on you, I want a complete answer', then pause for three to five seconds before you call on someone. Success lies in using questions which require longer and more thoughtful responses, pausing to allow ample time to organize those responses and reinforcing pupils for such responses.

If the pupil's response does not come up to the level you are seeking, you must be prepared to help him to develop a better answer. Good ideas however, should not be rejected simply because you did not previously consider them. You should always be prepared to evaluate and accept good answers, and to reinforce the pupil for them.

Prompting: This strategy is based on a series of questions containing hints that help the pupil develop his answer. Sometimes a single prompt will be sufficient to guide the pupil to a better answer. More commonly, it is necessary for the teacher to use a series of prompts which lead the pupil step by step to answer the original question. Teacher prompts may be in the form of intermediate questions, clues or hints that give the pupil the information he needs to arrive at a better answer. If the initial response is partly correct, first reinforce the correct part by telling the pupil what was right. Then begin by modifying the incorrect part. The exact questions used in a prompting sequence cannot be specified in advance, since each depends on the pupils' previous response. However, you should always have in mid the criterion response. Equally important, you should praise the final answer as much as if the pupil gave it at the beginning.

Seeking clarification: In some instances, a pupil may give a response which is poorly organized, lacking in detail or incomplete. Here you face a situation in which the pupil is not wrong, but in which his answer still does not match the response you seek. Under these circumstances you can use the probing skill of seeking clarification. Unlike prompting, seeking clarification starts at a different point on the response continuum. The teacher is not adding information; he is requesting the pupil to do so.

Refocusing: There are numerous occasions when the teacher receives a response that matches the one he wants. Refocusing may then be used to relate the pupil's response to another topic he has studied. The skill is used to help the pupil consider the implications of his response within a broader conceptual framework. He is asked to relate his answer to another issue. Refocusing is the most difficult form of probing since the teacher must have a thorough knowledge of how various topics in the curriculum may be related. You will be able to refocus more effectively if you study the content of your planned discussion beforehand, and note relationships with other topics the class has studied.

Improving the amount and quality of pupils' participation

Redirection: In using the technique of redirection, the same question is directed to several pupils. The question is neither repeated nor rephrased even though more than one pupil responds. To use redirection effectively, you must choose a question which calls for an answer of related facts or allows a variety of alternative responses. A poor question for redirection is one requiring only a single answer, such as 'What is the capital of France?' In this case, the first correct response effectively shuts off further questioning.

The first result of redirection is that you will talk less and the pupils will participate more. A second gain, which can be used to advantage later, is that by requiring several pupils to respond to the same question you can begin encouraging pupils to respond to each other.

Questions calling for sets of related facts: You undoubtedly encounter pupils in your classes who respond to almost any type of question as briefly as possible; that is, they answer 'yes' or 'no', or use only short phrases. Before you blame the pupils for not achieving more, be sure you are not at fault. You may be using types of questions associated with short answers that are not recognizable by their stem. When you ask, 'Isn't the purpose of your local police force the protection of life and property?' you are actually seeking a simple 'yes' or 'no' response. The question is so phrased that confirmation by the pupil is an acceptable answer. If on the other hand, you want discussion, you should phrase the same questions as follows: 'What are the duties of our local police force?' A 'yes' or 'no' response will not suffice here. But what if you have good questions and the pupils are still not responding adequately? Where do you start? As we have suggested, the question itself is only part of the story. Pupils previously allowed to respond briefly or to give memory-type responses are not likely to respond to your expectations at first. Praise the pupil for what he has stated and ask him to contribute more. Success lies in using questions which require longer and better responses and in reinforcing the pupils for their successively longer and better responses.

Higher-order questions: Besides encouraging pupils to give longer responses you should also try to improve the quality of their responses. Indeed, the kinds of questions the teacher asks will reveal to the pupil the kind of thinking which is expected of him. Since different kinds of questions stimulate different kinds of thinking, the teacher must be conscious of the purpose of his questions and the level of thinking they evoke.

An effective questioning sequence is one that achieves its purpose. When your purpose is to determine whether pupils remember certain specific facts, ask recall questions, such as: What is the capital of Canada? When did Henry VIII become King of England?

When your purpose is to require pupils to use information in order to either summarize, compare, contract, explain, analyse, synthesize or evaluate ask higher-order questions. For instance: Explain the kinds of problems caused by unemployment. How did life in the eighteenth century differ from life today?

Developing an overall questioning strategy

In order to be effective, skills must be appropriately incorporated into a questioning strategy planned to achieve particular learning objectives. The following summary indicates the relationships between functions and skills.

Figure 11.5.1
Relationships between functions and skills in questioning

Function	Skill	Participant
To increase readiness to respond	Pausing	Class
	Handling incorrect responses	Individual
	Calling on non-volunteers	Individual
To increase quantity of participation	Redirecting questions	Class
	Calling for sets of related facts	
To improve quality of response	Asking higher-order questions	Individual
	Prompting	Individual
	Seeking clarification	Individual
	Refocusing	Individual
To increase quantity of participation while improving quality of response	Redirecting higher-oder questions	Class

A common problem in questioning sequences is a lack of emphasis on higher-order questions. This may be due to failure in planning a strategy where the primary objective is the improvement of the quality of thought. It may also be related to the fact that questioning is taking place in a group situation where the teacher is concerned with the quantity of pupil participation. In his effort to increase the quantity of pupil participation a teacher might rely on redirecting a disproportionate number of multiple-fact questions. Such tactics tend to emphasize recall and decrease the time available for asking higher-order questions and probing.

A second problem relates to the teacher's failure to refocus. A primary task of the teacher is to help pupils relate what they are presently learning to what they have previously learned. Perhaps an even more significant task is to help pupils to understand that the idea which they are studying are often relevant to other situations. Refocusing is probably the most difficult probing skill. Although the use of this skill depends on the preceding answer of the pupil teachers who have clearly in mind the conceptual content of their lesson can plan for questioning sequences which enable them to use refocusing.

A third problem arises from the teacher's failure to have clearly in mind criteria for evaluating pupil responses. As previously mentioned, skills provide a means to an end.

Only by specifying a particular end can a teacher determine which means are appropriate. To increase the quality of pupils' answers teachers should:

Carefully plan questions which require higher-order responses.

Have in mind the criteria for an acceptable answer.

Identify previously learned facts which are essential to the initiation of the higher-order questions.

Review for essential information to determine what the pupils know.

Frame questions that can be used systematically to develop the original pupil response and meet the higher-order criteria.

Reading 11.6

'Applied', 'technical' and 'vocational': Constructions of knowledge in vocational education

Anne Marie Bathmaker

What is meant by 'knowledge' in vocational education qualifications? Who decides, and who should decide, what 'knowledge' is taught, learned and assessed on vocational programmes? Bathmaker's study indicates the complicated and unstable state of 'knowledge' in vocational education qualifications, in a context where 'skill' is the prevailing discourse. She argues that knowledge needs to be considered in greater depth as part of qualification design, so that vocational qualifications genuinely enable progression, whether to employment or to higher levels of education. Bathmaker reminds us that the issue of knowledge relates to questions of equity and justice.

Bathmaker's paper highlights the different ways people talk about vocational education by using the terms 'skill' and 'knowledge'. Thinking of your own practice where do ideas about skill and knowledge play a role in shaping or justifying current practice? Is one term more prominent than the other? What are the risks associated with this prominence?

Edited from: A. M. Bathmaker (2013) 'Defining "knowledge" in vocational education qualifications in England: an analysis of key stakeholders and their constructions of knowledge, purposes and content', *Journal of Vocational Education & Training*, 65 (1), 87–107.

Defining knowledge in vocational education qualifications

Debates in the literature on knowledge in vocational education start from differing 'ideal types' of vocational education and training, resulting in different imperatives shaping conceptualizations of knowledge. In relation to the focus of this paper, there are three prevalent ideal types, which vary in how closely they are connected to workplace practices. Firstly, there is workplace vocational education, which focuses on the knowledge and skills required for workplace performance (see for example Billett, 2006; Eraut, 1994). This ideal type contrasts with work-related vocational education, which involves broad, general education, embodied in a vocational area or an occupational interest, but which does not seek to meet the specific needs of workplace practices (see for example Pring, 2007; Pring et al., 2009; Young, 2008). A third ideal type involves pre-vocational education. Here the assumption is that learners do not have the necessary 'employability skills' to move into the world of work. The emphasis is therefore on low-level work-readiness skills and also literacy and numeracy skills (see Bates et al., 1984; Gleeson, 1989, 1990; Pollard, Purvis and Walford, 1988).

As this typology suggests, there is a tension in all debates about knowledge in vocational education between an emphasis on knowledge and an emphasis on 'skill', and it is skill rather than knowledge that has been the long-standing emphasis amongst policy-makers and employers in the UK. Moreover, what is meant by skill has both expanded and transformed, from a view of skill dating back to the 1950s as involving 'hard' technical abilities, combining physical dexterity, spatial awareness and technical 'knowhow' (Keep and Mayhew, 1999), to notions of skill at the present time as embracing generic, personal and any other skills deemed to enhance 'employability'. Payne (2000) suggests a number of different ways in which 'skill' is now understood, particularly in relation to education for young people. One meaning concerns attitudes and dispositions, associated with developing the 'right' outlook amongst young people preparing for transition to the labour market. A second meaning embraces all the skills deemed to enhance 'employability', including key or core skills of communication, numeracy and computer literacy; inter-personal or generic skills such as problem-solving and teamwork, as well as business and customer awareness (see Department of Children, Schools and Families [DCSF], 2009). A third version of skill centres around the need to ensure labour market flexibility and focuses on 'transferable' and 'learning' skills, so that people are capable of learning (or retraining) throughout life.

All these versions of skill appear to take precedence in employers' constructions of the purpose and content of vocational education. This is evident in a 2011 report by the UK's Confederation of British Industry (Confederation of British Industry [CBI], 2011), which stressed that:

> Over two thirds of employers (70%) want to see the development of employability skills among young people at school and college made a top priority [...] Two thirds of employers (65%) also see a pressing need to raise standards of literacy and numeracy amongst 14–19 year-olds. [...] Many young people are still leaving school and college with serious shortfalls in their employability skills. Over half of employers (55%) experience weaknesses in school leavers' self-management skills and two thirds (69%) believe they have inadequate business and customer awareness. (CBI, 2011: 6)

This overwhelming focus on 'skill' contrasts with recent debates about the importance of theoretical, abstract knowledge in vocational education amongst researchers such as Young (2008) in the UK and Wheelahan (2008, 2010) in Australia. These authors draw on the work of Bernstein, Durkheim and Vygotsky to distinguish between theoretical, context-independent and everyday, context-dependent knowledge. They use Bernstein's concepts of classification and framing to show the importance of learning abstract theoretical knowledge in vocational as well as academic education. They argue that all students need access to theoretical knowledge, so that they can navigate the boundaries between theoretical and everyday knowledge and between different areas of knowledge. For both Young and Wheelahan, theoretical knowledge represents 'powerful knowledge', where:

> Powerful knowledge provides more reliable explanations and new ways of thinking about

the world and it can provide learners with a language for engaging in political, moral and other kinds of debates. (Young, 2008: 14)

Their work centres on a critical analysis of the value of strongly classified disciplinary knowledge, which may involve either 'traditional' academic disciplines or 'occupationally recontextualised disciplinary knowledge' (Wheelahan, 2008: 23). Both these authors acknowledge that theoretical knowledge is not the only form of knowledge that is important in vocational education. Young (2008: 170) proposes that vocational education should have two purposes: 'providing access to the (disciplinary) knowledge that is transforming work, and acquiring job-specific skills and knowledge'. Wheelahan (2008) puts forward a detailed list of knowledge and skills that form part of vocational education, which includes:

- theoretical knowledge that is relevant to an occupational field of practice;
- knowledge that involves learning about the field of practice itself (e.g. what working in a science laboratory involves);
- knowing how, for example acquiring practical knowledge or technical skills, and the application of those skills and knowledge, to solve problems;
- the application of theoretical knowledge;
- the application of practical knowledge; and
- a wide range of transferable, personal and interpersonal skills and attributes that in themselves have 'underpinning' or related knowledge.

Nevertheless, their thinking and ideas are clearly oriented to 'work-related' vocational education, undertaken in a formal educational setting, rather than 'workplace' vocational education. Moreover, questions remain about the relationship between theoretical knowledge that might be learned through work-related vocational education, and how this connects to the knowledge that is embedded in the workplace, which is often tacit, and does not involve straightforward application of theory learned elsewhere. Guile (2006) argues that this relationship is central to conceptualising what is meant by knowledge in vocational education and how it should be learned.

The contrasting emphasis on knowledge and skill outlined above occurs against a context of widespread uncertainty about the legitimate purposes and content of academic as well as vocational education, and a retreat from talking about knowledge in other than very general, inclusive terms. Discussions of theoretical knowledge face particular challenges in the context of work-related vocational education and associated qualifications… Theoretical knowledge is perceived as alien and difficult, and associated with the disengagement of 'vocational' students from formal education. In England, this problem has historically been addressed by avoiding or reducing the amount of theoretical knowledge taught, rather than finding alternative ways to make it accessible (Atkins, 2009; Bates, 1998; Ecclestone, 2002). Moreover, a multiplicity of purposes means that a range of different stakeholders and experts, with their own particular interests, seek to influence the making and shaping of policy…

Confusion about purposes, the distinctiveness or otherwise of vocational education qualifications as opposed to other qualifications, and about the scope and remit of stakeholders were inextricably linked to wide-ranging views about what was meant by 'knowledge' in work-related vocational education, how it related to generic skills such as learning to learn, employability and so on, and what the respective importance or weighting of these areas should be. Stakeholders in both interviews and seminars were asked to define important knowledge in work-related general vocational education. This question generated a variety of different terms, which loosely grouped under three headings: workplace practice knowledge and skills; generic and transferable skills of various kinds; and subject knowledge or theory, as shown below:

Workplace practice knowledge and skills

- practice-focused knowledge,
- technical skills (e.g. using a piece of equipment) and,
- the skills and attitudes needed in the workplace.

Generic and transferable skills of various kinds

- non-technical skills (communication, planning, reporting, analysis and others),
- generic skills,
- personal learning and thinking skills,
- generic employability skills,
- employability skills,
- cognitive skills and
- generic concepts.

Subject knowledge and theory

- subject knowledge,
- a body of subject knowledge,
- pure knowledge and
- theory.

The diversity of knowledge discussed by participants in the study, spanning everything from workplace knowledge and skills through to academic, subject knowledge, in part reflected frequent, unnoticed slippage... The burgeoning list of knowledge and contentalso meant that discussions became trapped in arguments about too much or too little of different kinds of knowledge, rather than exploring the connections between different forms of knowledge as a distinctive focus for vocational education...

Discussion and conclusions

Repeated overhauls to funding, design and regulation, together with competition between qualification awarding bodies for market share over a considerable period of time in England, have done little to develop agreement about valuable knowledge to be learned by students taking these qualifications, and who should be involved in this process. This study shows a lack of consensus about the purposes of different forms of vocational education, and in particular, general, work-related vocational education, which is accompanied by tensions between the role of vocational education qualifications as preparation for work versus preparation for further study. There was a complex mix of stakeholders involved in designing and regulating vocational education qualifications, but it was difficult to discern which stakeholders take any responsibility for knowledge outside of qualification awarding bodies. For some respondents, the qualification awarding bodies were, and should be, seen as the most important determinant of what knowledge was included in qualifications and how that knowledge was developed. Yet, it was not clear from this study, how awarding bodies would engage with new developments and understandings of knowledge and maintain the currency of their qualifications without regular and structured engagement with outside experts.

Although employers were positioned as playing a central role, there was real uncertainty about defining who 'employers' were, or should be, in this context, and alongside this, ambiguity about their role as stakeholders in both design and day-today implementation of vocational education qualifications. Moreover, the employers and employer representatives who participated in the study tended to place the dominant emphasis on the development of generic and employability skills and had much less to say about specialist occupational knowledge, including relevant theoretical knowledge, in the context of vocational education qualifications. These are ongoing problems in English vocational education and training. A previous study by Young (2006: 111) found that while employer-led bodies continue to be seen as those who should take the lead in developing the vocational curriculum, 'despite the reality that in many sectors employers are reluctant to take on such a role and frequently lack the necessary expertise'. A further effect of the constant emphasis on employers in national policy is to disguise the absence of other important stakeholders, such as subject specialists from universities and subject associations, not to mention worker representatives, who might usefully contribute to evolving understandings of knowledge...

The questions raised about knowledge in this paper can also be asked about general, subject-based and workplace occupational qualifications: the issues encompassed by these questions are not ones that apply solely to vocational education qualifications. At the same time, this study raises questions that are particular to vocational education qualifications. The absence of important constituencies in qualifications development at national level in England sets considerable limitations on the possibilities for vocational education qualifications to be informed by new and evolving knowledge from research as well as occupational practice, or to be informed by the experience of practising teachers who work with students. Moreover, an emphasis on skill precludes serious engagement by those involved in vocational education qualifications with questions of knowledge, why knowledge may be important, and how it may best be learned. The 2011 Wolf review in England has not resolved these underlying issues.

Yet if, following Bernstein (1996), a key role of theoretical knowledge is to enable people to think the unthinkable and the not-yet-thought, and to imagine alternative futures, then a failure to engage with understandings of knowledge that reflect new thinking, in the context of 'vocational' as well as 'academic' education, unwittingly denies young people taking vocational education qualifications the opportunity to take part in society's debates and controversies (Wheelahan, 2010). As a crucial part of the education landscape, especially in a context of extended participation in full-time education, questions of knowledge are questions of equity and justice, which concern not just initial vocational education, but shape and constrain opportunities in young people's future working and learning lives.

Communication
How does language support learning?

12

Using examples and case studies for the teaching of adult reading (12.1), this chapter illustrates the importance of key issues including the maintenance of relationships of respect and dignity in communicating with our students. Gregson and Nixon (12.2) go on to show how the ways in which policy is implemented can distort communication in highly symbolic ways, which signal important tensions and contradictions in pedagogic practice. Thomson and Tuckett (12.3) highlight the importance to individuals and to the state of creating opportunities for people to learn throughout the life-course.

As a whole, these readings provide glimpses into some of the richness and educational potential of the contribution of communication to pedagogic practice and the shared responsibility of teachers for the development of communication skills. However, they also highlight the level and importance of the pedagogic expertise which is necessary to achieve this.

The associated chapter in *Reflective Teaching in Further, Adult and Vocational Education* considers the major characteristics of communication in FAVE contexts. At the end of the chapter suggestions for 'Key Readings' in relation to each of the topics covered are offered. These can be extended as with reference to the *reflectiveteaching.co.uk* website.

Reading 12.1

Foregrounding in adult literacy
Sam Duncan

In this reading edited from her 2012 book, Duncan writes about the role of reading in adult life. She traces the place of trade, history and empire in the history of reading and the 'shifting physicality' of how we read. She draws attention to how reading has been made a practice of social conformity or resistance as well as a choice, need or desire. Reading is strongly linked to democratic participation and is highly political. Duncan points to us reading for different reasons and in different ways and how this is the background against which we need to understand reading development and adult education.

Edited from: Duncan, S. (2012) *Reading Circles, Novels and Adult Reading Development.* London: Continuum/Bloomsbury, Chapter 2.

Reading and adult life

We read political manifestos and food packets, clothing websites and concert posters, street names and obituaries. We read because we want to and need to, because we are told to and sometimes because we are told *not* to. We read to learn, understand, escape, relax, be entertained, do our jobs, help our friends, communicate, cry, laugh and administer our lives. We read through arduous struggles and we read without realising that we have read anything.

I am using the pronoun 'we' to represent some experiences common to many people on this planet right now. Yet what would this picture have looked like five thousand years ago? One thousand? Five hundred? Two hundred? Even fifty? A quick glance at the history of reading seems at first to reveal a logical and inevitable path from antiquity – where reading was something oral, social and public, performed aloud by the few, male, experts reading from heavy pieces of stone or bulky scrolls – to our postmodern world where reading is predominantly a silent, private, solitary act which everyone does, at all times of day and night, reading from screens which will probably soon be implanted in our eyelids. In many ways this is not far from accurate, but these two end points create the illusion of a smooth and homogeneous development, obscuring the many twists and turns, blips, revolutions and contradictions that can provide us with the greatest insights into the role of reading in adult life.

Trade, religion and empire

Most historians agree that there were four independent birthplaces of writing: Mesopotamia, Egypt, China and Mesoamerica. Literacy practices moved to and from the Indian subcontinent through developments in religion and philosophy, as well as trade routes. Further west, the Phoenicians traded with the Ancient Greeks, bringing the alphabet which the Greeks, via the Etruscans, then brought to the Romans and the Romans to much of Europe. With both trade and religion, the Chinese brought their writing system to Japan, where the Japanese adapted it to write their evolving languages. The early Christians brought Latin and its alphabet to most of Western Europe, where the Celtic and Germanic peoples either converted or not, either started using the Latin language or not, but, regardless, used the Roman alphabet to produce written texts in their own languages on an unprecedented scale. The Greek alphabet also spread with the Eastern Orthodox Church, leading to the development of Cyrillic to write the Slavonic languages, while Islam brought the Arabic language and writing system to its conquered territories in Asia, Africa and southern Europe (Coulman, 2003; Ostler, 2005).

The European empires of France, Portugal, Spain, Holland and England/Britain brought their languages, religions and writing systems to their trading posts and colonies in Africa, Asia and the Americas. Along with the imposition of the vernacular European languages, the Roman alphabet began to be used as a writing system for native languages, some of which had been predominantly oral, or had used other systems of recording – such as the Quipu knot system of Peru and Ecuador (Coulmas, 2003: 20) – designed for administration rather than for narrative. With attempted religious conversion came new literacy practices, including the use of key religious texts translated into indigenous languages and written using the Roman alphabet. Invasion, religious conversion and economic empire-building continue to influence what, how and why we read and write.

The shifting physicality of reading

The first writing was probably done in cuneiform on clay tablets in the fourth millennium BC (Coulmas, 2003) and, for the next four thousand years, we read from stone or clay tablets, walls of buildings and statues, engraved pieces of wood, papyrus scrolls and pieces of animal skin. Over the past two thousand years we have moved from scrolls to the codex (the arrangement of bound pages we would now call a book) of parchment (sheep or goat skin) and then paper (Clanchy, 2009), from painstaking hand-copying to printing, and generally from larger to smaller volumes, a shift culminating in the paperback boom of the twentieth century. Kindles, iPads, smartphones, laptop screens and other electronic reading devices are probably even more revolutionary in terms of shifting the physical experience of reading, though it is still too early to say exactly how they have done this and to what extent.

Yet we certainly do not *only* read from screens now – or from books – but also from buildings, items of clothing, Zeppelins, the sides of trains and buses, each other's bodies (see Peter Greenaway's *The Pillow Book* (1996)), the walls of our homes and from billboards – Banana Yoshimoto first published her story *Newlywed* on a series of billboards on walls of the Tokyo Underground (Figes, 1996). We read standing up, sitting down, leaning on walls, lying on the floor, at tables, on tables and under tables. When completely alone in small flats, we shout poetry aloud for company, and when squashed on crowded trains we read silently to carve a private space. The physical nature of the texts we read, along with the material and immaterial conditions of our lives, continues to determine how we position our bodies, how we use our voices, and how, when and where we read.

Reading, civil rights and illiteracy

Learning how to read has often been seen as the basis for acquiring socially sanctioned moral behaviour, religious or otherwise. Yet at the same time, certain acts of reading, and certain texts, have been labelled as most definitely immoral. From the early Christian censorship of 'Pagan' (Classical and Muslim) texts to Henry Miller's *Tropic of Cancer*, the most common reason for text censorship is the claim of immorality. Further, a moral spotlight on reading identifies not only inappropriate texts but also inappropriate readers. Early modern scholars feared what teaching the poor to read could unleash (Houston, 2002). For similar reasons, there was a ban on teaching a slave or freed Black person to read in the United States before (and at a certain stage after) the Civil War (Salvino, 1989). Reading practices have been encouraged, enforced and banned by states and individuals in the name of morality, making reading a practice of social conformity or resistance as well as a choice, need or desire.

If, over the past five hundred years, the discourse linking reading and religion has been replaced with (or, in some contexts, joined by) a discourse linking reading and morality, then over the past hundred years this may well have been replaced with a discourse linking reading with democratic participation. Being able to read, the twentieth century proclaimed, means being able to participate in the democratic process. Reading, importantly, became a citizen's right. It became, as Brandt (2001) stresses, the responsibility of a democracy to equip its citizens with the tools for participation; chief among these was learning to read. This discourse provided a powerful argument for governments to supply the means for both adults and children to learn to read. It also, however, contributed to rising expectations of literacy and put in motion a dangerous slide, from literacy as every citizen's democratic right to literacy as an obligation, and illiteracy as a form of social irresponsibility (Brandt, 2001) – or even criminality.

Freire remembers talking with a Brazilian peasant about the difference between two hunters, an 'Indian' and a peasant:

> 'Between these two hunters,' he asserted, 'only the second can be illiterate. The first is not.' 'Why?' I asked him. [...] He answered, 'One cannot say that the Indian is illiterate because he lives in a culture that does not recognize letters. To be illiterate you need to live where there are letters and you don't know them' (Freire, 1985: 4).

The label of illiteracy comes with a literate society, and as expectations of literacy rise, so does the stigma of the 'illiterate'. The cycle of increased expectations wrongly assumes that if you teach everyone to read, then everyone will learn to read. It makes a deficit of those for whom reading does not come easily. Rising expectations of literacy can also become, as Brandt (2001) warns, a way to divide the population: the literate get more literate as the rich get richer. The role of reading in adult life has never been less than supremely political.

Summary

We have read from stone, wood, animal skin, our own skin and paper. Our languages, writing systems, textual artefacts, text types and associated reading practices have been passed around the globe with the best and worst products of the human imagination: stories, war, trade, dreams, religion and ideology. Our reading practices have been influenced by invention: paper, reading glasses, the printing press and libraries, inspiring and inspired by writing practices. We have read aloud and silently, alone and in groups, enacting and creating shifting notions of public and private. Our reading has been linked to our rights and obligations as members of religious communities and as national citizens, and our reading has reaped reward, punishment and judgement. The crucial point is that we read for very different reasons and in very different ways. This is the background against which we need to understand reading development and adult education.

Reading 12.2

Unlocking the potential for improvement in Skills for Life teaching and learning at the local level

Margaret Gregson and Lawrence Nixon

This reading draws on a range literature to explore how the instruments for the implementation and evaluation of SfL policy have operated in the past to shape English/literacy and Maths/numeracy (Skills for Life – SfL) practice in ways that produce unintended, negative consequences. For example, recent ways of using the 'Individual Learning Plans' have been shown to limit the choices of tutors to 'a limited range of procedural decisions' that marginalize so much that should be included in an education that prepares learners for the work of life. It is argued that in order to unlock the potential of this classroom practice, alternative 'democratic discursive spaces' need to be established where policy-makers and practitioners can share their knowledge and expertise to improve both policy and practice.

When reflecting on this reading, consider the following question: how could 'front-line' teachers of SfL be included in the evaluation and revision of implementation processes of English/literacy, Maths/numeracy and ESOL provision?

Edited from: Gregson, M., and Nixon, L. (2011) 'Unlocking the potential of Skills for Life (SfL) tutors and learners: a critical evaluation of the implementation of SfL policy in England'. *Teaching in Lifelong Learning,* 3 (1), 52–66. Huddersfield: University of Huddersfield Press.

ALLN Global and perspectives

Identifying the impact of any social policy upon practice is never simple or easy. The same educational policy can be implemented and evaluated in different ways in different contexts for a wide variety of reasons. This presents political, policy and educational professionals with the complex task not only of trying to make a educational policy 'work' in practice but also of understanding how well and why it is, or it is not, working. (Gregson and Nixon, 2009).

Approaches to the teaching, learning and assessment of Adult Literacy, Language and Numeracy (ALLN) remain contested and the field is populated by widely different understandings of what it means to be and/or to become literate and numerate and for what purpose. However, policy initiatives which overlook the contested nature of the field of ALLN continue to punctuate education policy discourse on a global scale.

In the *Education for All Global Monitoring Report* published by United Nations Educational Scientific and Cultural Organisation (Burnett, 2005), Burnett argues that inability to read, write and calculate not only prevents people from knowing their civil rights and how to demand and defend them but also limits their ability to participate politically in society. The same report emphasises that these abilities are essential human rights because they are the means through which people achieve other human rights, access other fields of vocational and disciplinary knowledge and provide individuals and groups with opportunities to participate in the economic and social development of the countries and communities in which they live. Drawing attention to the urgency of devoting increased policy attention and resources to literacy, language and numeracy development for both children and adults the report highlights the profound benefits of literate societies for individuals, communities and nations.

SfL unprecedented funding and policy achievements

The SfL strategy (2001) was the first national policy for ALLN in England. It attracted unprecedented levels of funding (£2 billion) to an important, long- neglected and under-resourced field of adult education. It raised the status and set standards of professional qualifications to which ALLN tutors were expected to work towards. The same policy introduced standardised initial and diagnostic assessment instruments, which aimed to bring greater rigour, coherence and structure to SfL practice. The National Core Curriculum (NCC) specified for the first time which aspects of literacy, language and number acquisition should be covered in ALLN programmes. SfL policy and strategy also served to raise the importance and increase the standing of ALLN teaching and learning. The SfL strategy also extended ALLN pedagogy beyond what were often well-intended but sometimes ad hoc practices of the past, towards standards of professional knowledge and practice resembling those already expected of teachers in other sectors of education (Hamilton and Hillier 2006).

The rise of cultures of compliance in SfL

The same authors track chronological trajectories in the ALLN policy process from the more holistic practices of ALLN in the 1970s through to the SfL policy agenda and strategy. They draw attention to the ways in which policy development and pedagogy in relation to ALLN in England became increasingly simplified, linked to SfL targets and wider economic concerns. Intensified by the economic crisis, the danger of these moves they argue is that they can lead to the privileging of the imperatives of the economy and the market over the more holistic educational concerns for democracy, civil and human rights, educational inclusion and social justice, which inspired early UK literacy campaigns.

In the field of compulsory education Morais (2001),Teese and Polesel (2003a, 2003b) show how top-down approaches to the implementation of education policy are increasingly pushing pedagogy towards compliance with externally set, centrally prescribed standards of performance. Ball describes this in terms of 'performativity' (Ball, 2003, 2004, 2010). Beck and Young (2005) and Clegg and Bradley (2006) reveal similar policy influences upon pedagogic practice in the field of higher education in England. Coffield et al. (2005), Coffield and Edward (2010a) and Coffield (1999, 2002, 2004, 2005, 2009, 2010b) extend the debate to include the nature of reforms in the Further Adult and Vocational Education (FAVE) sector in England.

Fenwick (2006), and Wheelahan (2005) identify similar pushes towards compliance and performativity in systems of education in Canada and Australia. The work of the above authors is important because it illustrates the way in which education policy not only shapes educational practice nationally and internationally but also frames what can and cannot be said, thought or enacted in particular pedagogic contexts.

From the outset the SfL policy strategy was characterised by the setting of challenging national targets for the achievement of improvements in ALLN. These targets were set centrally by UK policy makers and politicians. Staff across the FAVE sector worked extremely hard and dedicated considerable amounts of time, energy, money and resources to ensure, year on year that SfL targets were met. For example from April 2001 until July 2005 over 69,000 people in the North East of England (NE) alone achieved one or more of the national qualifications that counted towards the Government's SfL Public Service Agreement (PSA) targets for achievements in ALLN (DfES, North East Regional Office, 2006).

What is perhaps most remarkable about this achievement is that despite over 10 years of formal compulsory schooling, for many of these adult learners, achieving this qualification, was hugely significant … because it was their first!

The means through which SfL policy was implemented and evaluated involved the use of targets and 'outcomes', delivered through Individual Learning Plans (ILPs), framed in terms of the NCC. This development is significant because it signals the point at which the means of SfL policy implementation (ILP and qualification targets which levered funding) became the measures of its success.

Elliott (2001) contends that while the virtue of models of education based upon outcomes such as the ILP and targets for the achievement standards and levels of qualifications, on the face of it, seem to be a matter of 'common sense' and not open to question, such educational measures for evaluating the success of an educational policy reform actually rest upon some very questionable assumptions. Elliott argues that by specifying educational outcomes for all students; which are then referred to as 'standards' to be demonstrated as exit behaviours; which are then expressed as 'targets' to be measured against benchmarks of attainment (which in the case of SfL became a lever for funding), the mechanisms for the predictable and pre-determined failure of models of outcomes-based models of education are effectively locked in place.

Such educational reforms Elliott claims see the outcomes of teaching only as measurable outputs and render them as, not only predictable, but also amenable, to simplification by policy professionals and technical control by the teacher. Elliott illustrates how concerns with improving teaching then (simply) become a matter of increasing technical control over the production of increasingly predictable learning outcomes. The problem he claims becomes further compounded when evaluations of the success of educational outcomes and benchmarks of achievement are measured in inelastic ways, regardless of context and contingencies.

The means we use to evaluate education are therefore not neutral in relation to the ends we wish to achieve because they contribute qualitatively to the very character of the ends they produce. That is why Elliott (2001) argues education must be essentially more of a moral practice that a technological enterprise. Elliott points to the urgent need for the evaluation of education to become more educational for all concerned.

It is important to note how outcomes-based approaches to educational evaluation and improvement in the form of targets in SfL were centrally prescribed. This served to encourage pre-occupations with target-led activity and vertical accountability. In turn, these brought with them the high overheads associated with performative demonstrations of compliance which then require micromanaged regulation.

Hamilton is critical of how the implementation and evaluation of SfL policy was framed around the production of Individual Learning Plans (ILPs) and qualifications which were subsequently used as a key measure of success and a lever of funding. She illustrates how ALLN teachers widely expressed their concerns about ILPs in terms of,

> … a crisis of time, the inability of the ILP to represent the diversity of student experience, their needs or their narratives about their experiences and progress and constrain what counts as learning…tutors take up an enforced position as broker or mediator between student and demands and system requirements. This translation work is demanding and involves a high level of engagement that involves constrained manoeuvres within a tightly controlled framework drawn up by experts external to practice allowing tutors to make only a limited range of procedural decisions.
>
> (Mary Hamilton, 2009: 225).

The work of the above authors contributes to a growing body of literature which demonstrates in several fields of social and public policy including education, local government and medicine how government use of performance indicators and high stakes targets in public service reforms can have costly, perverse, unpredicted and even unwanted outcomes for teachers, learners and other stakeholders in the public domain.

In view of the expensive overheads of outcomes-based approaches to the implementation and evaluation of SfL policy and the limited effectiveness of such approaches to educational reform to date, we should know enough now to shun the offer of ready-made, centrally prescribed de-contextualised solutions for improving teaching, learning and assessment in ALLN in particular and in FAVE in general. Political, policy and education professionals should also know enough now to be able to muster the vision and courage to explore different approaches to education policy development and its implementation and evaluation. There is a clear and pressing need to design approaches to educational improvement capable of addressing the expensive shortcomings of outcomes-based models of educational and curriculum development which have proved to be so costly and have resulted in so little real improvement in education in the past.

Hajer and Wagenaar argue that many policy problems are now 'too complicated, too contested and too unstable to allow for schematic, centralised regulation' and that what is needed is 'deliberative policy analysis in order to help us to get to grips with the political phenomena of our time' (2003: 7). In the context of ALLN the challenge now facing us is to unlock the potential of ALLN of practitioners to improve educational practice in this important specialist branch of FAVE by opening up 'democratic discursive spaces' where policy makers and practitioners can share their knowledge and expertise to improve both policy and practice in this important field of education.

In closing we argue that there is never enough knowledge and there never will be enough time to make the perfect policy decision. However, as Scott (1999) and Keep (2006) point out, unless the state manages to find new ways of working and sharing power with those expected to implement its policies, then it is likely that it will find itself locked in a system of state control where the high costs and overheads of supervising unintended, ineffective and inefficient outcomes of public service policy will ultimately outweigh any potential benefits of those policies to its citizens and tax payers.

Reading 12.3

Reading 12.3

Lifelong learning in challenging times: An agenda for a new government

Alastair Thomson and Alan Tuckett

This paper was produced by NIACE, the National Institute of Adult Continuing Education, as a platform to shape its advocacy work with political parties ahead of the 2010 General Election. NIACE has enjoyed a voluntary sector compact with successive governments, recognizing its role as a critical friend – representing the interests of adult learners. It drew heavily on the independent Commission on the Future of Lifelong Learning, commissioned and funded by NIACE, following the loss of a million adult learners from public provision in England between 2002–8, and offers, we think, a continuing case for a lifelong learning strategy.

Alastair Thomson was Principal Advocacy Officer at NIACE from 1987–2014 and Alan Tuckett was Chief Executive Officer, NIACE, from 1988–2011.

Thomson A. and Tuckett A. (2010) *Lifelong Learning in Challenging Times: An Agenda for a New Government.* London. NIACE.

Introduction

The new government, of whatever political complexion, faces a range of challenges:

- *financial* – to ensure effective, sustainable recovery from global recession;
- *demographic* – to prepare for half a million fewer young people entering the labour market in the coming decade, a rapidly growing older population and greater international labour market flexibility;
- *technological* – to match the pace of innovation and entrepreneurialism of our trading partners;
- *environmental* – to secure a low carbon economy and greater sustainability;
- *social* – to secure social justice, community cohesion, and to minimise the negative impacts of inequality.

To meet these challenges the United Kingdom needs an adult population that is:

- confident and capable;
- engaged and empowered;
- enterprising and curious;
- cultured and reflective;

We need a society which ensures social justice for all, which is tolerant, inclusive and which celebrates diversity. In short, we need a learning society where:

- there is widespread understanding and confidence that we can learn our way out of our current difficulties, and lay the foundations for a future that values the contributions everyone can make to well-being and prosperity;
- everyone can see what they can contribute to make vibrant and inclusive communities, entrepreneurial, innovative and successful businesses and public services, and to making the world a better place for our children.

To that end NIACE, the National Institute of Adult Continuing Education, believes we need a national strategy for lifelong learning, backed by stable organisational structures, with national leadership combined with enough autonomy to support local decision making to fit local circumstances.

In 2007 NIACE commissioned an independent Inquiry into the Future of Lifelong Learning to look prepare the ground. Its final report, *Learning through life* was published in September 2009, and NIACE endorses its key recommendations, which are to:

- base lifelong learning policy formation on a new model of the educational life-course, with four key stages (up to age 25, 25–50, 50–75, and those aged 75+);
- re-balance resources fairly and sensibly across the different life stages;
- build a set of learning entitlements for adults;
- engineer flexibility by developing a system of credit across post-compulsory education and training, and by encouraging part-time study;
- improve the quality of work rather than the volume of qualifications;
- construct a curriculum framework for citizens' capabilities;
- broaden and strengthen the capacity of the lifelong learning workforce;
- revive local responsibility within national frameworks; and
- make the public system more intelligent.

Each recommendation was backed by detailed and none assumed an increase in spending overall.

Addressing the challenges highlighted above will involve major cultural change – to find ways of engaging everyone in learning at key points of change and development in their lives. The failures in the banking sector must not be allowed to deflect the UK from investing in lifelong learning that will help avoid such problems in the future.

Since 1997 government has increased spending on further education by 52 per cent, but that increase was concentrated in 1999–2003, and has been focussed overwhelmingly on those aged 18–25. For learning responsive to adults over 25, resources have stagnated or reduced, and there are more than 1,500,000 fewer publicly supported adult learners than there were in 2004. Meanwhile, employer investment overall remains concentrated on the already well-qualified.

In higher education there remains 'unfinished business' about the differential financial treatment of full- and part-time study, as well as how the UK pays for a mass system in an increasingly global higher education economy.

Reducing public expenditure on lifelong learning would be a wholly counterproductive measure. It would have the effect of reducing the UK's economic competitiveness as well as resulting in higher costs in such areas as health, criminal justice and community cohesion.

Existing resources can be better used by balancing them in a more sophisticated way to maximise a wider range of public benefits.

Three key principles

1. Inclusivity – every adult matters

NIACE evaluates policy proposals impacting on adult education and training by asking how far they benefit those adults who have benefited least from their initial learning and who face particular barriers to study. These include:

- part-time and temporary workers for whom time for formal learning is a major problem since employers seldom prioritise their skills development;
- those employed in businesses which are 'cool to training';
- people aged 45+ who are too often neglected when it comes to workplace training and development;
- migrants whose potential contribution may not be recognised by employers unfamiliar with a culturally and linguistically diverse workforce with skills but not qualifications recognised in the UK;
- women, especially from ethnic minority communities culturally resistant to high levels of female employment outside the home;
- people currently on welfare benefits – including those on Incapacity Benefits as a result of mental ill-health;
- ex-offenders;
- adults with the lowest levels of literacy and numeracy.

For these groups, further marketisation of lifelong learning won't help.

Because of the UK's changing demographic profile, NIACE believes special consideration must be given to educational opportunities for older people. For those aged 50–75, learning has a role to play in supporting prolonged economic activity; and for all older adults it can make a marked contribution to the quality of life – it has positive impacts on well-being and physical health which generate massive quantifiable savings in health and social care costs. For these reasons, **NIACE believes that the new government should consider introducing an older learners' entitlement.**

NIACE believes that policies which realise the contribution of people who are at risk of marginalisation and exclusion will be of both economic and social benefit to all.

2. Equitable contributions

Building a learning society will require increased investment by **everyone** – individuals, employers and government alike. But for this to happen there needs to be greater equity:

- in the distribution of opportunity across the whole lifecourse;
- between the resourcing of further and higher education;
- between the fees and support for part-time and full-time study;
- in the way employer and employees' contributions are recognised.

Although the general education of the adult population results in quantifiable public benefits, it also brings private benefits to individuals and for this reason, NIACE believes that adults who can afford to contribute to the cost of learning should do so in proportion to the benefit received and that public support should not further enhance the privileges of the most advantaged. A national system of learning accounts could form the basis of personalised entitlements.

NIACE also believes public money should not be used to displace existing private sector spending – and that it is the job of employers to train staff for their current and anticipated economic activities. State support for employers should focus on strategically important or emerging industries, innovation in the delivery of education and training and its dissemination; and widening participation.

NIACE is attracted to sectoral or occupational 'licence to practice' initiatives as means of raising levels of competence, standards and productivity in the workplace. The advantage of industry-wide approaches is that organisations committed to training suffer no competitive disadvantage against those which poach trained staff.

NIACE believes, too, that there should be a public commitment by government over the life of new Parliament to begin to develop a tertiary system that brings higher and further education closer together

3. Curricular breadth

The public benefits of education and training are not limited to particular subjects or levels of study. They can be measured through the behaviours and attitudes of adults who identify themselves as learners – whether that is through high-level formal study, vocational training, informal learning in community settings or independent study using new technology.

The state cannot be expected to meet all the learning aspirations of adults but neither should it presume to micro-manage resources. NIACE believes that it is reasonable for 80 per cent of public spending to focus on the government's priorities, the remaining 20 per cent should be determined by learners themselves (through the direction of resources through learning accounts) and by approved providers of education and training responding to local and regional need.

Building adults' capabilities

NIACE believes that the new government should introduce a common curriculum framework which would represent the state's offer to its adult population. This would include measures to build

- health capability;
- financial capability;
- civic capability; and
- digital capability.

This framework should be subject to local decision making to determine how such capabilities should be developed given local needs and aspirations.

The capability of adults to be good parents, grandparents or carers is the final part of this mosaic. Families have more impact on the educational success of children than do schools. And family and inter-generational learning has a positive impact on the life chances of children and adult alike so NIACE urges the new government to take an expansive approach to family policy in respect of learning by ensuring that the needs of adults are given parity with the learning needs of children.

Assessment
How can assessment enhance learning?

The readings in this chapter provide clarification on types of assessment and suggest the positive contribution assessment can make to teaching and learning. In the first reading (13.1) Hamilton and Hillier draw distinctions between assessment testing and accreditation in the context of the *Skills for Life* policy in England, which aimed to improve the language, literacy and numeracy skills of adults. They conclude that assessment in the field of adult basic education is at its best when done 'gently' in ways that not only encourage people to identify and gain confidence from their learning achievements but also manage to avoid the pedagogic perils of 'teaching to the test'. Harlen and colleagues (13.2) review the relationship between the form and purposes of different types of assessment. A key message here is that, if powerful forms of assessment are misaligned with educational purposes, then there is likely to be some distortion of teaching and learning. Major assessment purposes include formative assessment, evaluation of system-wide performance and educational accountability. Swaffield (13.3) emphasizes the responsiveness of assessment for learning to student progress and perspectives and draws attention to its unique role in the learning of teachers. The final reading (13.4) is a classic from the Assessment Reform Group and sets out its key features.

The parallel chapter in *Reflective Teaching in Further, Adult and Vocational Education* is also focused upon how assessment can enhance learning. It begins with a discussion of guiding principles of formative assessment and then provides detailed guidance on the main strategies involved. A final section affirms the principles of formative assessment, including a useful list of 'Key Readings'.

The *reflectiveteaching.co.uk* website provides sources for further study in 'Notes for Further Reading' and 'Reflective Activities'. Within the section on 'Deepening Expertise' a range of 'Expert Questions' on assessment are discussed and research highlights are showcased.

Reading 13.1

Mapping and tracking: Assessment and accreditation

Mary Hamilton and Yvonne Hillier

Hamilton and Hillier (2006) trace the development in England of the teaching and assessment of Adult Literacy, Numeracy and English for Speakers of Other Languages (sometimes described as ALNE), sometimes referred to as 'Basic Skills'. They point to important tensions and debates in this branch of adult learning and argue that assessment in this context is best undertaken when conducted in ways which are respectful of the lives and life histories of adult learners and do not involve formal 'testing', which may not only make learners anxious but also remind them of less-than-positive previous experiences of learning.

Edited from: Hamilton, M. and Hillier, Y. (2006) *Changing Faces of Adult Literacy, Numeracy and Language.* Stoke-on-Trent: Trentham Books.

We tend to channel them down certain paths now and … there's less emphasis on … just learning for learning's sake and writing for writing's sake … and it's more about skills … It's more sort of skills for work, skills for … life and things like that. (PW, LLN Tutor, Manchester)

If people want to improve their basic literacy, language and numeracy, how do they know they are making progress? How do the managers of provision know that the teaching and facilitation of learning is effective? If adults have experienced failure in their early lives, then are there better ways to help them make progress and find out their achievements than those they were exposed to in school? These questions inevitably lead to the hotly contested topic of assessment and accreditation.

The distinctions between assessment, testing and accreditation have become conflated in the current Skills for Life context. Assessment is a process of identifying what has been learnt, either recently or over a length of time, whereas accreditation is the award of credit, leading to qualifications, of learning which can be shown through the successful achievement of learning outcomes (Lavender et al., 2004). Assessment is not the same as testing which, as we will show, has particular connotations for learners who have failed in the past.

The early days of assessment

Adult Literacy, Numeracy and ESOL (ALNE) teaching and learning, whether in voluntary organisations, settlements or local authority provision, did not contain any formal assessment of learning as such, although it was conducted informally through discussion and feedback with learners. The non-formal nature of assessment was partly due to the fact that very few adult education courses involved formal assessment, unless they specifically led to qualifications. People either came to classes because they had a leisure interest in the subject or because they wanted to use it for specific purposes such as learning a language to use on holiday. It was accepted that classes comprised a range of levels and abilities, and the onus was on the teacher or tutor to find suitable ways to engage learners across this range. Adults who wanted to improve their literacy, language or numeracy were originally all treated in much the same way, although there was great sensitivity around the fact that they might feel shame or embarrassment about needing to attend classes, alongside an awareness that they might have found any assessment difficult, due to their experiences of failure in the past.

It was almost anathema for practitioners to assess people, either in the beginning through diagnostic tests, or at the end of a course. Indeed, the idea of *testing* learners and putting them back into categories they had been hoping to move away from, such as 'remedial' or 'special', was eschewed in favour of giving people a fresh start with no preconceptions about their ability. One of the tensions throughout the history of basic skills provision has arisen from respecting people's nervousness and helping them to overcome this.

Ongoing assessment

In some areas, good practice was being developed and then, typically, taken up and proselytised in the field, usually with the support of a range of practical guides regarding how to go about assessment in sensitive and ways often involving conversational methods of assessment. Here, tutors were encouraged to identify people's current level of skill and knowledge in a structured way, as well as identifying what could then be developed.

BSAI, Wordpower and Numberpower

In 1989, ALBSU (Adult Literacy and Basic Skills Unit), together with the BBC, began the Basic Skills Accreditation Initiative, and included consultations before defining the format of the qualification that was to become Wordpower and Numberpower. The BSAI proved to be one of the most contested aspects of ALNE in the 1990s. Learners might have liked the idea of working towards a qualification, but tutors were not convinced of its value, and some even argued that their learners hated it too.

One view of how the two qualifications came into being describes, additionally, the national context at the time. NVQs (National Vocational Qualifications) were being developed as a result of the 1981 White Paper on vocational qualifications and the setting-up of the NCVQ (National Council for Vocational Qualifications) in 1986 (see Hillier, 2002; Hyland et al., 2003). The driving force then, was through government but in the form of the MSC (Manpower Services Commission), or Training Agency as it had become.

Our interviewees identified a number of reservations about Wordpower and Numberpower. These included concerns about a curriculum that was being driven by the awards, the level of understanding and knowledge that the assessment process was attempting to demonstrate, and the value of the award. Some argued it was about time that learners gained credit for their learning, and others were vehemently against the competence-based movement, upon which these qualifications were founded.

At the point that they were introduced there was immense suspicion from the basic skills world of any concept of accreditation, and it was seen as introducing the possibility of failure, of destroying confidence rather than learning it. So then Wordpower and Numberpower were written explicitly to boost confidence and to address those concerns, they were written to be amenable to the evidence being created for individuals from the areas that they were motivated by; and they were written to be very practical and about the things learners would want and not the things that an employer would want. It was learner focused in that sense. (TF, Awarding Body)

Proponents argued that tutors who really loved doing Wordpower and Numberpower did it creatively, and their students liked it too. Tutors describe a 'softly softly' approach to encouraging their learners to work towards a qualification, perhaps by offering it as a possibility, rather than a requirement, often at the very first interview with a new learner. Wordpower and Numberpower could be used in different contexts, particularly in the workplace and through embedded basic skills, for example as part of a Good Hygiene Certificate. Detractors used strong language to describe their negative views, from saying it was 'nit-picking', 'fundamentally misguided' and 'utterly loathsome', usually on the basis that the criteria did not reflect accurately what people needed to be able to do, or that account could be taken of people's 'spikey profiles' of differing ability in writing, reading and speaking within any level of the award.

The slim evidence we have directly from learners (see Whitty, 1993), and from our own interviews with NCDS (National Child Development Survey) cohort members, indicates a broadly positive view and a clear appreciation of the differences between use and exchange value: that is, the value of certificates in validating learning and self-esteem as opposed to the instrumental value of having evidence to show employers and others, regardless of the real learning that has taken place.

Open College Network – an alternative framework

The first Open College began in the 1970s in the North West of England and quickly spread to all regions of the UK (Martin, 1998; Fieldhouse, 1996: 74). The Access movement had been established during this period, and the aim of the Open Colleges was to find an alternative means to accredit mature students, particularly those who did not have GCSE or 'A' Levels, but who wished to progress to further and higher education. The OCN courses, although nationally accredited, were developed and delivered locally through regional networks, providing local responsiveness. The approach to develop Open College accreditation was based on an underlying philosophy that was completely student-centred in focus, but which took account of the need for quality assurance and accountability.

> … it was important in terms of the ethos. It had to be sensitive, it had to be generated and focused very much on the learners' needs and experience but it also had to be rigorous, it had to be credible, and so that was a particular challenge. (JS, Manchester)

Progression

The underlying challenge throughout the development of assessment practices and accreditation frameworks for ALNE was how to establish progress. Articulation between qualifications, accreditation of prior experience and learning (APEL) and the identification of what, exactly, a qualification entitled someone to claim, in terms of their knowledge, skill and understanding, is an ongoing challenge, particularly in light of the status of academic versus vocational awards (see for example, Hodgson and Spours, 1997; Tomlinson, 2004).

Tensions and debates

Policy formation and implementation for assessment and accreditation in ALNE has been part of the move towards accountability, but has also been influenced by the wider competence-based movement adopted by the government from 1981 onwards, aiming to rationalise qualifications in the post-school sector. Moser reviewed the effectiveness of developments in assessment and accreditation in 1999 and the creation of *Skills for Life* was a direct consequence of his evaluation of the perceived lack of effectiveness of previous accreditation in the field. We can see that the problem of how learning can be measured has been stabilised through the use of accreditation and, latterly, testing.

What learners want

Throughout the history of accreditation for basic skills, there has been a difference of opinion at to whether certain qualifications are appropriate for the learners. The tutors and the learners have held opposing views and these views have occasionally erupted into volatile confrontations. In one community-run scheme, local black people accused the organisers of being patronising by not working towards the standard GCSEs. A practitioner working at this programme at the time recalls,

> 'What we want is GCSEs, what this community needs is GCSEs and you are offering us just basic education presumably you think because that's all that black people are fit for'. And we had to stand up in that room and defend what we believed, and also hearing what they were saying, so it was a very, very powerful experience. (AH, London)

The value of any basic skills accreditation

The early days of resistance to credit may have been overcome for tutors but also the learners. There is a problem with the status of a basic skills qualification, particularly for job seekers and those wishing to progress to further programmes of learning. A qualification carrying a title of basic skills labels the user as having low basic skills rather than as having improved them.

Why would I need a qualification to tell everybody that I can't read and write?

Moser and beyond

… In England, the manifestation of government action has been to develop a new accreditation system, based firmly on the use of external testing which would use the existing item bank of questions developed for a linked area, Key Skills. This decision once again demonstrates the permeability of policymaking, where a system is transferred to a parallel domain on the grounds that it is likely to be robust enough to work in the new context. However, not everyone on the committee agreed with Moser's resultant strategy, as one participant argued:

> You know from day one we argued about tests and qualifications. I believed very strongly that students need to assess their own learning and they need teachers to tell them where they are up to, that's absolutely bottom line. …What learners want is the same qualification as everybody else. (AZ, London)

As we noted earlier, testing is highly controversial in terms of its validity as a means to establish learners' achievement. The current regime is particularly criticised with its emphasis on reading, rather than writing, to establish that someone has a certain level of literacy (see Mace, 2002, 1992).

> There is a modern irony of course which is that the national tests, which I would say I support, have nevertheless required people to do no writing whatsoever. (JP, London)

Furthermore, testing is used as a means to meet targets and, as Alan Wells argued, 'if you attach targets you encourage fiddling', maintaining that he has never been in favour of single tests, and that continuous assessment provides a better indication of people's knowledge and skill. The *Skills for Life* system, then, has exploded the underlying tensions we have identified in assessment, because provision is strictly controlled through funding, attached to targets and outcomes, and permitted only if it offers certain prescribed curriculum. The field has moved a long way from the informal interviews, flexible programmes and voluntary nature of working towards qualifications of the 1970s.

A wider context

We have shown that accreditation is a highly contested area of ALNE. This was not the only field of education from the beginning in which assessment has been subject to debate. Vocational education had long been associated with accreditation, but employers and businesses were not always sure of the ability of education and training to provide them with people who had the necessary knowledge and skills to work in the labour market. The United Kingdom was not alone in its concern to produce qualified workers who would successfully contribute to the country's economy. European debate about up-skilling the workforce was also addressing the problems of high unemployment, particularly among young people, amid a growing backdrop of increasing use of technology and fears that countries outside Europe would become more highly competitive.

And for the future?

Testing and assessment is at its best when it is done 'gently', to encourage people and identify their achievements. Yet accreditation can become an obsession which dominates practitioners' energy. There is a danger of 'teaching to the test'. The awareness that there is greater focus and clarity with the current curriculum and qualification structure, coupled with significant resources, leads to lots of compromises (Lavender et al., 2004). The current *Skills for Life Strategy* relies heavily on accreditation for both staff and learners. The ongoing debate about the value of accreditation, and how best to represent the diverse needs of adults who wish to improve their basic skills, carries over into how practitioners should work within a curriculum which can only lead to credit.

> When I came back to basic education in 1994 I was really aware of how the teaching, the teachers were different, they had a different attitude … by then we had to have accreditation, it was a good thing, the students wanted it, we were beginning to realise that we should think about progression and progress and measuring distance of travel. What I realised was that teachers had become almost acclimatised, almost habituated to accreditation and there was a danger in that and there still is a danger in that …
> I do think in the 1970's and 1980's we tended to work for ourselves and for our own pleasure rather than for the student. (JD, London)

Reading 13.2

Assessment purposes and principles

Wynne Harlen, Caroline Gipps, Patricia Broadfoot and Desmond Nuttall

There are many types of assessment, but each is suited to particular purposes and cannot safely be used in other ways. This reading provides an excellent overview of assessment purposes, key principles and four of the most important types of assessment. Although this reading is set in schools, it is not difficult to see how the same issues are relevant to the FAVE sector.

Assessment purposes have often been conflated by policymakers, but what type would be most helpful to you in your work?

Edited from: Harlen, W., Gipps, C., Broadfoot, P. and Nuttall, D. (1992*)* 'Assessment and the improvement of education', *Curriculum Journal,* 3 (3), 217–25.

Assessment in education is the process of gathering, interpreting, recording and using information about pupils' responses to an educational task. At one end of a dimension of formality, the task may be normal classroom work and the process of gathering information would be the teacher reading a pupil's work or listening to what he or she has to say. At the other end of the dimension of formality, the task may be a written, timed examination which is read and marked according to certain rules and regulations. Thus assessment encompasses responses to regular work as well as to specially devised tasks.

All types of assessment of any degree of formality involve interpretation of a pupil's response against some standard of expectation. This standard may be set by the average performance of a particular section of the population or age group, as in norm-referenced tests. Alternatively, as in the National Curriculum context, the assessment may be criterion-referenced. Here the interpretation is in terms of progression in skills, concept or aspects of personal development which are the objectives of learning, and the assessment gives direct information which can be related to progress in learning. However, the usefulness of criterion-referenced assessment depends on the way in which the criteria are defined. Too tightly defined criteria, while facilitating easy judgement of mastery, require an extensive list which fragments the curriculum. On the other hand, more general criteria, which better reflect the overall aims of education, are much less easily and reliably used in assessing achievement.

The roles of assessment in education are as a means for:

providing feedback to teachers and pupils about on-going progress in learning, has a direct influence on the quality of pupils' learning experiences and thus on the level of attainment which can be achieved (formative role);

communicating the nature and level of pupils' achievements at various points in their schooling and when they leave (summative role),

summarizing, for the purposes of selection and qualification, what has been achieved (certification role);

recording information for judging the effectiveness of educational institutions and of the system as a whole (evaluative or quality control role).

There is an unavoidable backwash on the curriculum from the content and procedures of assessment. The higher the stakes of the assessment, the greater this will be. Multiple-choice and other paper-and-pencil tests provide results which are easily aggregated and compared but their used encourages teachers to ignore much of what pupils should learn as they 'teach to the test'.

Not all assessment purposes are compatible. Strong evidence from experience in the US, combined with that now accumulating in England and Wales, indicates that information collected for the purposes of supporting learning is unsuitable and unreliable if summarized and used for the purposes of quality control, that is, for making judgements about schools, and its use for this purpose severely impairs its formative role.

There is likely to be a trade-off between, on the one hand, cost and quality and, on the other, effectiveness. The cheapest assessment techniques, such as multiple-choice, machine-markable tests, may be convenient instruments to use but provide poor quality information for the purposes of communication and little or no support for the learning process itself.

Key principles

These issues are the purposes of assessment are borne in mind in proposing the following set of principles to inform policy-making on assessment:

assessment must be used as a continuous part of the teaching-learning process, involving pupils, wherever possible, as well as teachers in identifying next steps;

assessment for any purpose should serve the purpose of improving learning by exerting positive force on the curriculum at all levels. It must, therefore, reflect the full range of curriculum goals, including the more sophisticated skills and abilities now being taught;

assessment must provide an effective means of communication with parents and other partners in the learning enterprise in a way which helps them support pupils' learning; the choice of different assessment procedures must be decided on the basis of the purpose for which the assessment is being undertaken. This may well mean employing different techniques for different assessment purposes;

assessment must be used fairly as part of information for judging the effectiveness of schools. This means taking account of contextual factors which, as well as the quality of teaching, affect the achievement of pupils; citizens have a right to detailed and reliable information about the standards being achieved across the nation through the educational system.

Formative assessment

A major role identified for assessment is that of monitoring learning and informing teaching decisions on a day-to-day basis. In this role, assessment is an integral part of the interactions between teacher, pupil and learning materials. Because of this relationship, some teachers, who practise formative assessment well, may not recognize that what they are doing includes assessing.

What is required from a formative assessment scheme is information that is: gathered in a number of relevant contexts; criterion-referenced and related to a description of progression; disaggregated, which means that distinct aspects of performance are reported separately; shared by both teacher and pupil; on a basis for deciding what further learning is required; the basis of an on-going running records of progress.

A scheme of formative assessment must be embedded in the structures of educational practice; it cannot be grafted on to it. Thus there are implications in the foregoing for the curriculum, for teachers, in terms of required supporting materials and pre-service or in-service training, and for record-keeping practice.

Summative assessment

Summative assessment is similar to formative assessment in that it concerns the performance of individual pupils, as opposed to groups. In contrast with formative assessment, however, its prime purpose is not much to influence teaching but to summarize information about the achievements of a pupil at a particular time. The information may be for the pupils themselves, for receiving teachers, for parents, for employers or for a combination of these.

There are two main ways of obtaining summative information about achievements: summing up and checking up (Harlen, 1991).

Summing up provides a picture of current achievements derived from information gathered over a period of time and probably used in that time for formative purposes. It is, therefore, detailed and broadly based, encompassing all the aspects of learning which have been addressed in teaching. To retain the richness of the information it is best communicated in the form of a profile (i.e. not aggregated), to which information is added on later occasions. Records of achievement (RoA) provide a structure for recording and reporting this information, combining some of the features of formative assessment with the purposes of summative assessment in that they involve pupils in reviewing their own work and recognizing where their strengths and weaknesses lie.

Checking up offers no such additional benefits as an approach to summative assessment. It is generally carried out through providing tests or tasks specially devised for the purpose of recording performance at a particular time. End of year tests or examinations are examples, as are the end of module tests for checking performance in modular programmes and external public examinations.

Checking up and summing up approaches have contrasting advantages and disadvantages. Tests used for checking up are limited in scope unless they are inordinately long and so are unlikely to cover practical skills and some of the higher level cognitive skills. On the other hand, they do provide opportunities for all pupils to demonstrate what they have learned. Summative assessment which is based only on formative assessment depends on the opportunities provided in class for various skills and understandings to be displayed and, further, may be out of date in relation to parts of work covered at earlier points and perhaps not revisited.

This suggests that a combination of these two approaches may be the most appropriate solution. There are several advantages to having test materials available for teachers to use to supplement, at the end of a particular period, the information they have from on-going assessment during that time. The emphasis is on 'test materials' and not tests. These would ideally be in the form of a bank from which teachers select according to their needs. The items in the bank would cover the whole range of curriculum objectives and the whole range of procedures required for valid assessment. This provision would also serve the purposes of the non-statutory Standard Assessment Tasks.

The main advantages are that the availability of a bank of test material would provide teachers with the opportunity to check or supplement their own assessment in a particular area where they felt uncertain about what pupils can do. This would ensure that all aspects of pupils' work were adequately assessed without requiring extensive testing. Checking their own assessments against those arising from well-trialled and validated tasks would also build up teachers' expertise and lead to greater rigour in teachers' assessments.

Assessment for evaluative and quality assurance purposes

Information about pupils' achievement is necessary in order to keep under review the performance of the system as a whole – the quality assurance role of assessment. In the absence of such information it is possible for rumour and counter-rumour to run riot.

To serve this purpose, assessment has to be carried out in a way which leads to an overall picture of achievement on a national scale. It requires measures of achievement of a large number of pupils to be obtained and summarized. For this purpose testing in controlled conditions is necessary. However, if every pupil is tested, this leads to adverse effects on both teaching practice and on the curriculum and an over-emphasis on formal testing generally. Further, surveys which test every pupil cannot provide the depth of data required to provide a wide-range and in-depth picture of the system. Thus testing every pupil at a particular age is not appropriate for assessing performance at the national level.

To serve the evaluative role, assessment at the national level does not need to cover all pupils nor to assess in all attainment targets those who are included. The necessary rigour and comparability in assessment for this purpose can be provided by the use of a sample of pupils undertaking different assessment tasks.

Assessing school effectiveness

It is well established that the attainment of an individual is as much a function of his or her social circumstances and the educational experiences of his or her parents as it is of the effectiveness of the school or schools attended. To judge the effectiveness of a school by the attainment of its pupils is therefore misleading and unfair. What is wanted is a model that disentangles the effect on attainment of the school from that of the pupils' background. The value-added approach, that looks at the gain in achievement while the pupils is at a particular school (that is, the progress he or she makes there) offers a way forward and is, indeed, the basis of school effectiveness research such as that reported in School Matters (Mortimore et al., 1988; see also McPherson, 1992).

The assessments of attainment used (both on entry to the school and on leaving) should be as broad as possible to ensure that school effectiveness is not reduced to efficiency in teaching test-taking skills but reflects the full range of the aims of the school.

To counter the narrowness of outcomes implied by test results, even when shown in value-added form, it is suggested that schools should publish detailed reports covering such areas as: the aims of the schools; details of recent inspection reports (if any); particular areas of expertise offered; cultural and sporting achievements; community involvement; destinations of leavers. In short, the school should show its test results as part of its record of achievement.

Reading 13.3

Authentic assessment for learning
Sue Swaffield

In distinguishing assessment for learning from its commonly used synonym formative assessment, Sue Swaffield draws attention to some key features of AfL. These include its focus and prime beneficiaries, its timing, the role of learners, and the fact that AfL is in itself a learning process.

Are you clear about the principles underlying authentic AfL?

Edited from: Swaffield, S. (2011) 'Getting to the heart of authentic assessment for learning', *Assessment in Education: Principles, Policy and Practice,* 18 (4), 441–3.

The focus of Assessment for Learning (AfL) is on the enhancement of student learning.

The prime concern is with the here and now of learning, as it occurs in the flow of activity and transactions occurring in the classroom. This is what Perrenoud (1998) refers to as the regulation of learning, and what Wiliam (2008) describes as 'keeping learning on track'. The focus is on the learning of these students now, although there is also consideration given to their learning in the near future. The immediacy and clear focus on learners and their teachers are captured in the depiction of formative assessment by Thompson and Wiliam (2007: 6) as:

> *'Students and teachers,*
> *   … using evidence of learning,*
> *   … to adapt teaching and learning,*
> *   … to their immediate learning needs,*
> *   … minute-by-minute and day-by-day.'*

The emphasis is thus on everyday practice. Indeed, teachers are concerned with the learning of the pupils they are responsible for at the present, as well as for those they will teach in the future. When they review the results of periodic tests and assessments, they use that information to evaluate and revise provision, perhaps in terms of schemes of work and lesson plans, teaching approaches or classroom organisation. The information can also be used for longer-term curriculum improvement. Black et al. (2003: 122) point out that in this scenario, assessment is 'formative for the teacher'.

Assessment 'as' learning

AfL is, in itself, a learning process. Definitions often talk of seeking or eliciting evidence that is then used to enhance teaching and learning, but they don't always capture the constructivist, metacognitive and social learning elements of more sophisticated elaborations.

The strategies which are established as being central to assessment for learning have been presented in slightly different formulations by various authors but, in essence, the practices identified by Black and Wiliam in their 1998 review (see Reading 13.4) have been repeatedly affirmed.

Sharing criteria with learners, developing classroom talk and questioning, giving appropriate feedback, and peer and self-assessment are accepted as being at the heart of assessment for learning, and yet they are not always made explicit. Indeed, introductions to AfL often give less prominence to the learning aspects of these practices than their to their formative potential.

- Sharing criteria enables learners to develop a clear sense of what they are aiming at and the meaning of quality in any particular endeavour which, coupled with self and peer assessment, helps students learn not only the matter in hand but also to develop metacognition.

- Classroom talk and questioning are very good methods for teachers to elicit evidence of pupils' understanding and misunderstandings in order to inform the next steps in learning and teaching.

- Engaging in dialogue and listening to the flow of arguments enable students to construct their knowledge and understanding – irrespective of whether the teacher uses the information gleaned formatively.

- Dialogue and peer assessment help students learn socially, through and with others.

- When students are given appropriate feedback and the opportunity to apply it, they can learn through improving their work. More importantly, they learn that they can in effect 'become smarter' through judiciously focused effort.

Distinguishing assessment for learning from formative assessment

The terms 'assessment for learning' and 'formative assessment' are often used synonymously, but the discussion above suggests this is erroneous.

Assessment for learning differs from formative assessment in a number of ways:

- Assessment for learning is a learning and teaching process, while formative assessment is a purpose and some argue a function of certain assessments;

- Assessment for learning is concerned with the immediate and near future, while formative assessment can have a very long time span;

- The protagonists and beneficiaries of assessment for learning are the particular pupils and teacher in the specific classroom (or learning environment), while formative assessment can involve and be of use to other teachers, pupils and other people in different settings;

- In assessment for learning pupils exercise agency and autonomy, while in formative assessment they can be passive recipients of teachers' decisions and actions;

- Assessment for learning is a learning process in itself, while formative assessment provides information to guide future learning; and

- Assessment for learning is concerned with learning how to learn as well as specific learning goals, while formative assessment concentrates on curriculum objectives.

Making the distinction between formative assessment and assessment for learning clear is important particularly because the practice of using the terms synonymously has enabled assessment for learning to be misappropriated. An influential example of this was the English National Assessment for Learning Strategy introduced in 2008. For example, a list of adjectives used to describe 'good assessment for learning' was revealing, including as it did emphases on 'accuracy' and 'reliability' (DCSF, 2008: 5). But these are properties of summative rather than formative assessment. Although the strategy states that AfL 'focuses on how pupils learn' (DCSF, 2008: 5), its approach belies this by emphasising more formal and regular testing. Research has shown that frequent testing and assessment against national standards is detrimental to students' learning and motivation, especially for the lower attaining students.

Any misrepresentation of assessment for learning matters because of its power to affect people's view of the practice. Students, parents, teachers, school leaders, local authority personnel, and policy makers may be socialised into a flawed interpretation of AfL. It seems likely that this normalisation will be pervasive, self-reinforcing, and seen by the vast majority (if it is noticed at all) as unproblematic, even though enlightened teachers, school leaders and advisers undoubtedly mediate the strategy to remain as close as possible to authentic AfL.

We know from research and practice that authentic interpretations and enactments of assessment for learning improve pupils' learning – their engagement with learning, their attainment as measured by tests, and most importantly their growth in becoming more self-regulating, autonomous learners. Teachers' motivation and professional practice are enhanced. The relationships among pupils and teachers, and the culture of the classroom, are transformed.

Unless we get to the heart of authentic assessment for learning these precious prizes will not be widely realised. Teachers' professional lives will be impoverished, and the biggest and ultimate losers will be students.

Everyone committed to enhancing learning needs to strengthen and develop further our understanding of authentic assessment of learning. We need to take every opportunity to assert and explain the fundamental principles and features of AfL, including clarifying the similarities and differences between authentic assessment for learning and formative assessment. Academics, teachers, school leaders, policy makers, pupils, and parents should all be involved.

Learners, who as essential actors as well as beneficiaries are the beating heart of authentic assessment, deserve nothing less.

Reading 13.4

Assessment for learning
Assessment Reform Group

This extract comes from an influential pamphlet which helped to popularize the concept of 'assessment for learning'. Produced by a working group of educational researchers, it identified how feedback processes and active pupil engagement could have significant effects on learning, and how these could be embedded in routine classroom practice.

How could you investigate your own practice in respect of the 'five, deceptively simple key factors' (see below)?

Edited from: Assessment Reform Group (1999) *Assessment for Learning: Beyond the Black Box.* Cambridge: University of Cambridge School of Education, 5–8.

In a review of research on assessment and classroom learning, Paul Black and Dylan Wiliam synthesised evidence from over 250 studies (Black and Wiliam, 1998). The outcome was a clear and incontrovertible message: that initiatives designed to enhance effectiveness of the way assessment is used in the classroom to promote learning can raise pupil achievement. The scale of the effect would be the equivalent of between one and two grades at GCSE for an individual. The gain was likely to be even more substantial for lower-achieving pupils.

The research indicates that improving learning through assessment depends on five, deceptively simple, key factors:

- the provision of effective feedback to pupils;
- the active involvement of pupils in their own learning;
- adjusting teaching to take account of the results of assessment;
- a recognition of the profound influence assessment has on the motivation and self-esteem of pupils, both of which are crucial influences on learning;
- the need for pupils to be able to assess themselves and understand how to improve.

At the same time, several inhibiting factors were identified. Among these are:

- a tendency for teachers to assess quantity of work and presentation rather than the quality of learning;
- greater attention given to marking and grading, much of it tending to lower the self-esteem of pupils, rather than to providing advice for improvement;
- a strong emphasis on comparing pupils with each other which demoralises the less successful learners;

- teachers' feedback to pupils often serves social and managerial purposes rather than helping them to learn more effectively;

- teachers not knowing enough about their pupils' learning needs.

There is also much relevant evidence from research into the impact of National Curriculum Assessment in England and Wales during the 1990s, one of the most far-reaching reforms ever introduced into an educational system. That evidence suggests that the reforms encouraged teachers to develop their understanding of, and skills in, assessment. However, the very high stakes attached to test results, especially at Key Stage 2, are now encouraging teachers to focus on practising test-taking rather than on using assessment to support learning. Pupils are increasingly seeing assessment as something which labels them and is a source of anxiety, with low-achievers in particular often being demoralised.

Assessment for learning in practice

It is important to distinguish assessment for learning from other current interpretations of classroom assessment. What has become known in England and Wales as 'teacher assessment' is assessment carried out by teachers. The term does not imply the purpose of the assessment, although many assume that it is formative. This often leads to claims that what is already being done is adequate. In order to make the difference quite clear it is useful to summarise the characteristics of assessment that promotes learning.

These are that it:

- is embedded in a view of teaching and learning of which it is an essential part;

- involves sharing learning goals with pupils;

- aims to help pupils to know and to recognise the standards they are aiming for;

- involves pupils in self-assessment;

- provides feedback which leads to pupils recognising their next steps and how to take them;

- is underpinned by confidence that every student can improve;

- involves both teacher and pupils reviewing and reflecting on assessment data.

This contrasts with assessment that simply adds procedures or tests to existing work and is separated from teaching, or on-going assessment that involves only marking and feeding back grades or marks to pupils. Even though carried out wholly by teachers such assessment has increasingly been used to sum up learning, that is, it has a summative rather than a formative purpose.

The term 'formative' itself is open to a variety of interpretations and often means no more than that assessment is carried out frequently and is planned at the same time as teaching. Such assessment does not necessarily have all the characteristics just identified as helping learning. It may be formative in helping the teacher to identify areas where more explanation or practice is needed. But for the pupils, the marks or remarks on their work may tell them about their success or failure but not about how to make progress towards further learning.

The use of the term 'diagnostic' can also be misleading since it is frequently associated with finding difficulties and errors. Assessment for learning is appropriate in all situations and helps to identify the next steps to build on success and strengths as well as to correct weaknesses.

A particular point of difference with much present practice is the view of learning that the approach to assessment implies. Current thinking about learning acknowledges that learners must ultimately be responsible for their learning since no-one else can do it for them. Thus assessment for learning must involve pupils, so as to provide them with information about how well they are doing and guide their subsequent efforts. Much of this information will come as feedback from the teacher, but some will be through their direct involvement in assessing their own work. The awareness of learning and ability of learners to direct it for themselves is of increasing importance in the context of encouraging lifelong learning.

So what is going on in the classroom when assessment is really being used to help learning? To begin with the more obvious aspects of their role, teachers must be involved in gathering information about pupils' learning and encouraging pupils to review their work critically and constructively. The methods for gaining such information are well rehearsed and are, essentially:

- observing pupils – this includes listening to how they describe their work and their reasoning;
- questioning, using open questions, phrased to invite pupils to explore their ideas and reasoning;
- setting tasks in a way which requires pupils to use certain skills or apply ideas;
- asking pupils to communicate their thinking through drawings, artefacts, actions, role play, concept mapping, as well as writing;
- discussing words and how they are being used.

Teachers may, of course, collect information in these ways but yet not use the information in a way that increases learning. Use by the teacher involves decisions and action – decisions about the next steps in learning and action in helping pupils take these steps. But it is important to remember that it is the pupils who will take the next steps and the more they are involved in the process, the greater will be their understanding of how to extend their learning. Thus action that is most likely to raise standards will follow when pupils are involved in decisions about their work rather than being passive recipients of teachers' judgements of it.

Involving pupils in this way gives a fresh meaning to 'feedback' in the assessment process. What teachers will be feeding back to pupils is a view of what they should be aiming for: the standard against which pupils can compare their own work. At the same time, the teacher's role – and what is at the heart of teaching – is to provide pupils with the skills and strategies for taking the next steps in their learning.

part four

Reflecting on consequences

Outcomes
How do we monitor student learning achievements?

14

The focus in this chapter is on the summative use of assessment for monitoring achievement and evaluating education within and across educational organizations. Gregson and Nixon (14.1) argue that the social construction of assessment outcomes needs to be understood in terms of the shortcomings of technical–rational approaches to the improvement of teaching and learning which rely solely upon outcomes-based measures of educational evaluation. Drawing upon philosophical and sociological analyses of the interaction of policy implementation and assessment practice, they offer reasons why such models of improvement and evaluation of achievements in education are serving to distort rather than enhance teaching and learning. In closing, they suggest that more democratic and collaborative approaches to educational evaluation may be worthy of consideration as a possible alternative. Coffield (14.2) points to the phenomenon in England and elsewhere of teaching to the test and the increase of what Coffield describes in the title of his book as 'bulimic learning' among students in FAVE. Shain and Gleeson (14.3) trace similar problems in the FAVE sector in England back to the incorporation of Further Education colleges in the early 1990s, which they associate with the rise of managerialist practices and fabrications of achievement and compliance across the sector.

The parallel chapter in *Reflective Teaching in Further, Adult and Vocational Education* begins with issues of accountability and improvement, validity and reliability. It then considers summative assessment using statutory tests and examinations and teacher assessment and goes on to compare a number of approaches to the summative evaluation of educational achievement. Finally, there is a section on record-keeping and preparing for summative assessment, including external inspection and, of course, suggestions for 'Key Readings'.

On the *reflectiveteaching.co.uk* website, updated sources for further study are provided in 'Notes for Further Reading', including further 'Reflective Activities'. Within the section on 'Deepening Expertise' there is discussion of a wide range of issues in summative assessment.

Reading 14.1

Ways of seeing impact
Margaret Gregson and Lawrence Nixon

Decisions about what should be evaluated in education, how and by whom, have far-reaching consequences for systems of education and the societies which shape them and are, in turn, shaped by them. This reading raises concerns about the reliability, validity and impact of summative, 'technical–rational' approaches to the development, implementation and evaluation of educational policy. Gregson and Nixon argue that such 'technical–rational' approaches can all too easily overlook the processes of impact and 'softer' or more subtle indicators of impact, although difficult to measure or quantify, are often equally – if not more – important in educational contexts than their 'harder' counterparts.

Edited from: Gregson, M. and Nixon, L. (2009) 'Assessing effectiveness: ways of seeing impact', *International Journal of Interdisciplinary Social Sciences,* 21(3).

Introduction

Identifying the impact of any social policy upon practice is never a straightforward matter. There are no widely tested, universally accepted theories of public policy analysis and the same policy can be implemented in surprisingly different ways in different contexts for a wide variety of reasons. Furthermore competing claims can be made for gains or losses identified in the implementation of any policy. This presents policy makers, researchers and practitioners with the complex task not only of trying to make education policy effective in practice but also of understanding the extent to which a particular policy is, or is not, effective.

Debates about the purpose, use and value of identifying the impact of educational policy initiatives, raise serious issues in wider social and political arena. Decisions about what should be evaluated in education, how and by whom, have far reaching consequences for systems of education and the societies which shape them and, are in turn, shaped by them. Such decisions not only establish the measures through which an educational policy might be deemed to be 'successful' but also the degree to which a political administration might be considered by its citizens to be deserving of further public support at the ballot box. On these grounds alone, measures of impact in education are of paramount importance.

Contributions – the Education Evaluation Debate from the USA

The language we use to think and talk about education reforms and the ways in which we go about evaluating their impact, say much about what we consider to be real and true in the world and our understanding of our place within it. Our 'ways of seeing' impact in educational and in other contexts, signal what is viewed to be important and worthwhile and as well what is considered to be unimportant or even worthless.

A number of commentators in the USA have noted that education reform there has become dominated by a 'technical-rational' approach (see for example Malen and Knapp, 1997; Scott, 1999). This approach to policy development, implementation and evaluation is grounded in economics, and commonly looks to cost-benefit analysis to inform decision making and act as the main driver of policy choices. It begins with the assumption that all that needs to be known about the (educational) problem is or soon can be known. It then assumes that policy-makers have ready access to all of this information, it also assumes that time and expertise is available to make sense of this data in rational ways. In this situation, the best technical solution to the problem appears to be very obvious. In such instances discussions soon move on to a simple cost-benefit analysis of competing options in order to identify the most cost-effective means of realising the best envisaged solution, expected to have maximum impact. It is important to note how this approach requires policy makers to assume a particular prescient epistemological viewpoint and to regard the means of measuring progress as being straight-forward and unproblematic. In practice this technical-rational approach often begins with a very well intentioned educational goal. This educational intention then becomes part of a technical-rational transaction. In this transaction the problem is simplified and the solution rationalised into a series of sequential steps that can be easily followed and monitored. Once such measures have been identified, quantitative targets can be set for sectors, specific institutions and even individuals. Actual outcomes or impact are then judged against the set targets and local, regional and national progress gauged. Questions of how 'rational' this process actually is, how appropriate the 'technological solutions' arrived at really are and how useful the means chosen to measure their outcomes are in practice are seldom raised let alone addressed.

Sarason (1998) argues that what we choose to notice and what we choose to ignore in the highly charged political contexts and power relations of educational reform, are of enormous importance. Ignoring, or overlooking shortcomings in education reforms, he claimed, can have serious consequences, in situations where admitting or not admitting mistakes can be a dangerous and costly business for all concerned. Sarason draws attention to the high failure rates of education reforms in the USA and points out that despite continuing and extensive efforts of educational reformers, many of the long-standing declared aims of schooling in that country are still unmet. Such aims he contends have been reduced to hollow platitudes, which bear scant relationship to the social experiences of a large majority of students. Why he asked, despite over thirty years of unprecedented levels of funding,

... have our efforts – and they were many and expensive – met with intractability? Why should we expect that what we will now recommend will be any more effective than our past efforts? (Sarason, 1998: 3)

He attributes high failure rates in education reforms in the USA, to superficial conceptions of how complicated settings are organised. He emphasises the importance of paying attention to the dynamics and structures operating within education systems and the institutions which constitute them. According to Sarason, education reforms in the USA have largely failed because education reformers have not yet recognised the need to take power relationships seriously. In particular, he criticises those concerned with education reform for 'missing the point and ignoring the obvious' (p. 6). The 'point' being that power relationships influence and control activity at all levels of a system of education, influencing how people think and act in given situations, signalling what patterns of thought and behaviour are expected and are to be accepted and those that are not, thereby setting the parameters of what is imaginable and unimaginable. The 'obvious' is that to ignore these power relationships, to leave their rationales unexamined, is to effectively defeat efforts at reform or at least drastically reduce the prospect of achieving their desired outcomes,

... not because there is a grand conspiracy or because of mulish stubbornness in resisting change, or because educators are uniquely unimaginative or uncreative (which they are not) but rather because recognising and trying to change power relationships especially in complicated, traditional institutions, is among the most complex tasks human beings can undertake (p. 7).

To mistake activity for change, or to mistake change for progress, he argues is to confuse means with ends with potentially disastrous consequences. He advises policy makers to be wary of the dangers of allowing means to become ends in themselves and argues that, when the means of change in a reform become the instrument for the measurement of its effectiveness or success, then the possibilities of real educational change are seriously weakened from the outset. As the means become ends, so activity becomes increasingly focused upon the means and attention is drawn away from the educational ends originally intended by the reform. In this way, Sarason highlights how education reform can become effectively locked into a cycle of failure where, 'the more things change the more they remain the same, or (even get) worse' (p. 8) in such circumstances and situations the illusion of change, in the form of activity, masquerades as change itself.

Contributions – the debate from the UK

Technical-rational approaches to educational reform, based upon programmes and measures of outcomes-based education have also become particularly popular in England over the last thirty years. In recent years applications of the technical-rational approach there have come under increasing criticism. Fielding, one of the strongest critics of this approach, argues that the 'existential texture of a concept affects how we see the world, how we understand it, how we engage with it, and how we conduct our daily work within it' (2003: 292). He emphasises how the language we use to describe educational policy and its aspirations, matters a great deal because it influences how and how well we can identify and distinguish between levels of change in education and most importantly because the same language signifies the relays of power and control at work in the framing of notions of 'social justice' and a 'better' society. Fielding challenges current approaches to assessing the 'impact' of education in England and recognizes their deeper ontological and epistemological roots in the seventeenth and eighteenth century mechanical world view. Fielding (2003) also notes how the technical-rational approach to education reform, coupled with a 'fatuous' and 'hectoring' form of language, the language of 'performance, has come to pervade the discourse of educational policy in England through notions of 'impact' and its outcomes. The technical-rational language of 'hard outcomes' of impact in English education system, he claims have opened up some (largely superficial) possibilities but also closed down some very important others. He illustrates how this has operated to foreground 'what is short term, readily visible and easily measurable'. He also shows how the same language has marginalised qualities and phenomena which are 'complex, problematic, uneven, unpredictable, requiring patience and tenacity in order to bring them to light. According to Fielding, such qualities and phenomena, while difficult to measure, are crucially important aspects of the social and political realities which characterise sites of change at which educational policy is directed.

For Fielding, the blunt instruments of 'hard' outcomes combined with the language of impact currently being used in England have introduced commensurately crude, costly and in some cases very dubious measures of effectiveness. These are, he contends drawing us further into the machismo and the impatient mind-set and practices of 'performativity' which Fielding among others (see for example Ball, 2007, 2008) argue, necessitates the construction by teachers of defensive fabrications of 'performance' and 'compliance' in their work

He calls upon the academic community to accept that they have a major responsibility to challenge approaches to educational evaluation which portray human activity in purely mechanistic or mindlessly organic ways.

Impact names the new hegemony: its presumptions and pretensions need to be examined more closely than seems to have been the case thus far. (Fielding, 2003: 294)

Fielding concludes that a different intellectual model of educational change is needed, based upon different practical arrangements and different policies. Such a model he asserts would need to go beyond the mechanical technical-rational world view and be able to recognise that human beings are not machines or mindless organisms. Such a model of educational change would be able to acknowledge and respect the nature of our 'human being and becoming' (ibid.).

Elliott (2001) argues that evaluation in education needs to become more educational. He shows how technical-rational approaches to improving teaching then become matters of increasing technical *control* over the production of increasingly predictable learning outcomes and so the 'means-end' masquerade begins. This problem becomes further compounded when evaluations of the success of such educational outcomes and benchmarks of achievement are then measured in inelastic ways regardless of context. From this perspective, he illustrates how the means we use to evaluate education are not neutral in relation to the ends we wish to achieve because they contribute qualitatively to the very character of the ends they produce.

Through the above contributions to the education evaluation debate in the USA and the UK we have pointed to how the technical-rational approach to education reform is entrenched in a particular world view, underpinned by a particular set of power relationships. We argue that the technical-rational approach to educational change appear to gain much credibility from the apparent clarity and simplicity of its vision. The way it presents itself and the way it sees the problems set before it, the solutions it identifies and the ways in which it evaluates progress, simultaneously simplifies reality and takes on the appearance of objectivity. Implicated here, is the assumption that everyday experience is unreliable and/or biased. The work to be done then is to move beyond past surface impressions (of experience) in order to take up an objective view and thereby uncover the reality of the situation. The very plausibility of this view of 'objectivity' and the 'real' is we argue its 'fatal attraction'. By presenting itself as such a 'common-sense' view of the world it not only discourages challenge or criticism but indeed makes challenge or criticism to such a 'common-sense' view look strange and unnecessary thereby locking, in this case education reform, into a mechanical view of the world in which context, experience and fallibility have no place.

Reading 14.2

Students as learning partners within a community of learning

Frank Coffield

> In this second extract from Frank Coffield's *Beyond Bulimic Learning: Improving Teaching in Further Education*, two main themes are addressed. The first deals with different ways in which teachers can work in partnership with students and with each other to improve teaching and learning together. The second theme identifies three of the main characteristics of a learning community in which learning becomes the organizing principle, the central focus is upon teaching and learning and a climate of innovation is encouraged.
>
> *Edited from:* Coffield, F. (2014) in F. Coffield, with C. Costa, W. Muller and J. Webber, *Beyond Bulimic Learning: Improving Teaching in Further Education.* London: Institute of Education Press, 1–21.

In 2008 I wrote a booklet called *Just suppose teaching and learning became the first priority...* (Coffield, 2008), mainly because I thought this essential topic had slipped down the list of priorities of Senior Management Teams (SMTs). Understandably, when colleges were incorporated in the early 1990s, SMTs had to learn very fast to become successful business managers, while at the same time incorporation weakened the local identity of colleges and ended local democratic accountability. Many Principals became Chief Executive Officers and managed large groups of staff and students through the manipulation of copious amounts of data, data on recruitment, retention, student satisfaction, test scores, the tracking of students against targets, and on all other performance indicators. The responsibility for teaching, learning and assessment (TLA) was handed over to a middle manager, while the Principalship concentrated on what were considered to be the more important functions – keeping a large complex organisation afloat, maximising income from constantly shifting streams of government and private/commercial funding, and reconnoitring the horizon to spot trouble or financial opportunities coming over it.

That management style will no longer work because Ofsted has changed the rules of the game yet again. The Common Inspection Framework, which was revised in 2012, has made TLA the first priority, which will force colleges to change the very culture of their institutions. But what does it mean in practice to create a culture of learning? Let me quote the suggestion from Sir Michael Wilshaw, Chief HMI, who has some idiosyncratic ideas about motivating staff. As he put it: "If anyone says to you that staff morale is at an all time low, you know you are doing something right" (Wilshaw, 2011).

The problem is not, however, an occasional ill-judged remark by the Chief Inspector but the constant barrage of criticism directed at public education, which Stephen Ball neatly categorised as a 'discourse of derision' as far back as 1990. In a more recent formulation, he argues that "blaming teachers has become over the last 30 years a political blood sport ... Workplaces should be places where we flourish and grow and are encouraged and supported. They are social settings in which everyone deserves respect and has the right to feel valued. Just like students, teachers do not work well when they feel stressed. As *An Education Declaration to Rebuild Americal* puts it: 'The working conditions of teachers are the learning conditions of students'" (Ball, 2013: 23). I would also like to ask Sir Michael two questions: What theory of motivation suggests that it is a sensible strategy to denigrate, on a regular basis, the very people on whom you depend to enact your policies? And would Sir Michael be satisfied if the words "student morale" were substituted for "staff morale" in his infamous statement?

What are the three main characteristics of a learning community?[1] First, learning is *the* central organising principle of the college, which means that everyone from the youngest 14 year old student to the Principal demonstrates daily that they are still learning. If that were so, how did it come about that "many staff attending the LSIS Aspiring Principals and Senior Leadership Programme reported that neither the executive team nor the Principal ever discussed with them their learning from the programme or how it might suggest improvements in individual or organisational practices"? (Crowley, 2014: 139). One interpretation of that finding is that learning is something that students and teaching staff do, but not managers. On the other hand, I would like to know what structured support is available to help SMTs fulfil their multiple and multiplying responsibilities. The job has become virtually impossible, which helps to explain the reluctance of good candidates to come forward.

The second characteristic of a learning community that I would argue for is substantially more investment in the core activity of TLA, including an evidence-informed strategy to move students to higher levels of thinking and learning (not just to A*/Distinction). Students in such a community become not complaining customers but partners in learning, who are gradually drawn into the democratic life of the institution, which not only surveys their views but involves them in dialogue about TLA, trains them to sit on appointment panels and jointly to plan and teach lessons (and carry out research) with the guidance and support of their tutors (Fielding and Moss, 2012).

---

[1] This is not the first time I have tried to describe the main features of a learning community. In our book *From exam factories to communities of discovery: the democratic route,* Bill Williamson and I set out 13 characteristics of such communities. Instead of just repeating that list here, I offer in this chapter what I have learned since that book was published and I refer readers to it (pp. 49–54) for the earlier characterisation.

Box 14.2.1: Patterns of Partnership

Michael Fielding has produced a typology of seven different patterns of partnership by means of which adults not only listen to but learn with students. I have also added a final level. In an ascending ladder of democratic participation, the seven patterns can be briefly characterised as:

1 **Students as a source of data**, e.g. Staff use questionnaires to find out about students' satisfaction and well-being

2 **Students as partners in dialogue**, e.g. Staff involve students in discussions about TLA

3 **Students as fellow researchers**, e.g. Staff take the leading role in identifying plagiarism with active support from students

4 **Students as creators of knowledge**, e.g. Students take the leading role in studying bullying in college with active support from staff

5 **Students as joint authors**, e.g. Students and staff jointly plan the teaching of a section of the curriculum and jointly 'deliver' it

6 **Students and staff live and learn democratically together**, e.g. Students and staff share a commitment to and a responsibility for the common good

7 **Students and staff as equal learning partners**, e.g. Students and staff decide the key issues in the college, all with one vote.

Freely adapted from Fielding (2011)

(See Box 14.2.1 for a brief account of Michael Fielding's seven patterns of partnership between educators and students.) So the voices of students are heard loud and clear and are responded to appropriately. But so too are the voices of tutors (see Coffield, forthcoming).

There is now a solid and growing knowledge base on TLA which all tutors need to make their own, while acknowledging that "research can only inform practice because it can never replace other knowledge which teachers bring to bear on practical problems; and that even the best research evidence is not available as fixed, universal relationships between methods and outcomes, but as local, context-sensitive patterns which have to be interpreted by practitioners within their particular working environments" (Edwards, 2000: 301).

We will know we have created learning communities when SMTs start discussing which theory (or theories) of learning they espouse and what influence it has on their teaching, as fluently as they chat about whether Arsene Wenger's days at Arsenal are drawing to a close. Libraries need to be stocked with the latest research on TLA and the staff given time to read, reflect and discuss in their teaching groups how they will respond to it. A growing percentage of staff should be studying for higher degrees in TLA at their local university, which should be giving FE staff online access to its electronic library resources. TLA also become the first, standing item on the agenda of SMTs; and governors are appointed who are experts in TLA to complement those who are experts in finance.

In his book on visible teaching, John Hattie challenges classroom teachers with the question: "do the students believe that the climate of the class is fair, empathetic and trustworthy?" (2012: 165). I want to go further by asking a parallel question of SMTs: do your staff believe that the climate of the college is conducive to their learning?

The third characteristic of a learning community is one where the climate encourages tutors to innovate, take risks, fail and learn from their mistakes. Tutors are able to argue for their practices by citing evidence of the effectiveness of their teaching, and they have the freedom to debate different approaches openly and to see disagreements over practice as the basis for improving it. Principled dissent is therefore encouraged by SMTs and democratic, collaborative learning becomes the road to renewal. The more, however, that colleges and tutors are graded and inspected, the less welcoming the atmosphere will be to challenge, difference and dissent.

Quality in TLA becomes the desire of staff to be more than just employees, to get better for the sake of getting better rather than to get by or to outwit the inspectorate (Sennett, 2008); it is not something imposed from on high, something controlled and assured by management. The budgets for CPD will have to be doubled and perhaps trebled if FE tutors are to update their technical/vocational expertise with local companies as well as learning to be better teachers, course designers and assessors. This model of "dual professionalism" will help all tutors in FE to become powerful, democratic professionals.

Reading 14.3

Under new management: Changing conceptions of teacher professionalism and policy in the further education sector

Farzana Shain and Denis Gleeson

Teachers' work in the current Further Education (FE) sector in England and elsewhere is undergoing reconstruction through processes of marketization and managerial control. With reductions in public funding to FE and increased competition between institutions for students, many lecturers have experienced reductions in their pay, security, academic freedom and job satisfaction, accompanied by an increase in their workload. This reading seeks to understand how teachers make sense of the changing conditions of their work and, in doing so, explores the usefulness of professionalism as a conceptual tool for understanding contemporary educational change.

Shain and Gleeson raise the important question of how we can further enhance the support for classroom teachers to deliver a good education. The research identifies three ways in which practitioners viewed the professionalism of teachers. Resisters were critical of reform and sometimes used public sector discourses of professionalism as a defence against any change. Compliers uncritically embraced the enterprise culture and valued 'a technicist and conservative view of FE teaching'. Strategic compliers aimed to provide a good education for students within the constraints of the system. They often worked collaboratively to balance the sometimes competing demands of the classroom and managerialist discourses in ways that sought to open up quality spaces for teaching, learning and assessment.

Edited from: Shain, F. and Gleeson, D. (1999) 'Under new management: changing conceptions of teacher professionalism and policy in the further education sector', *Journal of Education Policy* 14 (4): 445–62.

Incorporation and marketization has reconstituted colleges as autonomous education and training enterprises. New funding arrangements and independence from local authority control has intensified competition between colleges and other providers including schools and universities, encouraging college management teams towards a greater market share and competitive advantage. Effective `facilities management' (FEFC, 1998) has been one such area, in encouraging competitive bidding for students, resources and funding in areas of defined local and national need. In addition to marketing campaigns, college budgets are spent on improving the physical or corporate appeal of colleges to attract new clients. As a consequence the physical appearance of many colleges has changed radically in the immediate post incorporation period. One of the case study colleges in the project, Oldhill College, spent vast sums of money on refurbishing the foyer, cafeteria, IT facilities, investing in new desks, chairs and uniforms for support staff in corporate colours…

According to one manager in Westgate College – an advocate of reform – this [new corporate discourse] had given the college a 'new professional air':

This college has had to wake up. It has had to realise that nobody will bail it out if it goes under. It has had to develop a professional air which in some areas [the lecturers] still don' t have. They still have the view that, `I'm the teacher and the student must put up with it'. In the main there is a growing feeling of professionalism. Now we are front of house. We look as smart as we can. We attempt to be as professional to our public as we can; we have a frontage … We have set up a new personnel office and new finance office, whereas we relied on the LEA before. (Monica: Manager, Westgate College)

Teachers' work and working practices are also being restructured in other ways under managerialist control. A number of features of teachers' work have been highlighted by critics of reform, as posing a threat to lecturers autonomy and control of the teaching process (Elliott, 1996; Randle and Brady, 1997) . These include:

- Competence based assessment that reconstructs the lecturer as trainer or assessor – its over prescriptive nature, it has been argued, is designed to introduce new forms of control over lecturers (Hodkinson, 1995; Randle and Brady, 1997)
- The shift to flexible IT-based learning when delivered by instructor or technicians rather than qualified teachers, threatens the expertise of the FE teacher and raises questions about the ownership of intellectual property
- The re-definition of quality from one based on process to outcome, measured by performance indicators or outcomes based primarily around recruitment, retention rates and exam results
- Increased monitoring and surveillance of teachers through internal and external control mechanisms including FEFC inspections, self assessment, teacher appraisal, observation, increasingly through student and employer evaluation forms – based primarily around the student and employer as both customer and consumer; and
- Competition between FE, schools, TECs, private trainers and employers which drive down teacher and student unit costs, with subsequent knock on effects for teacher autonomy and professionalism.

Teacher responses: shifting work identities

Rejection and resistance. A small but core group of lecturers in this study were extremely critical of the new reforms in FE. They found it difficult to identify with any positive aspect of Incorporation. In rejecting markets and competition they expressed a wish to return to the 'old days' of FE, the existence of which is questionable (Gleeson and Mardle, 1980). Such lecturers predominantly established contract staff, had often been in service for 10–20 years. Refusal to abandon the Silver Book agreement was their main way of expressing their resistance. Change was filtered through an existing commitment to 'old' public sector professionalism in defence of pedagogy (Randle and Brady, 1997)

Compliance. A section of recently appointed lecturers are more compliant toward the new enterprise culture of FE in that they are prepared to be flexible and identify real potential in the freedom which business values bring. For Alan who had taken the traditional part-time route into FE, his role promised creativity, autonomy and career development...

In the interview Alan compared his role as a lecturer to that of a salesman, having to sell courses to people on induction evenings. A smart 'professional' appearance and enthusiasm are necessary for this job. For Harvey, an ex-primary teacher, flexibility is the key quality for teachers in FE today:

> ... I have a very mixed bag of a job. I don' t have a clear role. I have actually realised, certainly in the last twelve months, that the less defined your role is it seems to be the safer you are or rather the more flexible you are. I have moved around in different educational sectors quite a lot and if you are prepared to chop and change without too much fuss...

Though this strategy of compliance is linked to the need for job security, it also anticipates the changing 'new realism' of FE. In the context of what is seen as the bullying of staff by a previous Principal and, in the wider context of unemployment, this strategy of compliance constitutes part of a conscious strategy of 'not rocking the boat'.

Strategic compliance. The vast majority of lecturers in the CTMC project were critical of some aspects of reform but accepting of others. Flexible learning, for example, was viewed as a positive option as long as it was not resourced 'on the cheap'; that is, through unqualified learning assistants in place of qualified lecturers, replacing direct contact teaching. These teachers draw on residual elements of public sector professionalism which is reworked in the current context to inform their practice. Of primary importance is the need to ensure that students receive a quality education within the constraints of the current system. The notion of quality is subject to competing definitions that are reflective of a tension between the 'new' official managerial discourse of professionalism and 'old' public sector professionalism.

Strategic compliers identify much more with their sector than with the college or institution. Indeed there is strong evidence of a growing sector identity with some lecturers talking of being in 'small pockets' (Pam: lecturer, Oldhill College), derived from devolved budgeting and related work intensification. Though common staff rooms still exist, there is less time for lecturers to socialise with colleagues outside their sector during break times. Breaks are increasingly being taken in busy workrooms in which work related issues are discussed. Such sector identity is further encouraged where devolved budgets are in operation, thereby avoiding potential conflict between sectors or schools or, as Hargreaves (1994) refers to it, as 'balkanization'. Where sectors are working with tightly devolved budgets the need to recruit and retain students is perceived as integral to the survival of the sector, (though in reality 'less successful' sectors are often effectively subsidized, causing further conflict and resentment from lecturers in 'successful' sectors). In some instances this can lead to students being given inappropriate advice and recruited onto courses for which they are not suited.

For strategic compliers the ethos of competition does not preclude cooperation or effective networking with colleagues and other institutions. Mike, the Sector head, for example, encourages his staff to take an active role in forums and discussion groups that involves meeting and working collaboratively with colleagues from comparative institutions. As a result there is a growing culture of collaboration within an overall competitive framework which allows Westgate and Oldhill General Education sections to share resources and write courses together.

… the lecturers here adopt a strategic view whereby they are able to offer 'alternative' measures within the system, to ensure that quality education is provided to a range of students. The regaining of ownership of enrolments is another such area. Under the previous Principal's regime this aspect of teachers' work was centralized resulting in a situation where that students were not always guided onto appropriate courses. Such was the inefficiency of centralization that, on one occasion, over 100 students had failed to be invited by central services to interview from a local school.

Reconstructing professionalism

The narratives presented in this paper suggest that changes are occurring in terms of what counts as being a 'good lecturer' in FE, through mediation of managerialist discourses that emphasise flexibility, reliability and competence. Though there is evidence of some incorporation of lecturers into this discourse (*Compliance*), it is by no means complete or uncontested. Rather, residual elements of 'public sector' or 'old' professionalism are drawn on and reworked through lecturer practice in order to 'make sense of' the changing conditions of work in managerial and competitive contexts. The responses across the colleges in this study are diverse but the vast majority of lecturers interviewed were strategically compliant in their approach to their work. The main element of this response suggests a commitment to ensuring that students receive a 'quality' education based on a definition of quality through *process*, rather than just output measures. This has encouraged lecturers in some sectors to share resources and place emphasis on developing collaborative modes of work within highly competitive environments. This growing climate of collaboration operates across colleges though, at this stage, it is contained within particular sectors and not others. There also exists apparent support for this growing atmosphere of collaboration at both local and national levels.

Inclusion
How do we manage equality and diversity?

15

The readings in this chapter reflect the prolific research that exists concerning inequalities in our societies and the importance of inclusive practice across all sectors of education. Richardson (15.1) reviews ten principles underpinning legislation on equality and diversity within the schools sector. Schuller (15.2) points to the importance of opportunities for people from all ages, backgrounds and experiences to be able to learn throughout their lives and of the right of each and every one of us to be included in education and in society. Spedding and colleagues (15.3) draw attention to the need for teacher education to equip student teachers and more experienced teachers with practical strategies and 'holding responses' which enable them to tackle prejudice, as and when it surfaces in FAVE contexts, in fair and pedagogically sound ways. Appleby (15.4) asks us to consider who our learners are as human beings, with all the richness and complexity that involves. This includes the recognition that teachers are learners too.

The parallel chapter in *Reflective Teaching in Further, Adult and Vocational Education* considers the social consequences of the educational experiences of students. It begins with a review of major dimensions of difference: disability, gender, social class, age, appearance, sexuality and learning capabilities. The chapter then moves on to consider how differentiation can occur in FAVE settings. Difference is discussed as part of the human condition – thus generating commitments to diversity and inclusion. Needs are discussed as a dimension of difference. Finally, the chapter focuses on practical ways of developing inclusive polices and practices and, of course, suggestions for 'Key Readings'.

The resources on the *reflectiveteaching.co.uk* website extend this discussion.

Reading: 15.1

Principles underlying UK legislation for equality and diversity

Robin Richardson

National legal frameworks work vary in some details, but in this reading Richardson picks out generic principles on which equality and diversity legislation in the UK is based. A key challenge for teachers, or any other provider of services, is to provide equality of treatment while also affirming difference. Guidance may come from consultation, participation and the use of evidence.

Considering particular individuals or groups who you teach, are there ways in which you could improve provision for equality and diversity?

Edited from: Richardson, R. (2009) *Holding Together.* Stoke-on-Trent: Trentham Books, 24, 26–8.

Legislation about equality and diversity in Great Britain is concerned with six separate strands or areas: age; disability; ethnicity; faith, religion or belief; gender, including gender reassignment; and sexuality. The ten principles summarised here apply to all six strands and each one is explicit in at least one piece of UK legislation.

Principle 1: Equality

All people are of equal value and should be treated with equal respect, dignity and consideration:

- whatever their age
- whether or not they are disabled
- whatever their ethnicity, culture, national origin or national status
- whatever their faith tradition, religion or belief
- whichever their gender
- whatever their sexual identity

Principle 2: Difference and reasonable accommodation

People have a range of different interests, needs and experiences. Treating people equally (Principle 1) does not necessarily mean treating them all the same. Policies, procedures and activities must not discriminate, but also must take account of differences of experience, outlook and background – one size does not 'fit all'. In particular policies must take account of the kinds of specific barrier, inequality and disadvantage which people may face, and must make reasonable adjustments and accommodation.

Principle 3: Cohesion

Positive attitudes, relationships and interaction should be fostered, and a shared sense of cohesion and belonging. Therefore, hate-crime and prejudice related incidents and harassment should be addressed and prevented. Policies, procedures and activities should promote:

- mutually positive attitudes between older people and younger, and mutually beneficial relationships
- positive attitudes towards disabled people, good relations between disabled and non-disabled people, and an absence of harassment of disabled people
- positive interaction, good relations and dialogue between groups and communities different from each other in terms of ethnicity, culture, national origin or national status, and an absence of racism-related bullying and incidents
- mutual respect and good relations between girls and boys, and women and men, and an absence of sexual harassment and bullying
- positive interaction, good relations and dialogue between groups and communities different from each other in terms of faith tradition, religion or belief, and an absence of racism-related bullying and incidents
- good relations between people regardless of their sexual identity, and an absence of homophobic incidents and bullying

Principle 4: Being proactive to create greater equality of outcome

Opportunities should be taken to reduce and remove inequalities of outcome and the barriers that already exist, with a view to producing not only equality of opportunity but also equality of outcome.

It is not enough just to avoid discrimination and negative impacts. In addition to avoiding or minimising possible negative impacts of our policies, we must take opportunities to maximise positive impacts by reducing and removing inequalities and barriers that may already exist.

Principle 5: Consultation and involvement

People affected by a policy or activity should be consulted and involved in the design of new policies, and in the review of existing ones – 'nothing about us without us'. Views and voices should be collected, directly and through representative bodies.

Principle 6: Participation

All people should be enabled to take a full part in economic, political, social and cultural life at local and national levels. Policies and activities should benefit society as a whole, both locally and nationally, by fostering greater participation in public life, and in the affairs of voluntary and community sector organisations and institutions.

Principle 7: Evidence

Policies should be based on reliable evidence. When new policies are proposed, and existing policies are monitored and reviewed, a range of quantitative and qualitative evidence should be collected and used about the likely impact.

Principle 8: Complexity

All people have multiple identities. No one is just one thing. All have a range of different affiliations and loyalties. Many of the terms and categories used in the equalities field are necessarily imprecise and have the potential to be misleading.

Principle 9: Social class

The inequalities cited above in respect to age, ethnicity, disability, faith, gender and sexuality should not be considered independently of inequalities of social class. Differences of wealth, income, occupation, status, educational qualifications, influence, leisure activities, consumption patterns, health levels, aspirations and outlooks are relevant when we are designing, implementing and improving services.

Principle 10: Action

Principles are not enough. There must also be action. Every public body must draw up an action plan or delivery plan showing the specific measures it will adopt to create greater equality in its sphere of influence.

Reading 15.2

Learning Through Life
Tom Schuller

This reading sets out the ten recommendations from the *Learning Through Life* Inquiry. The recommendations identify key issues that anyone thinking about an education system fit for the twenty-first century must address. The recommendations suggest an integrated 'intelligent' education system with strong links to local communities. It is suggested that such a system could offer all those with learning needs, split into four groups (up to 25, 25–50, 50–75, 75+), opportunities to study throughout their lives. In this way the reading offers a blueprint for a lifelong learning education system.

Do you agree with the blueprint? What amendments would you make? How could lifelong learning be better promoted?

Schuller T. and Watson D. (2009) *Learning Through Life. Inquiry into the Future for Lifelong Learning. A Summary.* Leicester. NIACE. This was a summary of the full report *Learning Through Life*, the main report of the Inquiry into the Future for Lifelong Learning.

Learning Through Life: our proposals

The UK's current system of lifelong learning has failed to respond to the major demographic challenge of an ageing society, and to variety in employment patterns as young people take longer to settle into jobs and older people take longer to leave work. We make ten recommendations for a lifelong learning strategy which will mark out the UK as a true pioneer in this field.

Ten recommendations

The details of our ten recommendations are set out below:

1. Base lifelong learning policy on a new model of the educational life course, with four key stages (up to 25, 25–50, 50–75, 75+)
Our current approach to lifelong learning is not responding adequately to two major trends: an ageing society and changing patterns of paid and unpaid activity.

A genuinely lifelong view means that a *four-stage model* – up to 25, 25–50, 50–75, 75+ should be used as the basis for a *coherent systemic approach to lifelong learning.*

People in the first stage (up to 25, but starting for our purposes at 18) should be looked at as a whole, with all of its members having claims to *learning and development as young people*. Learning in the second stage (25–50) should aim at sustaining productivity and prosperity, but also at building strong family lives and personal identity. This is part of a *new mosaic of time* with different mixes of paid and unpaid work and learning time. For those in the third stage, *training and education opportunities* should be greatly enhanced. Policy, including learning policy, should treat 75 as the normal upper age limit for economic activity (not linked to state pension age). The emergence of the Fourth Age means that we urgently need to develop a more appropriate approach to the curriculum offer in later life. 25, 50 and 75 should be identified and used as *key transition points*, each requiring access to advice and guidance about life planning.

2. Rebalance resources fairly and sensibly across the different life stages

Public and private resources invested in lifelong learning amount to over £50 billion, but their distribution does not match our changing economic and social context.

We need public agreement on the criteria for fair and effective allocation of resources for learning across the life course. As a start, we propose a very broad goal: to shift from the current allocation ratios of *86: 11: 2.5: 0.5* across the four stages outlined above, to *80: 15: 4: 1* by 2020. This means approximately *doubling the proportional support for learning in the third and fourth stages*. To counter any sense that we favour age segregation, we recommend redoubling efforts to support *family and intergenerational learning*.

3. Build a set of learning entitlements

A clear framework of entitlements to learning will be a key factor in strengthening choice and motivation to learn.

We need a clear overall framework of entitlements, with two key categories: general entitlements and specific 'transition' entitlements.

a) *General entitlements*

A *legal* entitlement of free access to learning for all who need it to acquire basic skills, i.e. literacy and numeracy, up to Level 1. A *financial* entitlement to a minimum level of qualification needed to be able to play a full contributing part in society; this is currently Level 2, but will rise and change over time. 1 Both these entitlements should extend to all, regardless of age. A '*good practice*' entitlement to learning leave as an occupational benefit to be developed flexibly and over time as part of mainstream employment conditions.

b) *Specific 'transition' entitlements*

These should be designed to help people use learning to make potentially difficult transitions, for example guaranteeing access to learning for those leaving prison or institutional care, moving between areas or countries, or retiring. The transition entitlements can be developed flexibly over time.

c) These entitlements should be underpinned by *infrastructure guarantees*: to universal access to advice and guidance (currently being developed in the adult advancement and careers service), and to a minimal level of digital technology (currently broadband at 2Mbps, but this will rise and change).

d) Funding of entitlements should be channelled through a *national system of Learning Accounts*, giving individuals the maximum control over how they are used. The Learning Accounts should be set up by the State for people reaching their twenty-fifth birthday. Fifty per cent of the public contribution to the Child Trust Fund should be allocated to this.

4. Engineer flexibility: a system of credit and encouraging part-timers

Faster progress is needed to implement a credit-based system, and to support people to combine study with other activities.

We should move quickly to implement fully a coherent system of credits as the basis for organising post-school learning. The funding for learning (both fees and student support) should be based on these credits and should not discriminate against part-time provision or part-time students. There should be greater fairness and consistency in funding for further and higher education.

5. Improve the quality of work

The debate on skills has been too dominated by an emphasis on increasing the volume of skills. There should be a stronger focus on how skills are actually used.

We need increased understanding of the kinds of work environment which encourage formal and informal learning as a means of raising performance and productivity. There should be a clearer set of standards for gauging employer engagement with learning. Claims to corporation tax relief for training should be linked to these standards. Data on training performance and expenditure, including on learning leave, should be published in the organisations' annual accounts of publicly quoted companies. Licence to practise requirements should be used more widely to promote the raising of the level and use of skills. Procurement policy should be used to drive up levels of training along the supply chain.

6. Construct a curriculum framework for citizens' capabilities

A common framework of learning opportunities should be created, aimed at enhancing people's control over their own lives.

An agreed framework for a citizens' curriculum should be developed, built initially around a set of four capabilities: digital, health, financial and civic, together with employability. In every area there should be a minimum local offer which guarantees access to the citizens' curriculum, locally interpreted to meet diverse needs.

7. Broaden and strengthen the capacity of the lifelong learning workforce

Stronger support should be available for all those involved in delivering education and training, in various capacities.

There should be a broad definition of who makes up the lifelong learning workforce, including school teachers and early years practitioners, and learning support staff. The work of union learning representatives and community learning champions should be further promoted and supported. Other people who play or could play roles as learning 'intermediaries' in 'non-educational' fields such as health, probation or citizens advice should be identified and supported.

8. Revive local responsibility...

The current system (in England) has become over-centralised, and insufficiently linked to local and regional needs. We should restore life and power to local levels.

Local authorities should lead the development of lifelong learning strategy at local level. They should develop the local infrastructure, including links to non-educational services such as health. FE colleges should be seen as an institutional backbone for local lifelong learning, with a predominantly local focus. Local strategies should embrace cultural institutions – including voluntary organisations, libraries, museums, theatres and galleries. Local employer networks should be promoted, as part of strengthening a culture of learning in and out of work. The idea of Local Learning Exchanges (LLEs) should be developed to connect people as socially networked learners, and to provide spaces for local groups to engage in learning. Higher education institutions should commit themselves to joining in local strategies for lifelong learning, and to disseminating their research knowledge to the community.

9. ... within national frameworks
There should be effective machinery for creating a coherent national strategy across the UK, and within the UK's four nations.

A single department should have the lead responsibility for promoting lifelong learning, with cross-government targets for lifelong learning. There should be a cross-departmental expenditure study as part of the next Comprehensive Spending Review, identifying cost efficiencies from a coordinated approach to lifelong learning. An authoritative body should be established to oversee and scrutinise the national system of lifelong learning, with suitable arrangements in the devolved administrations.

10. Make the system intelligent
The system will only flourish with information and evaluation which are consistent, broad and rigorous, and open debate about the implications.

A three-yearly *State of Learning* report should be published, covering major trends and issues, including evidence collected by and submitted to international bodies. Routine use should be made of external comparators, including a benchmark group of countries, together with a one-off OECD review of the UK's lifelong learning strategy. We need stronger and broader analysis of the benefits and costs of lifelong learning over time, and systematic experimentation on what works. There should be regular use of peer review and of inspections, and of 'learner voices'.

Reading 15.3

Tackling prejudice together: What are trainee teachers' experiences of prejudice in educational contexts?

Margaret Gregson, Lawrence Nixon and Patricia Spedding

This reading derives from a research and development project based around the ways in which teachers experience and deal with prejudiced behaviour. The research was conducted by the University of Sunderland's Centre for Excellence in Teacher Training (SUNCETT) in 2011 with student teachers on a PGCE programme in Post Compulsory Education and Training (PCET). Highlighted in this research, which is based upon an analysis of 76 case study accounts, is the concern that a significant number (43%) of experienced teachers ignored or made light of incidents of prejudice and that only a few (11%) had any pedagogical responses in place for dealing with incidents of prejudiced behaviour.

The key point to make is that teachers need practical strategies and support in order to improve their confidence to plan and develop teaching, learning and assessment activities in their own classrooms which enables them to 'tackle prejudice head-on'.

Gregson, M., Nixon L. and Spedding P. (2011) *Tackling Prejudice Together*. Presentation at University of Sunderland, Faculty of Education and Society Conference, 5 September.

Trainee teachers are concerned to develop their classroom management skills and to support their own students by having a range of strategies to help them deal with incidents of prejudiced and challenging behaviour.

In order to find out more about the ways in which teachers prepare and respond to incidents of prejudice in the classroom we conducted a small scale, case study research project with seventy six PGCE PCET student teachers in 2011 at the University of Sunderland's Centre for Excellence in Teacher Training (SUNCETT). We set out to identify the types of prejudice teachers' encounter and to identify the range of ways in which teachers commonly responded to these incidents. We then critically evaluated these responses and began to explore the ways in which teachers' can effectively address these types of prejudice in their own classrooms.

Trainee teachers were asked to produce a case study account of an incident of prejudice which had occurred in their teaching practice placement or from their own recent experience as a student in college or university. The case study accounts were used in the first instance as a focusing device for discussion and exploration at a practice based conference attended by the same seventy six trainee teachers. Following this conference event the case studies were analysed to identify both the types of prejudiced behaviour teachers' encountered (dimensions) and how teachers responded to these incidents (dynamics).

Dimensions of prejudice

The main categories of types or dimensions of prejudice were clustered around the charac-teristics of diversity identified in the Equalities Act 2010. These were sexism, racism, age, religion or belief, disability, sexual orientation and psychological bullying. The following figure illustrates the main categories and sub- categories identified from analysis of the student teacher case studies.

Figure 15.3.1
The types of prejudice we found

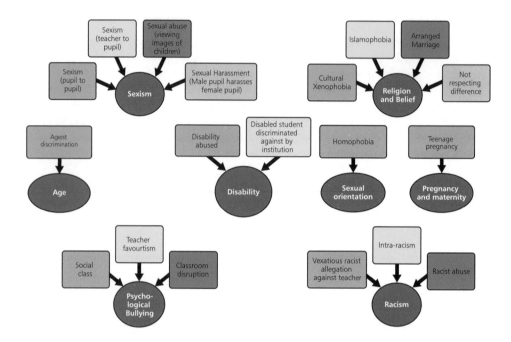

As can be seen from Figure 15.3.1 these categories were multi-dimensional. For example, sexism included incidents of sexist behaviour which was student to student and also teacher to student in addition to sexual harassment of male student to female student. Religion or belief included Islamaphobia and cultural xenophobia as well as a general disrespect for difference. A key point to make here is that potentially teachers are faced with a huge range of dimensions of prejudice and it would be difficult to have a well thought through strategy for each specific dimension but rather it requires that teachers need strategies based upon a best fit for a number of circumstances.

Dynamics of response

Following this identification of types or dimensions of prejudice the case studies were analysed in terms of the ways in which teachers responded to these incidents – in other words dynamics of response. Using categories developed from the discussion in "A holistic approach to racist incidents" available at **www.insted.co.uk** five key responses emerged from the case study analysis and identified that:

- 43% of teachers ignored or made light of the incident
- 30% of teachers rebuked or punished the instigator of the incident
- 15% of teachers reasoned with the instigator of the incident
- 11% of teachers developed a pedagogical response to the incident
- 1% took a whole organisational response to the incident.

It is important to acknowledge that this was a small scale study based upon the analysis of seventy six case study accounts drawn from a range of educational settings including schools, FE colleges, 6th Forms and private training organisations and therefore only 'fuzzy generalisations' (Bassey and Pratt, 2003) should be drawn from this data set.

That said the identification of these categories provides a helpful way of looking at how teachers in the sample responded to these incidents of prejudice and a subsequent framework for further thematic analysis.

Key themes

Analysing the case study data revealed some interesting themes which included:

- Sympathy for the teacher
- Teachers are potentially confronted with a very wide range of prejudiced behaviour
- This range can appear daunting to deal with (overwhelming even)
- It involves issues that are highly contested in society
- And it almost always involves our own personal attitudes beliefs and values.

Key Findings

The key findings to emerge from the thematic analysis were as follows:

- Students in the classroom want a serious response from their teacher to incidents of prejudice. Students did not want teachers to make light of these incidents.
- In some cases the victim of bullying came to blame themselves for the incident or situation.
- In all cases teachers were reacting to an unexpected incident.
- Teachers felt under pressure to react immediately.
- Many teachers did not handle these incidents effectively, although they almost always had the intention to do their best.

The most common response of teachers was to ignore and make light of incidents.

Sometimes it was difficult to know if this was because teachers simply didn't know how to deal with the incident.

This decision to ignore or make light of can be seen to be a particularly dangerous strategy when dealing with issues of racism as a number of the case studies showed that doing so almost always escalated into physical or verbal violence.

In only nine out of the seventy six case studies were teachers able to address the incident with a pedagogical response, that is, use teaching and learning activities which directly focused upon countering the prejudice and critically developing debate and 'understanding' of why such behaviour was 'unacceptable'.

Recommendations

The key recommendations from the study were:

- Teachers need to have practical holding responses to enable them to immediately deal with the incident. This holding response should show that the incident is being taken seriously.
- Teachers need the time, space and support to plan and develop learning and teaching activities to effectively address the specific type of prejudiced behaviour – in other words a thoughtful pedagogical response.
- Teachers need collaborative support to put these learning and teaching activities into practice.

When faced with incidents of prejudiced and by extension disruptive behaviour that requires more than a straight forward classroom response the value of having a 'holding response' was seen to be a very useful strategy. Trainee teachers appreciated the opportunity to discuss and develop holding responses together especially in the light of feedback from peers which promoted a positive encouragement for using holding responses in practice. Trainee teachers felt reassured by their peers' experiences in dealing with or considering how to deal with incidents in the future recognising that a holding response offered a tangible strategy they felt able to apply. A holding response is a short statement that has two purposes:

- To ensure the student stops this prejudiced and disruptive behaviour
- Signals to all learners that you will return to address this issue more fully in another session.

Preparing a holding response in advance was seen to allow teachers to deal effectively with the incident when it occurred and to buy them time to think about which pedagogical response would be the most appropriate to addressing this issue subsequently.

Trainee teachers worked in collaboration to identify and develop strategies to build a repertoire of pedagogical responses which directly addressed prejudiced behaviour and further to create classroom environments that valued diversity and promoted strong positive messages through relevant pedagogical interventions.

Most significantly this small scale study signalled the crucial role that organisational time and support has to play in the development of these key pedagogical skills. Teachers need opportunities to collaborate with colleagues to develop and apply strategies in practice. Perhaps most important of all was the recognition that creating pedagogy that gets to the very heart of tackling prejudice head on or better still preventing it from happening in the first place is a critical part of teachers' professional development.

Reading 15.4

Who are the learners?
Yvon Appleby

Looking at how the word learner is used tells us a lot about the relationship between policy and practice in adult education. It also enables us to critically examine access to provision and the relevance of that provision to adult lives. It is a label that can be used in policy terms to describe and define a category or a 'problem'; it can be used by teachers to frame their practice; and importantly, it can be used by learners themselves to describe their relationship to learning. Some definitions may provide increased opportunities for learning – for example, evidenced in greater enrolments. However, differences in learner definitions between policymakers, practitioners and learners raise fundamental questions about access to learning, what type of learning is made available, and for what purpose. These issues are discussed in the context of the national adult literacy strategy Skills for Life (DfEE 2001).

Edited from: Appleby, Y. (2010) 'Who are the Learners?'. In N. Hughes and I. Schwab (eds) *Teaching Adult Literacy: Principles and Practice*. London. Open University Press, 29–47.

Introduction

Who are literacy, numeracy and language learners – it's obvious isn't it? They are people who need to learn or improve these skills. You can see photographs and descriptions of learners on posters, in media campaigns and in policy documents. Surely we know how many learners there are, how many there should be and what levels they should be achieving? However, what seems a straightforward question to ask becomes less obvious in answering it.

In policy the term 'literacy learner' is used generally to define categories, groups and individuals who attend classes or some form of provision to improve their knowledge and literacy skill. The Moser report, *A Fresh Start* (DfEE, 1999) identified seven million adults who lacked adequate levels of literacy to be able to function effectively. Here people lacking necessary literacy skills were constructed as learners by policy in their absence. This labelling process is mainly external to individuals' lives and meanings around literacy. It relates strongly, though not exclusively, to social factors where the lack of literacy becomes defined by policy as an individual responsibility and as a 'social problem', one that can be remedied by learning literacy, numeracy or language. Whilst the term learner is useful in policy and overall planning of provision it does not tell us about these people as individuals, what they are learning, why they want to learn and how this fits in their everyday lives. It tells us who the policy spotlight falls upon, defining them as learners, at various points of its pendulum swing; a swing with a history (Hamilton and Hillier, 2006, Reading 9.1)

Listening to adult learners

From our research into adult learners' lives (see Barton et al., 2007) we found that when people self-identify as learners they have already made the first steps on a learning journey which relates to their individual history, current circumstances and future aspirations. Using a social practice approach enabled us to recognise learners as whole people who use these skills in a range of settings inside and outside the classroom: it is in contrast to a deficit view which sees learners as empty vessels to be filled with knowledge. By talking to a range of learners and teachers we identified that learning is the product of a dialogue between what the learners bring and what the teachers bring; that tutors need to respond to specific learning contexts and to individual learners; that good personal relationships are important for learning; that listening to learners takes time and resources; and, for some teachers there are tensions between different and possibly competing constructions of learner identity.

By looking at learners' situated in their own lives we see that they also bring much to learning. They often have existing knowledge and strategies; they have hobbies, interests and ruling passions (Barton and Hamilton, 2000). Many bring histories which inform their confidence or identity as 'a learner', for some these were negative and included bullying and intimidation. Others brought positive experiences and knowledge of their community and many supported learning for others, particularly within intergenerational learning and language communities. Many were managing complex lives and factors outside their control such as illness, long term unemployment or isolation.

Learners told us they wanted to learn for a mixture of social, economic and family reasons, some of immediate benefit and others were for the future. Individual motivation for learning was identified as: gaining particular subject knowledge; improving wider skills and learning about learning; making social contacts and developing new networks and skills; developing skills and confidence for employment; and, for overcoming school failure and negative experiences of learning. For some learning was for concrete everyday things like getting a job, for helping children with homework or being able to manage complicate forms and household bills. It could be for less concretely expressed reasons like overcoming a fear of maths, feeling better about oneself and gaining social confidence by being with others. Or, it could be managing to attend a course regularly, something not previously achievable within difficult life circumstances. Sophie (pseudonyms were used) shows the ping pong effect for some learners as they come in and out of learning whilst managing difficult life circumstances:

Sophie at 18 years old was a regular attender at Nightcare, a shelter for young homeless people. She had a troubled childhood, as her mother, a teacher, was drug and alcohol dependent. Although a bright child she hated school and often absconded. She was expelled for repeated assault and arson, leaving home at 15 and missing her exams.

Nightcare gave her life structure as well as safety, food people and activities. This included learning through art and craft. She had several attempts at going to college but didn't manage to complete a course because of the daily difficulties of finding food, shelter and safety. She left the last course, landscape gardening, when she became pregnant.

She found 'basic skill' stuff boring and easy but enjoyed reading, particularly Virginia Andrews, saying of her books 'Like it's real life...I can relate to the people, like the stuff that is going on'. Sophie writes Haiku poetry in French and English as well as free-writing. She was determined to go back to college after the baby was born to take her GCSEs and A levels to enable her to eventually study veterinary medicine or psychology.

By listening to learners like Sophie it is possible to see what people bring with them and what they want from learning as they tell us what they like and value about learning. People were active agents, not passive recipients, in the process of learning that occurred both inside and outside the classroom. The learners told us that to be able learn successfully it was important that it was: the right time in their lives to learn; that learning was useful and relevant to their everyday life; that learning was at the right pace; and, that the social dimension of learning was recognised. (See Appleby and Barton, 2008 and Appleby, 2008 for case studies from the study). Many registered surprise at being asked for their views about how they learned best and why they wanted to learn; these were seen as novel questions to ask learners.

Concluding remarks

Asking who literacy learners are shows the need to question the definitions we often unthinkingly use. Definitions used at a policy level are general and do not easily accommodate the experience of individuals and the complexity of their lives and learning. It makes it easy to categorise and generalise, often completely externally to the individual being labelled. Where learning is seen as part of everyday life it includes being in families, communities and workplaces as well as in the classroom or other learning environments. This learner, rather than learning, perspective can take account of things that people bring to learning, what they want to learn and how they learn best. People bring existing knowledge and skills as well as their histories, current circumstances and plans for the future – these need to be taken into account in any teaching environment and teaching relationship.

Through our collaboration with practitioners as co-researchers, who were working with and sometimes between competing institutional and personal definitions, we developed a social practice pedagogical approach. This took as the focus how best to respond to what the learners told us and to recognise them as active agents in their lives and learning. The approach has five principles based upon teacher inquiry and reflective practice where we asked teachers to look at their own literacy practices and learning experiences. These are: firstly, that it is important for teachers to research everyday practices to understand where learning occurs; secondly, to take account of people's lives including their histories, identities, current circumstances and imagined futures; thirdly, to support learning through participation using authentic materials for real purposes; fourthly, to enable safe and supported spaces that recognise and value the social aspects of learning including physical and emotional safety; lastly, to locate literacy in other forms of meaning making such as oral, visual, individual and groups ways of communicating.

The set of principles redefines who we mean when we talk of learners, asks how learning takes place and challenges us to change the focus from literacy learners as a generalised 'them' to a more inclusive one that includes all of us. This approach supports critical inquiry in teacher training and reinforces the need for ongoing critical professional development in adult education (Appleby and Pilkington, 2014) recognising that we are learners as well as teachers.

part five

Deepening understanding

Expertise
Conceptual tools for career-long fascination?

16

This chapter begins with a discussion (16.1) of how educational improvement and professional development in FAVE can be, supported through the application of an approach to the improvement of teaching, learning and assessment known as Joint Practice Development (JPD). Research in this approach to educational improvement was funded by the Education and Training Foundation (ETF) and developed and supported by the University of Sunderland's Centre for Excellence in Teacher Training (SUNCETT). The JPD model has been used to support practitioner research across the FAVE sector over the past five years. It has generated an incremental body of robust empirical research evidence, which demonstrates the positive impact of this approach.

Jameson and Hillier (16.2) highlight the scope and importance of small-scale practitioner research and reflective practice, while Hargreaves (16.3) explains an inherent conservatism which he argues is rooted in the practice of teaching. Finally, O'Leary (16.4) illustrates how more expansive approaches to teacher observation that do not require graded observations can help to establish more productive relationships and bring about significant improvements in practice.

The associated chapter in Reflective Teaching in Further, Adult and Vocational Education focuses on the structuring of expert knowledge which draws together themes discussed throughout the book, and relates these to enduring issues and principles in education.

'Key Readings' for this associated chapter suggest a number of classic studies on the development of teacher expertise. The approach to structuring expert knowledge is significantly extended in the 'Deepening Expertise' section of the reflectiveteaching.co.uk website. Advice and useful links to internet resources for evidence-informed expert practice can also be found there, together with links to a selection of TLRP publications.

Reading 16.1

Helping good ideas to become good practice: Enhancing your professional practice through Joint Practice Development (JPD)

Margaret Gregson, Patricia Spedding and Lawrence Nixon

This reading draws upon five years of empirical research at the University of Sunderland's Centre for Excellence in Teacher Training (SUNCETT). This work engages practitioners from across the Further Adult Vocational Education (FAVE) sector in HE-supported practitioner research which aims to improve practice. It offers insights into the practicalities of using a collaborative approach to improving teaching, learning and assessment, described as Joint Practice Development (JPD). Focusing upon a six-stage cycle, it illustrates different stages in using JPD as an approach to the improvement of teaching and learning. It also points to the importance of measuring the impact of JPD through both hard and soft indicators of change and improvement.

How might you use the joint practice development approach to improving teaching and learning as part of your CPD?

Edited from: Gregson, M., Spedding, T. and Nixon, L. (forthcoming 2015) *Helping Good Ideas Become Good Practice: Enhancing Professionalism through Joint Practice Development (JPD).* London: Bloomsbury.

Why Should Education Leaders and Teachers Use the JPD Approach to CPD?

It is customary for leaders of education to use continuing professional development (CPD) budgets to update the subject and pedagogical knowledge of their staff. Usually this involves attending time consuming, often expensive, courses, conferences or other events where someone who is considered (or considers themselves) to be 'an expert' tells everyone else in attendance what to do.

While such CPD events and networks might be helpful in raising awareness of new developments, exchanging ideas and sharing resources – arguably a necessary first step in improving practice, it is not enough to guarantee it. This is because a lot more 'new learning' (Eraut, 2004) has to take place before knowledge is 'transferred' well enough to bring about real changes in practice. Eraut uses the metaphor of an iceberg to explain how practice really changes. He argues that abstract, theoretical knowledge and information about a 'good practice' constitutes only one eighth of the knowledge needed to put a 'good idea' into practice and that the remaining seven eighths represents the amount of new learning needed to bring about real changes in practice. In view of this, education leaders need to think carefully about the extent to which existing, taken-for granted approaches to CPD can be justified in terms of value for money.

Central to Joint Practice Development (JPD) is the recognition that changing and improving practice involves more than the simple transfer of information. The JPD approach to CPD acknowledges that change takes time. It recognises that the reality of putting ideas into practice places greater demands upon the relationships of those involved in the processes of change and those responsible for the practices of improvement (Fielding et al., 2005).

How can JPD be organised and used to improve Teaching, Learning and Assessment ?

This reading deals with the practical issues of how to go about improving Teaching, Learning and Assessment (TLA) in straightforward, cost-effective and sustainable ways using JPD as an integral part of an organisation's CPD strategy. We describe a sequenced series of six workshops each with a distinct aim. We summarise the sequence in the Six-Step Cycle diagram below. This outline has been developed to help leaders of education and teachers get a further sense of what JPD could look like in practice. It is designed to stimulate and focus the discussions required to put JPD into practice. As such it is not a template or a 'recipe' but a stimulus and focus for discussion which can and should be adapted to suit particular circumstances.

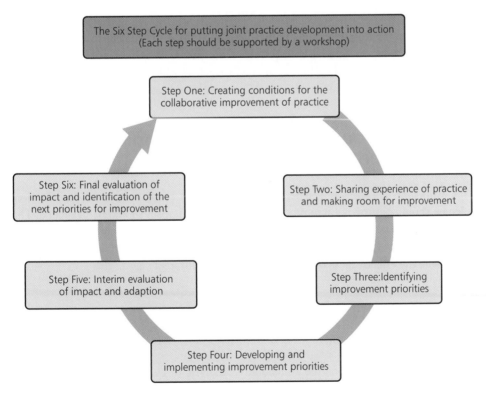

Figure 16.1.1
The Six Step Cycle for putting Joint Practice Development into action

Workshop One: Creating conditions for Joint Practice Development

This first Workshop will enable you to explain the need to take a new approach to CPD and help you to introduce ideas about JPD to colleagues in your organisation. This is why it's a good idea to think about how you can use existing collaborative relationships to lay the foundations for new ones and decide who might be responsible for the introduction, development and co-ordination of the project.

Workshop Two: Sharing experience of practice and making room for argument and improvement

This workshop can help participants to begin to talk about aspects of practice they would like to improve and to identify possible strategies that might be used to bring this about.

Workshop Three: Identifying improvement priorities

This workshop invites participants to discuss area(s) for improvement from the previous workshop in order to agree which priorities are the most important and need to be addressed first. The workshop then encourages teachers and learners to work together to identify possible interventions which could be used to address these.

Workshop Four: Developing and implementing improvement priorities

This workshop encourages teachers to work together to plan how the interventions selected should best be put into practice and how, their impact should be evaluated. This should include the identification of 'hard' and 'softer' measures of impact (**Gregson and Nixon** Reading 14.1) and how evidence of that impact can be collected, analysed and used to evaluate the effectiveness of the intervention(s) at different stages.

Workshop Five: Interim evaluation of impact and adaptation

This workshop focuses upon the collaborative analysis of evidence of the impact of the interventions selected for implementation at an interim stage of the process. Participants are given opportunities to consider if or how well the intervention is working and if it needs to be developed adapted or even abandoned in the light of emerging evidence.

Workshop Six: Final evaluation of impact and identification of next priorities for improvement

Workshop six brings together evidence of the impact and experiences of implementing the JPD interventions. Reviewing this evidence will help participants to evaluate the success of the intervention(s) in improving TLA and enable them to decide if the intervention is worthy of further development. This will include consideration of if/how the JPD community could be extended and what the next priorities should be.

Measuring impact: Hard and soft indicators of JPD

When you are setting up your JPD project it is really important that you take some time to agree upon some indicators of impact. These indicators need to play two closely related roles. First, to help you with your interim reflections and a final review of what is happening and what you need to adapt. Second, to help provide evidence of the positive or negative impact that the intervention is having upon TLA. It will therefore be well worth agreeing soft and hard indicators of impact that you understand and are happy to use. Remember to make time for this at the beginning of your JPD work and to review this together as you go along.

The questions below could help you to structure your discussion of which soft and hard indicators of impact to select:

- What positive outcomes do we expect this intervention to bring about?
- What hard indicators of impact could you use to demonstrate this impact? For example improvements in:
  - grade profile of a cohort for a specific assignment
  - retention rates
  - attendance rates
  - achievement rates
  - course reviews
  - inspection grades
  - staff motivation/ morale
  - student motivation/ morale
  - staff attitudes and interest in CPD

Other types of hard impacts could include:

- robust research evidence and more convincing arguments for the use of one pedagogical intervention over another
- greater cross-curriculum/departmental working
- beneficial links and collaboration with other providers/agencies
- robust evidence for subsequent funding applications
- establishment of a community of research and practice within your organisation
- FAVE staff active in the education research community
- closer links with HE colleagues
- students themselves being more "research active"

● What soft indicators of impact could you use to demonstrate this impact? For example,

- classroom atmosphere has changed – more settled, more questioning etc.
- students' are more willing to collaborate
- students more engaged with their learning
- teachers' being more creative in their approaches to TLA and prepared to experiment
- self-reported or observed autonomy of students
- staff willing and able to challenge taken-for-granted practices
- senior managers and other education managers more aware of the importance practitioner research
- senior managers and other education managers working collaboratively on joint practitioner research projects
- practitioner research projects within and across different departments/whole organisation.

Conclusion

In this reading we have described a cycle of six JPD workshops that you can use to develop teaching learning and assessment within your organisation and across organisations.

The research we have conducted with practitioners across the sector over the last five years demonstrates the potential of the JPD model to ensure the focus of activity remains squarely upon teaching and learning. This cycle of JPD workshops could therefore be a significant factor in extending an organisation's repertoire of strategies to improve TLA through CPD.

The key assumption underpinning this reading is that most people want to do a good job and want to get better at what they do. We have described how this model of JPD can provide a forum where teachers, education leaders and learners can work together to improve TLA. Many teachers in the sector are highly skilled artisans, artists, scientists, engineers, mathematicians, linguists, poets, dramatists, dancers, musicians, entrepreneurs etc., with much experience and highly qualified in their vocational or subject specialism. This model allows teachers and education leaders to devolve or share power to improve the experience and achievements of learners. We want to emphasise the significant role research plays in helping practitioners extend their thinking about improving TLA both in terms of the strategies they use and the quality of their reflections. Our experience also suggests that practitioners benefit greatly from being supported to explore the framing of their research, identifying its implications for practice and to use their experiences of research to effectively reflect upon what has happened. For these reasons, it is well worth considering using specialist support from HE colleagues at particular stages of the JPD cycle.

Finally, we hope this reading will encourage you to think seriously about trying out the JPD model with a colleague or colleagues within your team or across your organisation. For a more detailed discussion of JPD see Gregson et al. (forthcoming 2015).

Reading 16.2

Small-scale research: Action research and reflective practice

Jill Jameson and Yvonne Hillier

> In this reading, Jameson and Hillier explore the powerful possibilities of reflective practice in the development of an empowerment model for practitioners of further education research. A discussion of the differences between 'Reflecting in Action' and 'Reflecting on Action' provides the groundwork to help enable teachers to become truly reflective in their practice.
>
> Jameson and Hillier argue that by engaging in small-scale action research, teachers will be able to examine the ways in which they deal with their own learners in their own environments, with the intention of bettering their practice as they go along.
>
> How could the adoption of an action research model benefit you in your own practice?
>
> *Edited from:* Hillier, Y. and Jameson, J. (2003) *Empowering Researchers in Further Education.* Stoke-on-Trent: Trentham Books, Chapter 4.

Small-scale research in the context of further education

In developing an 'empowerment' model for practitioners in further education research, we draw on the varied roles people have and their communities and networks. These groups are often peer-group networks providing friendly support and help, sharing information, collaborating for problem-solving and generally providing a rich source of professional expertise that can be invaluable to staff in the sector. The concept of 'reflective practice' is intimately bound up with the specialist roles people hold in colleges, and the kinds of professional knowledge and skills they develop and share as 'communities of practice'.

Reflective practice

People who work in further education colleges have a wealth of professional knowledge. This knowledge is often tacit, unexplained and difficult to articulate. The problem with such knowledge is that it cannot be easily tested. Ideas and practices can become stultified, and 'taken for granted', resulting in resistance to change. A way forward is to be open to our assumptions, and actively to seek these out. This approach stems from a process called *reflective practice* (Schön, 1983, 1987).

Like Eraut, Schön was aware that professionals draw upon their tacit knowledge. People think about what they do, both at the time of any activity, called 'reflecting in action', and then later, called 'reflection on action'. Reflection in action is a bit like a running commentary, in which you note what is happening as you do something and adjust accordingly. For example, you may notice people 'switching off'' during a presentation, and decide to get people working in small groups to avoid them all dozing off. Reflection on action is retrospective, something you may do after the event. In this example, you may decide not to use the presentation in the same way in future, as it has not held people's attention. You therefore have 'reflected on your practice' and changed it as a result.

There are many ways to help us think reflectively, to 'reflect on action'. Peters (1994) provides a model that asks us to think of a concrete example and then to step back and allow ourselves to test out what are our assumptions about that situation. Brookfield (1995) suggests we can look at a situation from our own viewpoint, from our colleagues' viewpoints, from those of students, and also from perspectives derived from theoretical literature. He calls these the four critical lenses. Flanagan (1954), asks us to think of examples, perhaps with a particular characteristic, as exemplars of the phenomenon we are studying. We might want to think about sessions we have taught in which everything went well, and contrast these with sessions where things went badly wrong. These 'critical incidents' provide useful information for us to reflect upon. We can begin to uncover the characteristics about the two cases and perhaps identify trends.

We must be careful not to 'collude' with ideas that are comfortable for us, or let colleagues 'bump' us into taking up the latest teaching fad. Critical reflection is a key part of practitioner research, because it enables people to ask questions about 'the way we do things around here', and creates a space for conducting research.

If we are truly reflective, we are likely to want to change what we do as a result. Research aimed at change is something that is ongoing and active, rather than retrospective. We are not interested in analysing what has happened, but what *is* happening. In other words, we need to research our action, something that is called unsurprisingly action research! Let us consider an example

A course tutor's perspective

Mandy Williams teaches Care NVQs, and works with a variety of learners who are studying for a number of linked qualifications, including Nursery Nursing, Access to Nursing and Access to Social Work. There have been numerous initiatives introduced into the college in the last few years: competence based qualifications, problem based learning, information learning technology, widening participation for under represented groups. Mandy has hardly time to get used to running her programmes according to one set of regulations when another new procedure is introduced. She feels as though she is constantly changing the way she works without having the opportunity to find out if she is being effective. What could Mandy do to examine the way that she facilitates the learning of her different groups of people? What would help her identify what works, why she is being asked to adapt and change, how effective are these changes and what consequences follow from such changes?

Small-scale research

What do we mean by small-scale research? A large-scale study may examine retention of young learners across a number of colleges in different regions with different student groups. Imagine a course tutor is also interested in finding out how to improve the retention of her group of 14–16 year olds. This course tutor may use a similar methodology to the large-scale study but the *scale* of her research will be much smaller. This does not mean that her study is any less valid, or important. It does mean that she cannot claim that her findings and insights gained from the research will be generalised across all further education programmes of learning. What she does gain, however, is an understanding of *her* context, *her* learners, and *her* professional practice.

Action research

When people are researching into something that they are *doing,* with a view to making a difference as a result of their research, then they are engaged in something called *'action research'*. Action research does not only consist of people's reflections on what they have done. It is research while action is taking place. In other words, it is a deliberate attempt to examine the way in which something is being undertaken, with a view to making changes to that process as the research goes along. It is therefore a more fluid and iterative process than evaluation of past practice.

Lewin (1948) advocated that research that did not lead to any impact on improving people's lives was worthless. Habermas (1974), argued that one form of knowledge, *emancipatory*, is that which not only changes people's lives but also enables them to step out of their assumptions and challenge practices which are constraining of certain groups. Action research, then, is about making a difference but doing so in a way that is informed by careful research. It requires self-reflection because we cannot possibly ensure that we want to make changes to a current situation unless we begin to think analytically about it. Dewey (1933) argued that we should make *careful* observations, and then create hypotheses that we could test through action rather than rushing in on a trial and error basis.

Action research is participative and aims to enable people to improve their own practice, rather than have 'improvements' done to them. It is self-critical and develops practice through systematic enquiry and learning. It is iterative in the sense that someone may start with a thought, having reflected on a particular aspect of daily practice. A systematic enquiry into that practice may ensue, perhaps with colleagues' collaboration. The results of this may lead to a change that is monitored and evaluated. Throughout this process the action may be continually refined as a result of critical reflection.

Let us consider Mandy. Mandy has been asked to work with a revised curriculum. Learners in some programmes fared badly in their examinations and dropped out of the college. The Principal of the college has asked Mandy to work with a group of colleagues teaching Psychology and Sociology as well as the Access to Social Work and Access to

Nursing programmes. It appears that the Access programmes retain learners more effec-tively than the more 'traditional' academic programmes. What can the staff do to improve the retention and therefore achievement rates of the learners on the academic programmes?

Mandy could simply suggest a different teaching strategy and hope that her colleagues can implement it quickly. However, no one will know how well this strategy is doing until the retention figures are collected. By then, it may be too late and another group of learners will have dropped out. Mandy may not know why the Access learners stay on and success-fully complete their studies. She may attribute one way of working with them, perhaps working in small groups and fostering an autonomous approach to studying psychology, to the success of the programme, when it may simply be that the learners are all mature. How does Mandy know that her ideas will work? Can she afford to wait a year to find out?

Action research is an appropriate tool to help Mandy here. Essentially, Mandy and her colleagues, can investigate some of the factors that may contribute to the different success rates of the two programmes. They may try out new teaching methods, discuss any consequences of this early on in the project and make some changes which are then also subject to enquiry and debate. The underpinning rationale for this approach is one of continual examination, checking and rechecking what 'works', and if not, why not, and to reflect on the consequences of actions as they are taken. This iterative process, where one activity can lead to a different activity, which then is refined after further examination is not cyclical, in which a loop is followed around and repeated.

So action research has a fundamental and explicit aim to make a difference. It is inher-ently bound up with reflective practice, in which a group of colleagues challenge the taken for granted and try to create a rationale for their practice. Within this approach, we need to find out what is working for us and our students, what is happening as a result, and what is changing.

Reading 16.3

Contemporary change and professional inertia
Andy Hargreaves

> This reading discusses a tendency towards professionally conservative thinking by teachers – focused on present, practical realities. The nature of teachers' work is identified, and the ways in which this underpins a cautious approach to change are discussed. Hargreaves suggests that contemporary educational reforms increase pressure for short-term performance and thus reinforce 'addictive presentism'. He calls for inspiring vision and principled collaboration to build expertise for long-term improvement (see also Hargreaves and Fullan, 2012).
>
> How do you feel about your work, and your future in the profession?
>
> *Edited from:* Hargreaves, A. (2007) *The Persistence of Presentism and the Struggle for Lasting Improvement,* Professorial Lecture. Institute of Education, University of London, 24 January.

Dan Lortie's *Schoolteacher* (1975) is a great classic of the field. At the core of the book lay a simple but compelling argument: that teaching is characterised by three orientations which impede educational improvement – conservatism, individualism and presentism.

Conservatism is the most evident obstacle to change. The only changes that teachers deemed desirable, Lortie argued, were ones that amounted to 'more of the same'; confirming current 'institutional tactics' by 'removing obstacles and providing for more teaching with better support'. Teachers had 'a preference for doing things as they have been done in the past' (1975: 209).

Individualism, Lortie claimed, was reinforced and rewarded by a job that had uncertain criteria for successful performance and which led them to align their goals with their 'own capacities and interests' (Lortie, 1975: 210). Teachers therefore had a stake in their own autonomy and were likely to resist changes in conditions that would threaten it.

Presentism springs from what Lortie termed the 'psychic rewards' of teaching:

Teachers perceive their psychic rewards as scarce, erratic and unpredictable. They are vulnerable to the ebb and flow of pupil response; even highly experienced teachers talk about 'bad years'. Uncertainties in teaching inhibit the feeling that future rewards are ensured, and such doubts support the position that it is unwise to sacrifice present opportunities for future possibilities. (1975: 211)

Presentism reinforces individualism and conservatism. Teachers at the time of Lortie's study showed little enthusiasm 'in working together to build a stronger technical culture' (Lortie, 1975: 211). They 'punctuate their work' into small study units, 'concentrating on short-range outcomes as a source of gratification', and they 'do not invest in searching for general principles to inform their work' (Lortie, 1975: 212).

In the decades following Lortie's classic study, there has been an accumulating assault on individualism in teaching. There have been significant efforts to re-culture schools so as to develop greater collaboration among teachers, in cultures of interactive professionalism. More recently, this has acquired greater precision through the idea of schools becoming strong professional communities where teachers use achievement data and other evidence to guide collective improvement efforts. These communities promote cultures of continuous and shared learning, distributed teacher leadership, and professional learning and assistance across schools through networked learning communities that expand school-to-school lateral capacity for improvement.

Lortie's legacy has therefore been to highlight the existence of and connection between individualism and conservatism in teaching as interrelated obstacles to improvement and change, and to inspire antidotes in the form of teacher collaboration and collegiality.

However, Lortie's legacy in relation to presentism has been much less urgent or evident, and antidotes to its effects on teaching, learning and educational change are weak or absent.

Three forms of presentism

Endemic presentism: Lortie's classic explanation of presentism is that it is an ingrained feature of teaching that results from the way teaching is organized. Jackson referred to this quality as one of immediacy: the pressing and insistent nature of classroom life for teachers who are responsible for organising, orchestrating and reacting to the needs and demands, the vagaries and vicissitudes, of large groups of energetic children gathered together in one place (Jackson, 1968).

Events at school-level may also breed cynicism towards long-term thinking. For example, missions collapse when headteachers leave and others replace them in rapid succession; whole-school self-evaluation exercises are often experienced as so exhausting that teachers do not want to endure them more than once; and after repeated failures at long-term, whole-school change, teachers in mid-to-late career become cynical and concentrate on immediate issues in their own classrooms even more than they did before (Hargreaves, 2005; Huberman, 1993).

Adaptive presentism: In recent years, presentism has changed from being an endemically 'natural' condition of teaching to an acute and unwanted one. Years of encroaching standardisation of teaching, characterised by increasingly detailed and prescribed curriculum and assessment systems, have separated teachers from their purposes and pasts (Helsby 1999; Woods et al., 1997).

This process was described by Apple (1989) and others as one of increasing intensification in teachers' work, where teachers were expected to respond to increasing pressures and comply with multiple innovations. Intensification and initiative overload led to reduced time for relaxation and renewal, lack of time to retool skills and keep up with the field, increased dependency on externally prescribed materials, and cutting of corners and of quality.

The age of standardisation and marketisation also placed many schools in increasingly competitive relationships with each other, in relation to criteria determined by high-stakes tests, along with serious sanctions for those who do not make satisfactory progress on the short-term targets measured by the tests.

A pervasive and predictable consequence has been the proliferation of a calculative approach to meeting short-term, high-stakes targets. Such success in delivering short-term targets may be achieved at the price of long-term sustainability in lifelong learning and higher-order proficiencies within a broader curriculum.

Addictive presentism: The major reason for the persistence of presentism lies in an emergent and professionally appealing variant that shows signs of becoming even more potent than its predecessors. Indeed, short-term improvement measures are at risk of acting like lids on efforts to attend to longer-term, more sustainable transformation. Instead of building people's confidence to break out of the existing culture, the affirming success of short-term strategies seems to entrench schools in the culture of presentism even more deeply. Schools become almost addicted to them.

The logic of short-term funding, of a policy culture characterised by immediacy and a teaching culture steeped in endemic presentism, along with a performance-driven discourse that addresses itself more to short-term targets of achievement and improved management of pupil learning than to long-term transformations of teaching and learning, all exert a combined pressure to preserve and perpetuate the short-term orientation as a substitute for, rather than a stimulant of, long-term transformation.

The persistence of presentism in teaching in an era of more collaborative teacher involvement in data-informed improvement and educational reform, is therefore not merely professionally endemic, nor even organisationally and politically adaptive. It is now also personally, professionally and institutionally addictive.

To understand the persistence of presentism as an educational phenomenon poses the challenge of how to deal with it. Perhaps, most important of all, is a need at all levels for an inclusive, inspiring vision and discourse of educational improvement that connects the learning of individuals to the lives of their communities and the future of their societies – a vision that does not merely personalise the curriculum through increased management, monitoring and mentoring, but that connects pupils' learning with who they are, where they are from, where they are headed, and how they will live among and contribute to the welfare of others in a prosperous, just and secure world.

Reading 16.4

Measurement as an obstacle to improvement: Moving beyond the limitations of graded lesson observations

Matt O'Leary

In this reading Matt O'Leary questions the need to measure teacher performance in terms of numbers or grades awarded to teachers following observations of their lessons. He points out that this stems from a relatively recent rise in neo-liberal preoccupations with being able to quantify all forms of human activity. He exposes the limitations of such practices and offers an alternative.

Edited from: O'Leary, M. (2014) *Classroom Observation: A Guide to the Effective Observation of Teaching and Learning.* London: Routledge.

Introduction

Lesson observation has a longstanding tradition in the training, assessment and development of teachers. However, in recent years it has come to be viewed quite narrowly as a performative tool of managerialist systems fixated with measuring teacher performance rather than actually improving it. This position is symptomatic of a wider neo-liberal obsession of wanting to quantify all forms of human activity, epitomised in education by the reliance on graded observations. In exposing some of the limitations of such practice, this short piece discusses ways in which lesson observation can be engaged with in a more meaningful way.

Performance-driven models of observation

One of the most hotly contested practices to affect FE teachers over the last decade is the use of graded lesson observations. These summative assessments of a teacher's classroom competence and performance are typically undertaken annually and culminate in the award of a grade (1–4) based on Ofsted's 4-point scale. These grades are then fed into employers' quality management systems, where they are used to manage the performance of staff as well as providing evidence for inspection purposes. Yet recent research has argued that such practice is no longer fit for purpose, as it is based on a pseudo-scientific approach to measuring performance that gives rise to a range of counterproductive consequences that ultimately militate against professional learning and teacher improvement (e.g. O'Leary, 2013; O'Leary and Gewessler, 2014).

A key finding to emerge from a recent national project into the use and impact of lesson observation on the FE workforce as a whole was the widespread discontent felt towards it as a form of teacher assessment (UCU, 2013). Graded models of observation were particularly singled out for criticism, often regarded as little more than 'box-ticking exercises' and a 'disciplinary stick' with which 'to beat staff', with explicit links between the outcome of annual observations and the triggering of formal capability procedures in some instances. As far as practitioners were concerned, performance management models of observation were of little relevance to their professional needs and failed to improve their practice. For them, such models existed purely to furnish senior managers and external agencies like Ofsted with quantifiable data that could be used to exercise managerial control over judgements about the effectiveness of teaching and learning. They were also identified as a major cause of increased levels of stress and anxiety, as well as impacting negatively on the self-esteem and self-efficacy of some teaching staff. In contrast, there was a consensus that low-stakes, peer-based models of observation were most conducive to sustainable change and professional learning and thus should be at the forefront of most providers' use of observation and wider CPD strategy.

Development-driven models of observation

Development-driven models of observation such as ungraded peer observation tend to operate under the radar of metric-driven activity in many FE providers with little evidence of the data generated from them being formally acknowledged or contributing to performance-related data. This does not mean that they are any less valuable or have less of an impact on improving the quality of teaching and learning than those that seek to measure performance. On the contrary, the adoption of a more formative approach to the use of observation is arguably likely to yield more meaningful and sustained improvements, as the emphasis is on developing staff with the goal of improving learning outcomes for students rather than generating performance management data. In the remainder of this article, I would like to touch briefly on two specific aspects: 1) differentiated observation and 2) the importance of feedback and forward

Differentiated observation

Differentiated observation runs counter to conventional models in that it involves identifying a specific focus to the observation rather than carrying out an all-inclusive assessment of the lesson based on a generic template, as is currently the norm in most institutions. The observee is given greater ownership and autonomy in deciding the focus and negotiating which session they wish to be observed, though it can also be negotiated and/or discussed with the observer and even the wider team/department depending on the underlying purpose and context of the observation. The purpose and context thus shape the way in which the focus is decided. So, for example, in the case of the trainee or less experienced teacher whose practice is being assessed as part of an on-going programme, it makes more sense for the observer to play a more decisive role in the focus than they would if they were observing experienced colleagues, who have identified a specific area of practice that is of particular relevance to their on-going development.

What are some of the advantages and reasons for using a differentiated approach to observation? Firstly, a differentiated approach is built on the premise that each teacher is likely to have differing strengths and weaknesses in their pedagogic skills and knowledge base in the same way that a group of learners is likely to differ. Just as the most effective teachers differentiate in their teaching, so too does it make sense to apply this approach to the way in which teachers' practice is observed. Secondly, maximising teacher ownership of the observation process is an important feature of facilitating professional learning that is likely to endure. All teachers have a responsibility for their CPD and they are likely to value this more highly if they feel they are given some ownership of the decision making process. Thirdly, the collaborative nature of professional learning means that it is not an individual act or the sole responsibility of the teacher but one that involves colleagues working together. So, for example, there may be times when the focus of differentiated observation is driven by wider objectives across a department such as a departmental improvement plan. These objectives may stem from a range of sources e.g. self-assessment, inspection reports, appraisal meetings etc and may be divided into separate strands or themes (e.g. use of formative assessment, use of ICT, behaviour management) to address through observation. In this instance a team/department of teachers may choose particular themes to focus on.

The importance of feedback and feed forward

Feedback is regarded by many as the most important part of the observation process. Yet less than a third of respondents in a national study agreed that feedback was well managed in their workplace (UCU, 2013: 51–2). Over three quarters of respondents from a smaller study revealed that feedback typically lasted no longer than twenty minutes (O'Leary, 2014: 83–4). It is difficult to imagine a professional dialogue of any substantive conse-quence for a teacher's developmental needs occurring in such a short space of time. But why is so little time given to feedback if it is recognised as being the most important part of the observation process?

The answer is that so much of the time spent carrying out observations is taken up with the completion of the accompanying paper trail and performance data, with the result that the time available for feedback and professional dialogue between observer and observee ends up being squeezed and often rushed. This is further exacerbated by insufficient time being allocated to the observation process from the outset, which means that as feedback falls at the end of the process, it invariably ends up losing out. But this needn't be the case as there are more long term gains to be made from allocating adequate time to feedback in the observation process.

My research has found that those providers that attach more significance to the feedback and feed forward stages than the observation itself are often those that prove themselves to be most successful in improving the quality of teaching and learning, along with fostering a culture of continuous improvement amongst their staff. What those providers have in common is that the importance of feedback and feed forward is not just paid lip service to, but is enacted in practice. Providing both observees and observers with opportunities to engage in substantive professional dialogue as part of the observation process is vital, though if this is going to work in practice then sufficient time needs to be allocated and embedded into teachers' workloads at the start of each academic year. At the very least, this time allocation needs to allow for: 1) a pre-observation meeting; 2) feedback and 3) feed-forward meetings as well as the observation of the lesson itself as a minimum commitment.

Conclusion

There can be little doubt that lesson observation has an important role to play in improving the quality of teaching and learning as well as contributing to a greater understanding of these processes. Yet to ensure we maximise its potential to do so, there needs to be a significant shift in focus away from how it is currently used in the sector. Such a shift should concentrate less on the pseudo-scientific practice of graded observations and more on how it can be harnessed to stimulate the sustained professional development of teachers. It should not simply be seen as an assessment tool to be used episodically, but a method of inquiry that contributes to on-going professional dialogue based on self-reflection, action research, feedback, peer coaching and experiential learning.

Professionalism

How does reflective teaching contribute to society, and to ourselves?

17

The readings in this chapter are concerned with teacher professionalism and society. Wiliam (17.1) argues that participation in teacher learning communities is particularly suited to supporting teachers in their development. Through participation in learning communities, he claims, teachers can experiment, share, discuss, network and so improve their expertise. Debate within the Republic of Ireland is conveyed by Sahlberg, Furlong and Munn (17.2), who report the findings of an international panel advising on the importance of combining theory and practice in teaching. Menter and colleagues (17.3) discuss a range of approaches to teacher education and show how these relate to educational purposes and aspirations. Finally Hodgson and Spours (17.4) reminds us of the multi-dimensional purposes of education and the importance of teacher judgement.

The parallel chapter in *Reflective Teaching in Further, Adult and Vocational Education* begins with a review of professions and professionalism. The aims of education in relation to social development are then discussed. Wealth creation, cultural reproduction and social justice are identified as particular goals .The chapter highlights the value issues which reflective teachers face when they recognize the ways in which their actions contribute to the future identities and life-chances of their students. Reflective teaching is then related to the democratic process and to the importance of teachers contributing their professional voice to policy debates and public decision-making on educational topics.

Of course, there is a list of suggested 'Key Readings', and more support is available on the *reflectiveteaching.co.uk* website.

Reading 17.1

Improving teacher expertise

Dylan Wiliam

> This reading focuses on the development of teacher expertise and on professional development activity. Wiliam suggests how professional understanding develops through practice, and argues that the content of professional development should focus on teaching strategies of proven effectiveness and on practical processes of classroom application. The lecture from which this reading is drawn describes Wiliam's collaboration with Paul Black on Assessment for Learning (Black et al., 2003).
>
> Thinking of your own development plans, do you first analyse what is likely to be most effective, as Wiliam suggests?
>
> *Edited from:* Wiliam, D. (2007) *Assessment for Learning: Why, What and How?* Inaugural lecture. Institute of Education, University of London, 24 April.

In England, there is a four-fold difference in the speed of learning between the most effective and least effective classrooms. The obvious factors – class size or grouping strategies – make relatively little difference. What matters is the quality of the teacher.

Aristotle's perspective on the nature of expertise (or intellectual virtue as he called it) is informative here. Aristotle identified three main intellectual virtues: episteme, techne, and phronesis. The first of these, episteme (science), is the knowledge of timeless universal truths. For example, the base angles of an isosceles triangle are always equal. Once you have proved this to be true, there is no need to check it tomorrow, it will still be true. The second intellectual virtue, techne (craft), deals with the realm of things that are variable. For example, there is no one perfect form for a table, but the ability to make a table for a specific purpose is an important virtue. Yet it is the third intellectual value, phronesis (practical wisdom), that Aristotle regarded as the highest. As an example of phronesis, Aristotle gave the leadership of the state. For this task a person needs to be aware of important principles, but these must always be tempered by the knowledge of specific contexts.

This perspective is fruitful when thinking about the nature of expertise in teaching because governments, and agencies employed by governments, are often engaged in a search for 'what works'. However, in education 'what works' is a particularly useful question to ask because almost everything works somewhere, and nothing works everywhere. The important question is, 'Under what conditions does a particular initiative work.' Expertise in teaching would therefore appear to be mainly a matter of phronesis rather than episteme or indeed, techne. This is why so much educational research appears to teachers either to tell them what they already know or something they know to be inappropriate to their particular circumstances.

Promoting 'practical wisdom'

If expertise in teaching is 'practical wisdom', how can we promote its development? The organizational theorists Nonaka and Takeuchi (1995) looked at processes of knowledge creation and knowledge transfer in commercial organizations. In particular, they explored the interplay of explicit and implicit or tacit knowledge (often described as the kind of knowledge that an organization does not know it has until the people who have it leave).

Nonaka and Takeuchi outline four basic modes of knowledge conversion (see Figure 17.1.1). Perhaps the most familiar is the process they call 'combination' where one person communicates their explicit knowledge to another, for example, when one person tells another that lessons in a particular school are all of 40 minutes' duration. A second form of knowledge conversion occurs when one person's implicit knowledge is picked up by others, implicitly, through a process of socialization. An individual learns, 'That's the way things are done round here.'

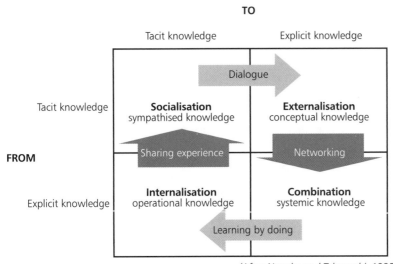

Figure 17.1.1
Processes for transferring professional knowledge

(After Nanaka and Takucuchi, 1995)

Externalization is a process in which one person's implicit knowledge is made explicit for the purpose of communication to another. When I started training teachers in the 1980s, I wasn't particularly helpful to the student teachers I was supporting because I had no way of describing what it was that I was doing. I had been reasonably successful as a practitioner, but had not developed a language for describing what I was doing. However, as a consequence of being forced to reflect on practice, and being forced to develop a language of description, I was developing a deeper understanding of my own practice.

Complementary to this is internalization – the process of moving from explicit to implicit knowing. One example of this process is what happens when one is told how to do something, which creates a basic knowledge of the process, only for a much deeper understanding to emerge later – often months later. A friend of mine is a very keen golfer, and his coach was telling him that in order to improve his swing, he needed 'to quieten his lower body'. For weeks, he worked on trying to put this into practice, and eventually, he understood what his coach had meant, but only when he could actually do what his coach was suggesting. The phrase 'to quieten his lower body' looked like an instruction, but it was really a description of what it would feel like to have internalized this new knowledge, and make it into operational knowledge.

As well as these four modes of knowledge conversion, Nonaka and Takeuchi propose a 'knowledge spiral' that is generated by moving around the four modes of knowledge conversion through four processes: sharing experience, dialogue, networking and learning by doing. It is this model of knowledge creation and knowledge conversion that drives our approach to teacher professional development.

The fundamental insight contained in the Nonaka and Takeuchi model is that knowing something is not the same as being able to do it. In our conversations with teachers, Paul Black and I realized that many of the teachers knew the research we were talking about quite well. What they did not do was to enact this knowledge in their practice. The problem was not lack of knowledge but a lack of understanding of what it meant to do this in the classroom.

That is why I do not believe we should tell teachers what to do. This is not out of some misguided sense of wanting to be kind to teachers or to value their experience. If there were something that we could tell teachers to do with a guarantee that it would improve student outcomes, then there would be a strong case for telling them what to do (and perhaps even sacking those who refused!). After all, schools are there for students, not teachers. But telling teachers what to do doesn't work because it is impossible to prepare teachers for every situation they are going to face in the classroom. Teaching is just too complex.

On the other hand, we also know that experience alone is not enough. Just leaving teachers to their own devices does not work either – if it were then the most experienced teachers would generate the greatest progress in their students, and we know that is not true. Instead, what is needed are ways to support teachers to reflect on their practice in systematic ways, to build on their accessible knowledge base and, perhaps most importantly, to learn from mistakes.

Twenty years ago this would have resulted in a very gloomy prognosis, because there was relatively little evidence that it was possible to improve teacher practice. However, in recent years, it has become clear that the relative ineffectiveness of teacher professional development efforts in the past means nothing for what we might to in the future, because we have not engaged consistently in the kinds of activities that the research indicates are necessary in order to help teachers change their practice.

Content, then process

If we are to help teachers improve student outcomes, the starting point must be on those things that make most difference to student outcomes. In other words, we start from the changes in teacher practice that make the most difference to students, and only then work out how to help teachers make the change – content, *then* process.

The content and efficacy of teaching

The first element of our content model is evidence of efficacy. This is essential because without such evidence, teachers say, 'I would love to teach this way, but I can't because I've got to raise my test scores.' For example, if Assessment for Learning (AfL) is being promoted, it is essential that teachers know that their students are likely to have higher achievement on tests and examinations. Fortunately, as discussed above, the evidence in favour of AfL is strong.

The second content element of the model is a number of practical techniques for implementation in classrooms. Here are some examples associated with AfL.

To highlight learning intentions, a very simple technique is to discuss examples, before students are asked to complete a task themselves. So, if the task is to write a story, examples of stories from last year's class might be considered – some good, some middling, and some weaker ones. There can then be discussion, either in pairs, groups or as a whole class, about what is good about the good ones.

Techniques for effective feedback typically involve ensuring that the feedback creates more work for the student. For example, a mathematics teacher once said to me, 'If you're marking a student's work and tick 15 of the answers as correct and mark five of them as incorrect, then the child can work out for themselves that they've got 15 out of 20.' So I suggested that instead, the teacher could explain an error and then tell the student, 'Five others are also wrong for the same reason. Find them and fix them.'

Teachers can increase the extent to which students act as learning resources for one another. For example, secondary science teachers typically have a number of requirements for laboratory reports, including a margin for each page, headings being underlined, diagrams drawn in pencil and labelled and so on. One way to engage students in supporting each others' learning is to insist that before students are allowed to submit their report to the teacher they have to get a 'buddy' to certify that all the basic requirements have been satisfied by signing the 'pre-flight checklist'. The teacher then marks the assignment, and reports back to the student who wrote the report on the quality of the report, and to the 'buddy' on the extent to which they accurately assessed their partner's work in terms of how well the basic requirements had been met.

The process of teaching to improve outcomes

The second part of our professional development model focuses on the process. For example, how we can support teachers in making greater use of AfL in their classrooms? From work with teachers over a ten-year period, five aspects of the process seem to be particularly important: choice, flexibility, small steps, accountability and support.

First, teachers need to be given a choice about what aspects of practice to develop. It is often assumed that to improve, teachers should work on the weakest aspects of their practice, and for some teachers, these aspects may indeed be so weak that they should be the priority for professional development. But for most teachers, students will benefit more from teachers becoming even more expert in their strengths. In our work with teachers in Oxfordshire and Medway, one of the teachers, Derek, was already quite skilled at conducting whole-class discussion sessions, but he was interested in improving this practice further. He is now one of the most skilled practitioners we have ever observed in this regard. A colleague of his at the same school, Philip, was much more interested in helping students develop skills of self-assessment and peer-assessment and he too is now highly skilled at these aspects of practice. To make Philip work on questioning, or to make Derek work on peer-assessment and self-assessment, is unlikely to benefit their students as much as supporting each teacher to become excellent in their own way. When teachers themselves make the decision about what it is that they wish to prioritize for their own professional development, they are more likely to 'make it work'.

Second, teachers need the flexibility to be able to modify the AfL techniques they use to fit their own classroom context. The danger in this is that a teacher may so modify an idea that it is no longer effective.

The third element of the process model is that of taking small steps (Reading 16.1). In implementing this professional development model, we have to accept that teacher learning is slow. This is, to borrow a rather well-known phrase, an 'inconvenient truth'. Social inequalities are everywhere, and the knowledge that high-quality education can largely alleviate many of these inequalities means that policymakers are understandably in a hurry to make a difference. However, for changes in practice to be lasting, they must be integrated into a teacher's existing routines, and this takes time. Many of those involved in professional development are familiar with the experience of encouraging teachers to try out new ideas, and seeing them being enacted when they visit teachers' classrooms only to hear that as soon as they have left, the teachers revert to their former practices.

Any kind of change in one's teaching practice is hard. But the kinds of changes I am calling for here are particularly hard, because they go 'against the grain' of current educational orthodoxy. In our pre-service courses with teachers, we talk about the importance of 'opening up' the classroom, providing space for students to talk, both because it is beneficial to their development, but also because by careful listening to what the students say, teachers can gain insights into their development. However, opening up the classroom in this way is seen by many teachers as 'giving up control' – faddish ideas being advocated by ivory tower academics who don't know what real teaching is. AfL practices would be hard to develop even in the most supportive climate, but are even harder when there is active hostility to their introduction. That is why, even if we are in a hurry to help teachers improve their practice, we should 'hasten slowly'.

The last two elements of the process model are support and accountability, which can be thought of as two sides of the same coin: supportive accountability. The idea here is that we create structures that while making teachers accountable for developing their practice, also provide the support for them to do this. Developing one's practice of formative assessment is different from learning new facts. It requires developing new habits, and traditional models of teaching are much better at imparting knowledge than changing habits. If we want to change teachers' habits, we would do well to look at organizations such as Weight Watchers. After all, everyone who wants to lose weight knows they have to do two things: eat less and exercise more. The knowledge base for weight loss is actually very simple. What is hard is changing the habits that result in weight gain. In the same way, if we are going to change what teachers do in classrooms then helping teachers change habits is as important as giving teachers new knowledge.

Clearly, creating this 'supportive accountability' could be done in a number of ways, but one particular mechanism – teacher learning communities within school and beyond – is particularly suited to supporting teachers in their development. Through participation in learning communities, teachers can experiment, share, discuss, network – and thus develop their expertise.

Reading 17.2

Combining research and practice in teaching

Pasi Sahlberg, John Furlong and Pamela Munn

This report, commissioned by the Irish Government, highlights an international pattern linking high performance of national systems with recruitment of capable teachers and research-informed teacher education. Such training is often provided from university bases in association with partnership schools, but it can also be located in 'teaching schools' in association with partnership universities. Either way, provision must be made to develop educational understanding in, and of, practice.

Considering a teacher education programme you know well, how does it combine research and practice, evidence and experience, theory and application?

Edited from: Sahlberg, P., Furlong, J. and Munn, P. (2012) *Report of the International Review Panel on the Structure of Initial Teacher Education Provision in Ireland.* Review conducted on behalf of the Department of Education and Skills. Dublin: Higher Education Authority of Ireland, 5, 14–15.

Initial teacher education is probably the single most important factor in having a well-performing public education system. Evidence from the OECD countries is consistent with this notion. Singapore, Korea, Canada and Finland, countries that the OECD labels as having 'strong performing' education systems, have systematically invested in enhancing the initial education of their teachers. In all of these education systems, teachers are educated in academic universities where theory and practice are combined to form a foundation for teaching that is on a par with other academic professions. In all of these high performing education systems, teaching is also perceived by young people as an attractive career choice which makes admission to teacher education highly competitive and intellectually demanding.

Ireland has several advantages in its current system of teachers and teacher education that distinguish the Irish education system from many others. Most importantly, among young Irish people, to be a teacher is a popular choice that carries strong social prestige unlike in most other countries in Europe. Teacher education is widely accessible throughout Ireland and numerous initial teacher education programmes are serving diverse needs of communities and regions in the State. Finally, due to Ireland's economic and social structures, education has a central role to play in the future strategies of the nation. This brings teachers and how they are educated to the core of the implementation of national programmes for sustainable economic growth and prosperity.

One of the priorities of the European Union is to improve teacher quality and teacher education. It has made a number of proposals on areas such as: teachers' knowledge, attitudes and pedagogic skills; coordinated, coherent, and adequately resourced teacher education; reflective practice and research among teachers; the status and recognition of the teaching profession and the professionalisation of teaching. The EU proposals indicate that

Initial Teacher Education (ITE) needs to be upgraded in many countries and that transition from teacher education to school needs to be made smoother through effective mentoring, induction and school leadership.

The EU aspirations have been actualised in Finland which is highly acclaimed for its education system due especially to the quality of its teachers. There is a rigorous selection process for entry to teacher education and the competition for places adds to the attraction of teaching. ITE is research-based and extends to five years leading to a Masters level award. On being employed, teachers assume professional responsibility for curriculum planning, student assessment and school improvement, enjoying a high level of autonomy in their work and high status in society.

In Singapore, the National Institute of Education (NIE) is the sole provider of ITE. Evidence-based and research-informed learning underpins NIE's programmes. NIE's strategic plan for 2007–12 sets out its ambition to be an institute of distinction, excelling in teacher education and teacher research. It has formed partnerships with other universities in Asia and also in Europe and the USA for the purpose of research collaboration and staff and student exchanges.

It has been found that in high-performing education systems, such as Canada, South Korea, Finland and Singapore, policy on teacher education is a national priority. Teachers are educated in academic universities where theory and practice are combined to form a foundation for teaching that is on a par with other academic professions. Teacher education is research-based and internationalisation is high on the agenda. Also, in these systems, teaching is perceived by young people as an attractive career choice which makes admission to teacher education highly competitive and intellectually demanding.

The main international trends in initial teacher education are the following.

First, teaching is increasingly viewed as a high status profession similar to the work of lawyers, doctors and engineers. Teachers have similar access to Masters and Doctoral studies and thereby to a career path in academic universities and research institutions as well as in schools and classrooms.

Second, as a consequence of the former trend, teacher education is increasingly relying on research knowledge on the one hand and focusing on preparing teachers to use and do research on the other. Research-based teacher education expands conventional teacher competences so that teachers are able to use educational research as part of their work in school. They diagnose their own teaching and learning by using educational research knowledge and methodologies to find the best methods of work, and understand their professional development through critically reflecting on their own thinking and behaviour.

Third, many teacher education programmes are having a more systematic focus on linking theory and practice during the initial preparation of teachers. In some countries, practical learning is also becoming an integral part of Masters' degree studies for ITE, similar to the way in which doctors or lawyers practise during their studies. School placements are giving way to clinical learning in special teacher training schools or carefully assigned regular schools where highly trained master teachers supervise the learning of student teachers. These features are seen as contributing to a continual spiral of improvement in pupils' learning which is the key objective of high quality ITE and continuous professional development.

Reading 17.3

Teacher education and professionalism
Ian Menter, Moira Hulme, Dely Elliot and Jon Lewin

This reading is derived from a literature review on the contribution that teacher education can make to the quality of educational experience and personal development of young people in the twenty-first century. Commissioned by the Scottish Government, it identifies four models of teacher education: the effective teacher, the reflective teacher, the enquiring teacher and the transformative teacher. Each of these has an important rationale. In practice, most forms of provision for initial training and continuing professional development, whether school- or university-led, seek to combine these elements.

How would you characterize the teacher education programme which you experienced or are experiencing?

Edited from: Menter, I., Hulme, M., Elliot, D. and Lewin, J. (2010) *Teacher Education in the 21st Century*. Edinburgh: The Scottish Government, 21–5.

Four conceptions of teacher professionalism underlie policy and research literature on teacher education.

The effective teacher

This model has emerged as the dominant one in much official government discourse across the developed world over the last thirty years. It is closely associated with an economically led view of education. The emphases are on technical accomplishment and measurement for an age of accountability (Mahony and Hextall, 2000). Such an approach may be aligned with a nationally prescribed curriculum and a national assessment system, which extends down to the earliest stages of schooling.

This particular aspect of education in the UK has seen considerable recent variation in policy across the four nations, with the effective teacher model being most fully adopted in England. In Scotland, there has not been a national curriculum as such and, with Curriculum for Excellence, introduced from 2010, there is even more scope for professional autonomy. In Wales and Northern Ireland there has been much relaxation of the National Curriculum since devolution, especially in the earlier years of schooling.

In contrast to the politically driven 'effective teacher' model, the other three approaches emerged more from within the teaching profession and teacher education itself. The notion of teaching as a reflective activity emerged strongly in the UK, partly in response to the growing influence of the effective teacher model, which was seen by some as restricting teacher professionalism, rather than enhancing it (Stronach et al., 2002; Hartley, 2002).

The reflective teacher

The philosophical roots of the reflective teaching model lie in the work of the American educator John Dewey. Early in the twentieth century he developed an approach to teaching based on teachers becoming active decision-makers. Similar ideas were later developed by Donald Schön who wrote about *The Reflective Practitioner* (1983), stressing the significance of values and of theory informing decision-making.

In the UK, such ideas were developed in a very practical way by Andrew Pollard and his collaborators who from the late 1980s onwards, produced a series of books on 'reflective teaching' (e.g. Pollard and Tann, 1987). At the centre of this model was a cyclical approach to planning, making provision, acting, collecting evidence, analysing the evidence, evaluating, reflecting and then planning next steps. Built into such a model is a commitment to personal professional development through practice.

The model took a firm hold in teacher education institutions across the UK during the latter parts of the twentieth century. Indeed, the largest scale studies of initial teacher education undertaken in England by Furlong et al. (2000) found that about 70 per cent of teacher education programmes led from universities and colleges were informed by some version of 'reflective teaching'.

The reflective teaching approach also has significance for experienced teachers. In their Teaching and Learning Research Programme study 'How teachers value and practise professional learning' Pedder et al. (2005) found that there were opportunities for considerable teacher learning to take place in the classroom context, through applying research, collaborating with colleagues (Reading 16.1), or consulting with pupils. However, reflective teaching does not in itself imply a research orientation on the part of the teacher.

The enquiring teacher

In the UK the origins of the notion of 'teacher as researcher' is usually associated with the groundbreaking work of Lawrence Stenhouse (1975), who argued that teachers should indeed take a research approach to their work. He described this as a form of curriculum development.

In this model, teachers are encouraged to undertake systematic enquiry in their own classrooms, develop their practice and share their insights with other professionals. Such ideas have been taken up, developed and enhanced through a range of subsequent initiatives, often associated with university staff working in partnership with teachers and lecturers in schools and colleges (Reading 16.1).

At various times, such approaches have received 'official' endorsement through funded schemes (see McNamara, 2002; Furlong and Salisbury, 2005; Hulme et al., 2010). Teacher enquiry frequently figures within contemporary approaches to professional development (Campbell et al., 2004; Campbell and Groundwater Smith, 2009) and has been found to 're-energise' teachers (Burns and Haydn, 2002).

Ponte et al. (2004) conducted case studies in the USA, Australia and UK, of programmes that aimed to introduce action research in initial teacher education. They concluded that there is a need to introduce student teachers to inquiry-oriented approaches to teaching during initial training in order to provide a firm foundation for career-long professional learning – i.e. to develop a disposition towards thoughtful and critical self-study.

The transformative teacher

The final model incorporates and builds upon elements of the previous two. However, its key defining feature is that it brings an 'activist' dimension into the approach to teaching. If the prevalent view of the teacher is someone whose contribution to society is to transmit knowledge and prepare pupils for the existing world, the view here is that teachers' responsibilities go beyond that; they should be contributing to social change and be preparing their pupils to contribute to change in society.

The most cogent articulation of this model is that set out by the Australian teacher educator, Judyth Sachs (2003), who talks of 'teaching as an activist profession'. Those who advocate teaching as a transformative activity will suggest that some challenge to the status quo is not only to be expected but is a necessary part of bringing about a more just education system, where inequalities in society begin to be addressed and where progressive social change can be stimulated (Zeichner, 2009; Cochran-Smith, 2004). In aspiring to achieve greater social justice through education however, those such as Clarke and Drudy (2006) have argued that it is important to consider the influence of teachers' own beliefs and values, which they bring to their work at whatever stage of their career they are at.

The future of teacher professionalism

Eric Hoyle suggested that models of teaching exist at some point on a spectrum between 'restricted' and 'extended' versions of teacher professionalism (Hoyle, 1974). Crudely speaking, the first model depicted above, the effective teacher, rests at the 'restricted' end of the spectrum, where teaching is largely defined in terms of a range of technical skills. The other three models are at various points towards the 'extended' end of the spectrum, where teachers are seen as more autonomous and their own judgement is called upon to a much greater extent (Adams, 2008).

In considering the future of teacher education in the 21st century, Edwards et al. (2002) argued that teachers should be given increased control over the professional knowledge base of teaching, and should be seen as:

Users and producers of knowledge about teaching, in communities of practice which are constantly refreshed through processes of professional enquiry, in partnerships between practitioners and researchers. (p. 125)

Reading 17.4

Towards a universal upper secondary education system in England: A unified and ecosystem vision

Ann Hodgson and Ken Spours

In this extract Hodgson and Spours consider how we should go about reforming 'upper secondary' (post-16) education. At present, they suggest, little more than 'a set of arrangements' determine the often 'truncated' educational opportunities the FAVE sector offers to post-16 students. Hodgson and Spours argue for the long-term development of a 'unified' FAVE 'ecosystem' that appreciates interdependence of a wide range of factors, in order to maximize educational opportunities for *all* students. The five recommendations, considered in this extract, identify the practical steps that should be taken to achieve inclusive reform.

When reflecting on this reading, it might be useful to consider the expanded role for teachers implied by the reforms Hodgson and Spours recommend. How do you think these reforms would extend the professional role of teachers in the upper secondary sector?

Edited from: Hodgson, A. and Spours, K. (2012) *Towards a universal upper secondary education system in England: A unified and ecosystem vision.* Inaugural professorial lecture, Institute of Education, University of London, 27 June.

Is it now appropriate to talk about an upper secondary education system in England? The term 'upper secondary' is more commonly used at the international level when describing the phase that precedes higher education or entry to the labour market. We think it is useful to use this term and, moreover, to argue for a *universal* upper secondary education system. Thinking about the education of 14–19-year-olds in this way brings considerable demands and requires a new form of critical analysis. Currently upper secondary education in England remains a truncated experience for many, often with little extra to show for any additional years of study beyond 16, and without significantly better employment prospects. Moreover, it is a set of arrangements, rather than a system as such. The underlying assumption of this lecture is that England needs to develop a universal upper secondary education system that develops the potential of all, enhances the life chances of young people and goes well beyond the aim of current government policy to raise the participation age to 18 by 2015.

Our vision of a universal upper secondary education system is explored through a discussion of two related concepts: first, a 'more unified' 14–19 phase that addresses head-on the academic/vocational divide and, second, an 'ecosystem' approach to reform that links changes in the curriculum and qualifications to a range of other factors – organisational, social, political and economic – at national, regional and local levels.

In the current global and national economic context we suggest that policy-makers … build a new, more inclusive and unified system … Only [this] … option has the potential to address what we see as the major challenges for 14–19 education in England – inadequate performance, lack of equity for different groups of young people and a weak relationship between education, the economy and the democratic process in this country.

… We assert that the upper secondary education system in England should reflect and promote the more equal and democratic society that we want to build rather than reinforce its current inequalities and divisions. We want to foster a sense of optimism for young people, for those who work with them, and for society at large, about the power of education to transform lives at a time of deepening crisis in the economy, the environment and social relations …

The alternative – a unified and ecosystem approach

We will now suggest … a new type of system dynamic in order to build a universal upper secondary education system. Here we try to connect two ideas: first, the concept of unification that supports the development of broad underlying capacities in all learners… Second, the concept of 'ecosystems', that appreciates that interdependence of a wide range of factors are required for successful reform.

The notion of 'unified' is not about uniformity and 'one size fits all'. In exploring unification in relation to what young people learn and achieve – curriculum and qualifications – we will argue that any form of specialisation should involve a strong relationship between the practical and theoretical, regardless of previous levels of attainment. Relating thinking and doing is inherently human, and an upper secondary curriculum for the age in which we live, and the future we anticipate. should reflect this. We also wish to apply the concept of unification to system-building more broadly. This involves recognising that upper secondary education should be seen as part of a complex and interdependent ecological system that requires collective deliberation and action to promote the sustainable participation, development and progression of all 14–19-year-olds. The concept of unification applied in this way also suggests a dialectical relationship with concepts of diversity –individual need, institutional autonomy and devolution of responsibility.

In building this more unified and dynamic concept of system change, we adapt David Finegold's concept of a 'high skill ecosystem'… to argue for the creation of a national 'high-opportunity-progression ecosystem' (HOPE) for upper secondary education in England that can respond to both the challenges of history and the new context. We will argue that such an ecological approach will require a number of related dimensions of reform that embrace unity and diversity, national and local, leadership and professionalism, change and stability. In this sense, the concepts of unification and ecosystem constitute both means and ends. This reform approach would require:

1. An overarching vision and set of purposes that speak to all young people, their parents, educators and wider social partners, and that provide the 'cultural glue' of the ecosystem.

… We would suggest that all 14–19-year-olds undertake a balance of general and vocational activity in upper secondary education, that will enable them to see themselves as both preparing for, and playing, an important role in their locality and wider society. Therefore, regardless of their specialisation, they would share certain common experiences, be empowered to ask the 'big questions' and contribute towards the building of what has been termed the 'good society'. At its deepest, this particular concept of unification is associated with the human condition and the ability to relate thinking and doing.

2. A unified curriculum, assessment and qualifications framework for enhanced general and vocational education.

… We want to respond to the knowledge challenge [the challenge of giving young people from all social groups access to what Michael Young refers to as 'powerful knowledge'] by suggesting a four-fold reform of general education – first, promoting an idea of subjects that contain not only established knowledge but also the means to question that knowledge; second, the experience of different dimensions of general education, including a research project to encourage greater in-depth understanding and exploration of interdisciplinary knowledge; third, the opportunity to apply knowledge to life as it is experienced and to the major problems that face society; and, finally, an acceptance that an 'educated 19 year old' requires the acquisition of and participation in different types of knowledge. These four proposals could be seen as extending our A level academic tradition by developing a more 'connective specialisation' that reaches out beyond the boundaries of traditional subject knowledge to other forms of general and vocational education …

3. A more supportive and engaged role for employers and higher education providers, which would involve greater regulation of the labour market and a move towards the concept of a social partnership.

… Strong vocational education relies on specialist knowledge and skill fostered by expert institutions and professional communities of practice that have a close relationship with employers and employment. … A full national system of social partnership will take decades to develop and would involve some difficult political decisions … but we could start locally. Here we suggest the formation of what we have called a 'devolved social partnership' in which specialist vocational institutions, such as further education colleges, collaborate with vocational higher education providers, employer organisations and schools through regional and sub-regional networks …

4. A strongly collaborative local learning system of providers that combines institutional autonomy with a strong sense of shared professionalism, locality and region, and is capable of supporting 14+ participation, progression and transition for all learners in an area.

… We would suggest – somewhat counterintuitively – that a strong local approach to support the participation, progression and transition of all 14–19-year-olds in a locality will depend on strong national frameworks. By this we are referring to the need to reinforce local vision and voluntary collaborative working with a set of frameworks that makes it easier to achieve an active consensus and to bring everyone to the table … [This is about] providing social partners in localities with parameters within which equity is assured and in which they have the space to exercise local discretion …

5. A gradual and more deliberative policy process in which national leadership is focused more on providing a framework for professional and economic action at the local and regional levels and less on political micromanagement

… Policy is not just about its content but also about how it is made and enacted. Policy that is made quickly and is imposed from the centre has proved remarkably ineffective. It is expensive in terms of bureaucratic accountability and transaction costs, is prone to serious error, and produces unintended outcomes, because the conditions on the ground are far more complex than central policymakers appreciate. As Lawrence Angus reminds us, 'education is, first and foremost, a relational [and certainly not a managerial] enterprise'.

There are very strong arguments for a different style of policy process in which democratically elected politicians set the general tone … and leave spaces for its mediation at the lower levels, confident in the knowledge that those on the ground are better informed.

Working for sustainable change

… We have noted how the upper secondary phase in England is still in a process of formation with no clear consensus about its purpose, shape or future direction. As a result of its historical roots, the default setting had been selection rather than learner progression, and it is this that has produced the low-opportunity-progression equilibrium. Recent economic and policy developments appear only to be reinforcing this situation.

A universal upper secondary phrase that promotes effective participation, progression and transition to higher study and employment for all learners – an essential educational goal in the twenty-first century – will, in our view, only be achieved when the culture of selection and division is addressed by an alliance of social and political partners to bring about sustainable change. This is why we have argued for the vision of a more unified approach to the 14–19 phase, and a comprehensive ecosystem reform strategy, that relates different policies, practices and structures, builds on historic strengths, and directly addresses fundamental weaknesses.

List of figures

Bibliography

Adams, P. (2008) 'Considering 'best practice': the social construction of teacher activity and pupil learning as performance', *Cambridge Journal of Education*, 38 (3), 375–92.

Ainley, P. and Bailey, B. (1997) *The Business of Learning: Staff and Student Experiences of Further Education in the 1990s.* London, Cassell.

Alexander, R. J. (2008) *Essays on Pedagogy.* London: Routledge.

Apple, M. (1989) *Teachers and Texts.* New York: Routledge and Kegan Paul.

Appleby, A. (2010) 'Who are the Learners?'. In N. Hughes and I. Schwab (eds) *Teaching Adult Literacy: Principles and Practice.* London. Open University Press, 29–47.

Appleby, Y. (2008) *Bridges into Learning for Adults Who Find Provision Hard to Reach.* Leicester: NIACE.

Appleby, Y. and Barton, D. (2008) *Responding to People's Lives.* Leicester: NIACE.

Appleby, Y. and Pilkington, R. (2014) *Developing Critical Professional Practice in Education.* Leicester: NIACE.

Armitage, A. Bryant, B., Dunnil, R., Hammersley, M., Hayes, D., Hudson, A. and Laws, S. (1999) *Teaching and Training in Post Compulsory Education.* Buckingham: Open University Press.

Arnold, M. (1874) *High Schools and Universities in Germany.* London: Macmillan.

Assessment Reform Group (1999) *Assessment for Learning: Beyond the Black Box.* Cambridge: University of Cambridge, Faculty of Education.

Bailey, B. (1990) 'Technical Education and Secondary Schooling'. In Summerfield, P. and Evans, E. J. (eds) *Technical Education and the State since 1850.* Manchester: Manchester University Press.

Bakhtin, M. (1986) *Speech Genres and Other Essays.* Austin, TX: University of Texas Press.

Ball, S. (2003) 'The teacher's soul and the terrors of performativite', *Journal of Education and Policy*, 18 (2), 215–28.

—(2004) 'Performativities and Fabrications in the Education Economy: Towards the Performative Society'. In *The Routledge-Falmer Reader in Sociology of Education.* London: Routledge-Falmer, 143–55.

—(2004) *Education for Sale! The Commodification of everything?* The Annual Education Lecture 2004, Institute of Education, University of London.

—(2007) *Education PLC. Understanding Private Sector Participation in Public Sector Education.* London: Routledge.

—(2010) 'New voices, new knowledges and the new politics of educational research: the gathering of a perfect storm?', *European Educational Research Journal*, 9 (2), 124–37.

—(2008) *The Education Debate.* Bristol: The Policy Press.

Ball, S. J. (2013) *Education, Justice and Democracy: The Struggle over Ignorance and Opportunity.* London: Routledge.

Barton, D. (1994) *Literacy: An Introduction to the Ecology of Written Language.* Oxford: Blackwell.

Barton, D., Ivanic, R., Appleby, Y., Hodge, R. and Tusting, K. (2004) *Adult Learners' Lives Project: Setting the Scene, Progress Report.* Lancaster: Lancaster University: NRDC.

—(2007) *Literacy, Lives and Learning*. London: Routledge.

Barton, D. and Hamilton, M. (1998) *Local Literacies: Reading and Writing in one Community*. London: Routledge.

—(2000) *Local Literacies: Reading and Writing in One Community*. London: Routledge.

Bassey, M. (1999) *Case Study Research in Educational Settings*. Bucks: Open University Press.

Bassey, M. Pratt J. (2003) *How General are Generalisations? Educational Research in Practice. Making sense of Methodology*. J. Swann and J. Pratt. London: Continuum, 164–71.

Beck, J. and Young, M. (2005) 'The assault on the professions and the restructuring of academic and professional identities: a Bernsteinian Analysis', *British Journal of the Sociology of Education*, 26 (2), 83–197.

Bennett, T. (2012) *Teacher: Mastering the Art and Craft of Teaching*. London: Continuum.

Berliner, D. (1990) 'What's all the Fuss about Instructional Time?'. In M. Ben-Peretz and R. Bromme, (eds) *The Nature of Time in Schools*. New York: Teacher College Press.

Bernstein, B. (2000) *Pedagogy, Symbolic Control and Identity: Theory, Research, Critique*. Oxford: Rowman and Littlefield.

—(1971) *Class, Codes and Control, Vol. 1*. London: Routledge and Kegan Paul.

Biesta, G. (2011) 'The future of teacher education: evidence, competence or wisdom?', 2020 The Future of Teacher Education' Conference, Vienna, 3–4 March 2011.

Biesta, G. J. J. (2004) 'Against learning: reclaiming a language for education in an age of learning', *Nordisk Pedagogik*, 23.1, 70–82.

—(2007) 'Why "what works" won't work: evidence-based practice and the democratic deficit of educational research', *Educational Theory*, 57.1, 1–22.

—(2006) *Beyond Learning: Democratic Education for a Human Future*. Boulder, CO: Paradigm.

—(2010) *Good Education in an Age of Measurement: Ethics, Politics, Democracy*. Boulder, CO: Paradigm.

—(in press/2014) 'How does a Competent Teacher become a Good Teacher? On Judgement, Wisdom and Virtuosity in Teaching and Teacher Education'. In R. Heilbronn and L. Foreman-Peck (eds) *Philosophical Perspectives on the Future of Teacher Education*. Oxford: Wiley Blackwell.

Biesta, G. and James, D. (2007) *Improving Learning Cultures in Further Education*. London: Routledge.

Black, P., Harrison, C., Lee, C., Marshall, B. and Wiliam, D. (2003) *Assessment for Learning: Putting it into Practice*. Maidenhead: Open University Press.

Black, P. and Wiliam, D. (1998) *Inside the Black Box – Raising Standards Through Classroom Assessment*. London: Kings' College School of Education.

Bourdieu, P. (1991) *Language and Symbolic Power*. Cambridge, MA: Harvard University Press.

Bourdieu, P. and Passeron, J. (1977) *Reproduction in Education, Society and Culture*. London: Sage Publications Ltd.

Brandt, D. (2001) *Literacy in American Lives*. Cambridge: Cambridge University Press.

Bransford, J. D., Brown, A. L. and Cocking, R. R. (eds) (1999) *How People Learn: Brain, Mind, Experience and School*. Washington, DC: National Academy Press.

Britten, J. (1975) *The Development of Writing Abilities 11–18*. London: London Schools Council.

Brookfield, S. (1995) *Becoming a Critically Reflective Teacher*. San Francisco. Jossey Bass.

Brophy, J. and Good, T. (1974) *Teacher-student Relationships: Causes and Consequences*. New York: Holt, Rinehart and Winston.

—(1986) 'Teacher Behaviour and Student Achievement'. In M. C. Wittrock (ed.) *Handbook of Research on Teaching*. New York: Macmillan.

Bruner, J. (1972) *The Relevance of Education*. London: George Allen and Unwin. Luria 1962.

—(1996) *The Culture of Education*. Cambridge, MA: Harvard University Press.

—(2006) *In Search of Pedagogy Volume II: The Selected Works of Jerome S. Bruner*. New York.

Burbules, N. and Hansen, D. (1997) *Teaching and its Predicaments*. Oxford: Westview Press.

Burnett, N. (2005) *Education for All Global Monitoring Report: Literacy for Life*. Paris: United Nations Education and Scientific Cultural Organisation (UNESCO).

Burns, B. and Haydn T. (2002) 'Engaging teachers in research: inspiration versus the daily grind', *Pedagogy, Culture and Society*, 10 (2), 301–21.

Calderhead, J. (1994) 'Can the complexities of teaching be accounted for in terms of competences? Contrasting views of professional practice from research and policy'. Mimeo produced for an ESRC symposium on teacher competence.

Campbell, A., McNamara, O. and Gilroy, P. (2004) *Practitioner Research and Professional Development in Education*. London: Sage Publications Ltd.

Campbell, A. and Groundwater-Smith, S. (eds) (2009) *Connecting Inquiry and Professional Learning in Education: International Perspectives and Practical Solutions*. Abingdon: Routledge.

Carr, W. (1987) 'What is an educational practice?', *Journal of Philosophy of Education*, 21 (2), 163–75.

Carter, R. and McCarthy, M. (1997) *Exploring Spoken English*. Cambridge: Cambridge University Press.

Chaplain, R., (2003) *Teaching Without Disruption in the Primary School*. New York: Routledge.

Clanchy, M. T. (2009) 'Parchment and Paper: Manuscript Culture 1100–1500'. In S. Eliot and J. Rose (eds) *A Companion to the History of the Book*. Oxford: Wiley-Blackwell, 194–206.

Clark, D. (1996) *Schools As Learning Communities*. London: Cassell.

Clarke, M. and Drudy, S. (2006) 'Teaching for diversity, social justice and global awareness'. European Journal of Teacher Education. 29 (3), 371–86.

Clegg, S. and Bradley, S. (2006) 'Models of professional development planning: practice and process', *British Educational Research Journal,* 32 (1), 56–76.

Cochran-Smith, M. (2004) *Walking the Road – Race, Diversity and Social Justice in Teacher Education*. New York: Teachers' College Press.

Cockroft, W. (1982) *Mathematics Counts*. London: HMSO.

Coffield, F. (1999) 'Breaking the consensus: lifelong learning as social control', *British Educational Research Journal*, 25 (4), 479–99.

—(2002) 'Britain's continuing failure to train: the birth of a new policy', *Journal of Education Policy*, 17 (4), 483–97.

—(2004) 'Alternative routes out of the low skills equilibrium: a rejoinder to Lloyd and Payne', *Journal of Education* Policy, 19 (6), 733–40.

—(2007) *Running ever Faster down the Wrong Road: An Alternative Future for Education and Skill*. London: Institute of Education, Inaugural Lecture, 5 December 2006.

—(2008) *Just Suppose Teaching and Learning Became the First Priority…*. London: Learning and Skills Network.

—(2009) *All You Ever Wanted to Know About Teaching and Learning But Were too Cool to Ask*. London: Learning and Skills Network.

—(2010b) *Yes, But What has Semmelweis to do with my Professional Development as a Tutor?* London: Learning and Skills Network.

Coffield, F., Costa, C., Muller, W. and Webber, J. (2014) *Beyond Bulimic Learning: Improving teaching in Further Education*. London: IOE Press.

Coffield, F. and Edward, S. (2010a) 'Good best and now "Excellent" practice: what next "perfect" practice?', *British Educational Research Journal*, 35 (3), 371–90.

Coffield, F., Moseley, D., Hall, E. and Ecclestone, K. (2004) *Learning Styles and Pedagogy in Post-16 Learning: A Systematic and Critical Review*. London, Learning and Skills Research Centre.

Coffield, F., Steer, R., Hodgson, A., Spours, K. and Finlay, I., (2005) *A New Learning and Skills Landscape?: The Central role of the Learning and Skills Council'*. London: London University.

Coffield, F. and Williamson, B. (2012) *From Exam Factories to Communities of Discovery: The Democratic Route*. London: Institute of Education.

Cole, M. (1996) *Cultural Psychology: A Once and Future Discipline.* Cambridge, MA: Harvard University Press.

Conole, G., Dyke, M., Oliver, M. and Seale, J. (2004) 'Mapping pedagogy and tools for effective learning design', *Computers & Education*, 43 (1/2), 17–33.

Cooper, B. and Baynham, M. (2005) 'Rites of passage: embedding meaningful language, literacy and numeracy skills in skilled trades courses through significant and transforming relationships. *National Research and Development Centre for Adult Literacy and Numeracy.* London: NRDC.

Cornelius-White, J. (2007) 'Learner-centred teacher-student relationships are effective: a meta-analysis', *Review of Educational Research*, 77 (1), 113–43.

Coulmas, F. (2003) *Writing Systems: An Introduction to their Linguistic Analysis.* Cambridge: Cambridge University Press.

Cowley, S. (2010) *Getting the Buggers to Behave.* London: Continuum.

—(ed.) (2014) *Challenging Professional Learning.* London: Routledge.

Davie, R., Bulter, N. and Goldsein, H. (eds) (1972) *From Birth to Seven.* Harlow: Longman.

Denbo, S. (1988) *Improving Minority Student Achievement: Focus on the Classroom.* Washington, DC: Mid-Atlantic Equity Center Series.

Department for Children, Schools and Families (2008) *The Assessment for Learning Strategy.* Nottingham: DCSF Publications.

Department for Education and Employment (DfEE) (1999) *Improving Literacy and Numeracy: A Fresh Start. The Report of the Working Group Chaired by Sir Claus Moser.* London: HMSO.

—(2001) *Skills for Life: The National Strategy for Improving Adult Literacy and Numeracy Skills.* London: DfEE.

Department for Education and Skills (2006) *North East Regional Office Annual Report*: Newcastle- upon Tyne: NE Regional Basic Skills Department, March 2006.

Dewey, J. (1916) *Democracy and Education.* New York: Macmillan.

—(1933) *How We Think: A Restatement of the Relation of Reflective Thinking to the Educative Process.* Chicago: Henry Regnery.

Douglas, J. (1964) *The Home and School.* London: Macgibbon and Kee.

Doyle, W. (1977) 'Learning the classroom environment: an ecological analysis', *Journal of Teacher Education*, XXVIII (6), 51–4.

Duckworth, V. (2008) *Getting Better Worksheets, Adult Literacy Resources.* Warrington: Gatehouse Books.

—(2013) *Learning Trajectories, Violence and Empowerment amongst Adult Basic Skills learners. Monograph: Educational Research.* Routledge: London.

—(2014) 'Literacy and Transformation.' In V. Duckworth and G. Ade-Ojo (eds) *Landscapes of Specific Literacies in Contemporary Society: Exploring a Social Model of Literacy.* Monograph: Routledge Research in Education (forthcoming): London.

Duncan, S. (2012) *Reading Circles, Novels and Adult Reading Development.* London: Continuum/ Bloomsbury.

Dunne, P. (1993) *Back to the Rough Ground.* Notre Dame, IN: University of Notre Dame Press.

Dylan, W. and Thompson, M. (2007) 'Integrating Assessment with Instruction. What Will it Take to Make it Work?'. In Dwyer, C. A. (eds) *The Future of Assessment: Shaping Teaching and Learning.* Mahwah, NJ: Lawrence Erlbaum Associates.

Edmunds, R. (1979) 'Effective schools for the urban poor', *Educational Leadership*, 37 (3) 15–27.

Edwards, A. (2012) *New Technology and Education.* London: Continuum.

Edwards, T. (2000) '"All the Evidence Shows …": reasonable expectations of educational research', *Oxford Review of Education*, 26 (3/4), 299–311.

Elliott, G. (1996) 'Educational management and the Crisis of Reform', *Further Education and Training*, 48 (1), 5–23.

—(1996) *Crisis and Change in Vocational Education and Training*. London: Jessica Kingsley.

Elliott, J. (2001) 'Making evidence based practice educational', *British Educational Research Journal*, 27 (5), 555–73.

Eraut, M. (2004) *Transfer of Knowledge between Education and Workplace Settings. Workplace Learning in Context*. A. Fuller, A. Munro and H. Rainbird. London: Routledge, 211–20.

Fawbert, F. (2003) *Teaching in the Post-compulsory Education: Learning, Skills and Standards*. London: Continuum.

FEFC (1998) *Effective Facilities Management: A Good Practice Guide*. London: The Stationery Office.

Fenwick, T. (2006) 'The audacity of hope: towards poorer pedagogies', *Studies in the Education of Adults*, 38 (1), 9–24.

Fielding, M. and Moss, P. (2011) *Radical Education and the Common School: A Democratic Alternative*. Abingdon: Routledge.

Fielding, M. (1999) 'Radical collegiality: Affirming teaching as an inclusive professional practice', *Australian Educational Researcher*, 26 (2), 1–34.

—(2003) 'The impact of impact', *Cambridge Journal of Education*, 33 (2), 289–95. London: Routledge.

—(2011) 'Patterns of Partnership: Student Voice, Intergenerational Learning and Democratic Fellowship'. In Mockler, N. and Sachs, J. (eds) *Rethinking Educational Practice through Reflexive Research*. Berlin: Springer, 61–75.

Fielding, M., Bragg, S., Craig, J., Cunningham, I., Eraut, M., Gillinson. S., Horne, M., Robinson, C. and Thorp, J. (2005) *Factors Influencing the Transfer of Good Practice*. London: Department for Education and Skills RR 615.

—(2005) *Factors influencing the Transfer of Good Practice. D.f.E. and Skills*. London: University of Sussex and Demos.

Fieldhouse, R. (ed.) (1996) *A History of Modern Education*. Leicester: National Institute of Adult Continuing Education.

Figes, K. (ed.) (1996) *The Penguin Book of International Women's Stories*. London: Penguin Books.

Fisher, R. (2013) *Teaching Thinking: Philosophical Enquiry in the Classroom*. London: Bloomsbury.

Flanagan, J. C. (1954) 'The critical incident technique', *Psychological Bulletin*, 51 (4), 327–58.

Freire, P. (1985) *The Politics of Education: Culture, Power, and Liberation* (trans. D. Macedo). New York: Bergin and Garvey.

Freire, P. (1993) *Pedagogy of the Oppressed*. New York: Continuum.

Fuller, A. and Unwin, L. (2004) 'Expansive Learning Environments: Integrating Organizational and Personal Development'. In H. Rainbird, A. Fuller and A. Munro (eds) *Workplace Learning in Context*. London: Routledge.

Furlong, J. and Salisbury, J. (2005) 'Best practice research scholarships: an evaluation', *Research Papers in Education*, 20 (1), 45–83.

Gee, J. P. (1996) *Social Linguistics and Literacies: Ideology in Discourses*, 2nd edn. London: Routledge Falmer.

Gipps, C. (1992) *What We Know About Effective Primary Teaching*. London: Tufnell Press.

Gipps, C. and MacGilchrist, B. (1999) 'Primary School Learners'. In P. Mortimore (ed.) *Understanding Pedagogy and its Impact on Learning*. London: Paul Chapman Publishing.

Gleeson, D. and Mardle, G. (1980) *Further Education or Training? A Case Study in the Theory and Practice of Day-release Education*. London. Routledge.

Gleeson, D. and Shain, F. (1999) 'Managing Ambiguity: Between Markets and Managerialism: A Case Study of Middle Managers in FE'. *The Sociological Review* (forthcoming).

Goleman, D. (1996) *Emotional Intelligence – Why it Matters More than IQ*. London: Bloomsbury.

Green, A. (1990) *Education and State Formation*. London: Macmillan.

Green, A. and Janmaat, J. G. (2011) *Regimes of Social Cohesion: Societies and the Crisis of Globalisation*. London: Palgrave.

Greenaway, P. (1996) *The Pillow Book* (film).

Gregson, M. and Nixon, L. (2012) *Discussion Papers Presented to CAVTL at Consultation Seminars in 2012*.

—(2009) 'Assessing effectiveness: ways of seeing impact', *International Journal of Interdisciplinary Social Sciences*, 21 (3).

Gregson, M., Nixon, L. Spedding, P. and Kearney, S. (2015) *Helping Good Ideas Become Good Practice*. London: Bloomsbury.

Grosz, S. (2013) *The Examined Life*. London: Chatto and Windus.

Guile, D. (2006) 'Learning across contexts'. *Educational Philosophy and Theory*, 38 (3), 251–68.

—(2010) *The Learning Challenge of the Knowledge Economy*. Rotterdam: Sense Publishers.

Habermas, J. (1974) *Theory and Practice* (trans. J. Viertel). London: Heinemann.

Hajer, M. and Wagenaar, H. (2003) *Deliberative Policy Analysis: Understanding Government in the Network Society*. Cambridge: Cambridge University Press.

Hamilton, M. (1996) 'Adult Literacy and Basic Education'. In R. Fieldhouse (ed.) *A Modern History of Adult Education*. Leicester: National Institute for Adult Continuing Education.

—(2009) 'Putting words in their mouths: the alignment of identities with system goals through the use of Individual Learning Plans', *British Educational Research Journal*, 35 (2), 221–42.

Hamilton, M. and Hillier, Y. (2006) *Changing Faces of Adult Literacy, Language and Numeracy: A Critical History*. Stoke-on-Trent: Trentham Books.

Hargreaves, A. (1994) *Changing Teachers, Changing Times*. London: Cassell.

—(2005) 'Educational change takes ages: life, career and generational factors in teachers' emotional responses to educational change', *Teaching and Teacher Education*, 21 (8), 967–83.

—(2007) *The Persistence of Presentism and the Struggle for Lasting Improvement, Professorial Inaugural Lecture*. Institute of Education: University of London.

Hargreaves, A. and Fullan, M. (2012) *Professional Capital: Transforming Teaching in Every School*. Boston: Teachers College Press.

Hargreaves, A. and Shirley, D. (2009) *The Fourth Way: The Inspiring Future of Educational Change*. Thousand Oaks, CA: Corwin.

Harlen, W. (1991) 'National Curriculum Assessment: Increasing the Benefit by Reducing the Burden'. In *Education and Change in the 1990s, Journal of the Educational Research Network of Northern Ireland*, 5, February, 3–19.

Harlen, W., Gipps, C., Broadfoot, P. and Nuttall, D. (1992) 'Assessment and the improvement of education', *Curriculum Journal*, 3 (3), 217–25.

Harper, H. (2013) 'Outstanding Teaching – the Reality'. In *Tuition Issue 15*. London: Institute for Learning (IfL), 16–17.

Hartley, D. (2002) 'Global influences on teacher education in Scotland', *Journal of Education for Teaching*, 28 (3), 251–5.

Hattie, J. (2009) *Visible learning: A Synthesis of Over 800 Meta-Analyses Relating to Achievement*. London: Routledge.

—(2012) *Visible Learning for Teachers: Maximising Impact on Learning*. London: Routledge.

Haynes, A. (2010) *The Complete Guide to Lesson Planning and Preparation*. London: Continuum.

Heilbronn, R. (2008) *Teacher Education and the Development of Practical Judgement*. London: Continuum.

—(2011) 'Practical Judgement and Evidence-informed Practice'. In R. Heilbronn and J. Yandell (eds) *Critical Practice in Teacher Education: A Study of Professional Learning*. London: IOE Press.

Heron, J. (1996) *Co-operative Inquiry: Research into the Human Condition*. London: Sage Publications Ltd.

Helsby, G. (1999) *Changing Teachers' Work: The Reform of Secondary Schooling*. Milton Keynes: Open University.

Herrington, M. (1994) 'Learning at Home: Distance Learning in Adult Basic Education'. In M. Hamilton, D. Barton and R. Ivanic, *Worlds of Literacy*. Clevedon: Multilingual Matters. pp 182–7.

Hillier, Y. (1998) 'Informal practitioner theory: eliciting the implicit', *Studies in the Education of Adults*, 30 (1), 35–52.

—(2002) *Reflective Teaching in Further and Adult Education*. London. Continuum.

—(2005) *Reflective Teaching in Further and Adult Education*. London. Continuum.

—(2006) 'An analytical framework for policy engagement: the contested case of 14–19 reform in England', *Journal of Education Policy*, 21 (6), 679–96.

—(2008) *Education and Training 14–19: Curriculum, Qualifications and Organisation*. London: Sage Publications Ltd.

Hillier, Y. and Jameson, J. (2003) *Empowering Researchers in Further Education*. Stoke-on-Trent: Trentham Books, Chapter 4.

Hodgson, A. and Spours, K. (1997) *Dearing and Beyond. 14–19 Qualifications, Frameworks and Systems*. London. Kogan Page.

Hodkinson, P. (1995) *The Challenge of Competence*. London: Cassell.

—(2012) 'Towards a universal upper secondary education system in England. A unified and ecosystem vision'. Inaugural professorial lecture, Institute of Education, University of London, 27 June.

Hodkinson, P., Biesta, G. and James, D. (2007) 'Understanding learning cultures', *Educational Review,* 59 (4), 4115–427.

Hodkinson, P., Biesta, G., Postlethwaite, K., and Maull, W. (2007) 'Learning Cultures across Sites'. In D. James and G. Biesta (eds) *Improving Learning Cultures in Further Education*. London: Routledge, 60–84.

Hogan, P. (2003) 'Teaching as a way of life', *Journal of Philosophy of Education*, 37 (2), 207–24.

Houston, R. A. (2002) *Literacy in Early Modern Europe: Culture and Education 1500–1800*. London: Longman/Pearson Education.

Hoyle, E. (1974) 'Professionality, professionalism and control in teaching', *London Education Review*, 3 (2), 13–9.

Huberman, M. A. (1993) *The Lives of Teachers*. New York: Teachers College Press.

Hulme, M., Menter, I., Kelly, D. and Rusby, S. (2010) 'Schools of Ambition: Bridging Professional and Institutional Boundaries'. In R. Ravid and J. J. Slater (eds) *Collaboration in Education*. New York: Routledge.

Hyland, T. and Merrill, B. (2003) *The Changing Face of Further Education: Lifelong Learning. Inclusion and the Community*. London. Routledge Falmer.

Ivanic, R. (1998) *The Discoursal Construction of Identity in Academic Writing*. Amsterdam: John Benjamins.

Jackson, P. (1968) *Life in Classrooms*. New York: Holt, Rinehart and Winston.

Jameson, J., Hillier, Y. and Betts, D. (2004) *The Ragged-trousered Philanthropy of LSC Part-time Staff*. Presented at the British Educational Research Association Conference, UMIST, Manchester. 16–18 September.

Johnson, C., Duckworth, V., McNamara, M. and Apelbaum, C. (2010) 'A tale of two adult learners: from adult basic education to degree completion', *National Association for Developmental Education Digest*, 5 (1), 57–67.

Keep, E. (2006) 'State control of the English education and training system – playing with the biggest train set in the world', *Journal of Vocational Education and Training*, 58 (1), 47–64.

Keep, E. and Mayhew, K. (1999) 'The assessment: knowledge, skills and competitiveness', *Oxford Review of Economic Policy*, 15 (1), 1–15.

Keogh, B. and Naylor, S. (2014) Concept Cartoons in Science Education. Available from: www.millgatehouse.co.uk (last accessed June 2014).

Kohl, H. (1976) *On Teaching*. London. Methuen and Co.

Kress, G. (2010) 'The Profound Shift of Digital Literacies'. In J. Gillen and D. Barton (eds) *Digital Literacies*. TLRP TEL. London: Institute of Education.

Kuykendall, C. (1989) *Improving Black Student Achievement*. Washington, DC: The Mid-Atlantic Equity Center Series.

Laurillard, D. (2008) 'Digital technologies and their role in achieving our ambitions for education' (Inaugural Professorial Lecture). London: Institute of Education.

Lave, J., and Wenger, E. (1991) *Situated Learning: Legitimate Peripheral Participation*. New York: Cambridge University Press.

Lavender, P. Derrick, J. and Brooks, B. (2004) *Testing, Testing ... 123: Assessment in Adult Literacy, Language and Numeracy*. A NIACE Policy Discussion Paper. Leicester: NIACE.

LeDoux, J. (1996) *Emotional Brain*. New York: Simon and Schuster.

Lemke, J. L. (2002) 'Becoming the Village: Education Across Lives'. In G. Wells and G. Claxton (eds) *Learning for Life in the 21st Century: Sociocultural Perspectives on the Future of Education*. Oxford: Blackwell.

Lewin, K. (1948) *Resolving Social Conflicts*. New York. Harper and Row.

Lingard, B. (2009) 'Pedagogizing Teacher Professional Identities'. In G. Gewirtz, P. Mahony, I. Hextall and A. Cribb (eds) *Changing Teacher Professionalism. International Trends, Challenges and Ways Forward*. London: Routledge, 81–93.

Lucas, B., Claxton, G. and Webster, R. (2010) *Mind the Gap. Research and Reality in Practical and Vocational Education*. London: Edge Foundation.

Lortie, D. C. (1975) *Schoolteacher: A Sociological Study*. Chicago: University of Chicago Press.

MacLellan, E and Soden, R (2012) 'Successful learners, confident individuals, responsible citizens and effective contributions to society: exploring the nature of learning and its mplications in curriculum for excellence', *Scottish Educational Review*, 1, 29–37.

Mace, J. (1992) *Talking about Literacy: Principles and Practices in Adult Literacy Education*. London: Routledge.

—(2002) *The Give and take of Writing: Scribes, Literacy and Everyday Life*. Leicester: NIACE.

Mahony, P. and Hextall, I. (2000) *Reconstructing Teaching*. London: Routledge Falmer.

Malen, B. and Knapp, M. (1997) 'Rethinking the multiple perspectives approach to education policy analysis: Implications for policy-practice connections', *Journal of Education Policy*, 12, 419–45.

Martin, P. (1998) 'Open College Networks: success against the odds?', *Journal of Further and Higher Education*, 22 (2), 183–92.

McLaughlin, F. (2013) *It's about work ... Excellent adult vocational teaching and learning*, London: Learning and Skills Improvement Service (LSIS).

McNamara, M. (2007) *Getting Better*. Warrington: Gatehouse Books.

McNamara, O. (ed.) (2002) *Becoming an Evidence-Based Practitioner: A Framework for Teacher Researchers*. London: Routledge.

McPherson, A. (1992) *Measuring Added Value in Schools, National Commission on Education Briefing No. 1*. London: National Commission on Education.

Menter, I., Hulme, M., Elliot, D and Lewin, J. (2010) *Teacher Education in the 21st Century*. Edinburgh: Scottish Government.

Merton, K. (1968) *Social Theory and Social Structure*. New York: Free Press.

Mills, C. W. (1959) *The Sociological Imagination*. New York: Oxford University Press.

Morais, A. and Neves, I. (2001) 'Pedagogic Social Contexts: Studies for a Sociology of Learning. "Towards a Sociology of Pedagogy". The Contribution of Basil Bernstein to Reseach'. In

A. Morais, I. Neves, B. Davis, and H. Daniels. *Pedagogic Social Contexts: Studies for a Sociology of Learning.* New York: Peter Lang.

Mortimore, P. (1993) 'School effectiveness and the management of effective learning and teaching', *School Effectiveness and Improvement*, 4 (3), 290–310.

Mortimore, P and Mortimore, J. (1986) 'Education and Social Class'. In R. Rogers (ed.) *Education and Social Class.* London: Falmer Press.

Mortimore, P., Sammons, P., Stoll, L., Lewis, D. and Ecob, R. (1988) *School Matters: The Junior Years.* Open Books: London.

Noddings, N. (2003) *Happiness and Education.* Cambridge: Cambridge University Press.

Nonaka, I. and Takeuchi, H. (1995) *The Knowledge-creating Company: How Japanese Companies Create the Dynamics of Innovation.* New York: Oxford University Press.

Nuffield Review of 14–19 Education and Training. (2008) 'Issues Paper 9. Applied learning: The case of applied science'. Available from www.nuffield14–19review.org.uk (accessed August 2011).

Ostler, N. (2005) *Empires of the Word.* London: Harper Perennial.

O'Leary, M. (2013) 'Surveillance, performativity and normalised practice: the use and impact of graded lesson observations in Further Education Colleges', *Journal of Further and Higher Education,* 37 (5), 694–714.

—(2014) *Classroom Observation: A Guide to the Effective Observation of Teaching and Learning.* London: Routledge.

O'Leary, M. and Gewessler, A. (2014) 'Changing the culture: beyond graded lesson observations'. *Adults Learning – Spring 2014*, 25, 38–41. Available from http://www.niace.org.uk/sites/default/files/documents/adults-learning/2014-spring/AL-Spring-2014-Vol25-pg38-41.pdf

Palincsar, A. S. and Brown, A. L. (1984) *Reciprocal Teaching of Comprehension Fostering and Monitoring Activities: Cognition and Instruction.* Hillsdale, NJ: Lawrence Erlbaum.

Payne, J. (2000) 'The unbearable lightness of skill: the changing meaning of skill in UK policy discourses and some implications for education and training.' *Journal of Education Policy*, 15 (3), 353–69.

Pedder, D., James, M. and Macbeath, J. (2005) 'How teachers value and practise professional learning', *Research Papers in Education*, 20 (3), 209–43.

Perrenoud, P. (1998) 'From formative evaluation to a controlled regulation of learning: towards a wider conceptual field', *Assessment in Education: Principles Policy and Practice*, 5 (1), 85–102.

Perrot, E. (1982) *Effective Teaching: A Practical Guide to Improving Your Teaching.* London: Longman.

Pillings, D. and Pringle, M. K. (1978) *Controversial Issues in Child Development.* London: Paul Elek.

Pollard, A., Purvis, J. and Walford, G. (1988) *Education, Training and the New Vocationalism: Experience and Policy.* Milton Keynes: Open University Press.

Pollard, A. and Tann, S. (1987) *Reflective Teaching in the Primary School.* London: Cassell.

Ponte, P., Beijard, D. and Ax, J. (2004) 'Don't wait till the cows come home: action research and initial teacher education in three different countries', *Teachers and Teaching*, 10 (6), 591–621.

Pring, R. (2000) *Philosophy of Educational Research.* London: Continuum.

—(1995) *Closing the Gap. Liberal Education and Vocational Preparation.* London: Hodder and Stoughton.

—(2007) '14–19 and Lifelong Learning. Distinguishing between Academic and Vocational Learning'. In L. Clarke and C. Winch (eds), *Vocational Education. International Approaches, Developments and Systems.* London: Routledge, 118–32.

Pring, R., Hayward, G., Hodgson, A., Johnson, J., Keep, E., Oancea, A., Rees, G., Spours, K. and

Wilde, S. (2009) *Education for All. The Future of Education and Training for 14–19 Year Olds.* London: Routledge.

Randle, K. and Brady, N. (1997) 'Managerialism and professionalism in the Cinderella service', *Journal of Vocational Education and Training,* 49 (1), 121–39.

Reason, P and Heron, J. (1995) 'Co-operative Inquiry'. In J. A. Smith, R. Harre and L. Van Lagenhove (eds) *Rethinking Methods in Psychology.* London: Sage Publications Ltd.

Reynolds, D. (1982) 'The search for effective schools', *School Organization*, 2 (3), 215–37.

Richardson, R. (2009) *Holding Together.* Stoke-on-Trent: Trentham Books.

Robinson, K. (2009) *The Element: How Finding your Passion Changes Everything.* London. Penguin Books.

Rogoff, B. (2003) *The Cultural Nature of Human Development.* New York: Oxford University Press.

Rosen, C. and Rosen, H. (1973) *The Language of Primary School Children.* Harmondsworth: Penguin.

Rosenthal, R. and Jacobson, L. (1968) *Pygmalion in the Classroom: Teacher Expectation and Pupils' Intellectual Development.* New York: Holt, Rinehart and Winston.

Rudduck, J., Chaplain, R. and Wallace, G. (1996) *School Improvement: What Can Pupils Tell Us?* London: David Fulton.

Rutter, M., Maughan, B., Mortimore, P. and Ouston, J. (1979) *Fifteen Thousand Hours: Secondary Schools and Their Effects on Children.* London: Open Books.

Sachs, J. (2003) *The Activist Teaching Profession.* Buckingham. Open University Press.

Sahlberg, P. (2011) *Finnish Lessons: What Can the World Learn from Educational Change in Finland.* New York: Teachers College Press.

Sahlberg, P., Furlong, J. and Munn, P. (2012) *Report of the International Review Panel on the Structure of Initial Teacher Education Provision in Ireland: Review conducted on behalf of the Department of Education and Skills.* Dublin: Higher Education Authority of Ireland, 5, 14–15.

Salmon, G. (1993) *Distributed Cognitions: Psychological and Educational Considerations.* Cambridge: Cambridge University Press.

Salvino, D. N. (1989) 'The Word in Black and White: Ideologies of Race and Literacy in Antebellum America'. In C. N. Davidson (ed.) *Reading in America: Literature and Social History.* Baltimore, ML: The Johns Hopkins University Press, 140–56.

Sammons, P. Hillman, J. and Mortimore, P. (1995) *Key Characteristics of Effective Shcools: A Review of School Effectiveness Research.* London: Institute of Education.

Sarason, S. B. (1998) *The Predictable Failure of Educational Reform.* San Francisco: Jossey-Bass.

Schon, D. (1983) *The Reflective Practitioner: How Professionals Think in Action.* London: Temple Smith.

Scott, J. C. (1999) *Seeing Like a State.* New Haven: Yale University Press.

Searle, C. (1982) 'Five Girls: Classroom Interaction and Informal Speech'. In J. Eyers and S. Richmond. *Becoming our own Expects. The Vauxhall Papers.* London: ILEA English Centre.

Sennett, R. (2008) *The Craftsman,* London: Allen Lane.

Shain, F. and D. Gleeson (1999) 'Under new management: changing conceptions of teacher professionalism and policy in the further education sector', *Journal of Education Policy*, 14 (4), 445–62.

Simon, B. (1981) 'Why no pedagogy in England?'. In B. Simon and W. Taylor (eds) *Education in the Eighties: The Central Issues.* London: Batsford.

Skinner, B. F. (1954) 'The science of learning and the art of teaching', *Harvard Educational Review*, 24, 86–97.

Smith, A. (1998) *Accelerated Learning in Practice.* Stafford: Network Educational Press.

Smith, D. and Tomlinson, S. (1989) *The School Effect: A Study of Multi-racial Comprehensives.* London: Policy Studies Institute.

Smith, F. and Miller, G. A. (1966) *The Genesis of Language: A Psycholinguistic Approach.* Cambridge, MA: MIT Press.

Somekh, B. (1994) 'Inhabiting each other's castles: towards knowledge and mutual growth through collaboration', *Educational Action Research.*

Stanton, G. (2008) *Learning Matters: Making the 14–19 Reforms Work for Learners.* London: CfBT Education Trust.

Stenhouse, L. (1975) *An Introduction to Curriculum Research and Development.* Oxford: Heinemann.

Stones, E. (1979) *Psychopedagogy: Psychological Theory and the Practice of Teaching.* London: Methuen.

Street, B. (1984) *Literacy in Theory and Practice.* Cambridge: Cambridge University Press.

Stronach, I., Corbin, B., McNamara, O., Stark, S. and Warne, T. (2002) 'Towards an uncertain politics of professionalism: teacher and nurse identities in flux', *Journal of Education Policy,* 27 (2), 109–38.

Swaffield, S. (2011) 'Getting to the heart of authentic Assessment for Learning', *Assessment in Education: Principles, Policy and Practice,* 18 (4), 441–3.

Teese, R., and Polesel, J. (2003a) *Undemocratic Schooling: Equity and quality in Mass Secondary Education in Australia.* Melbourne Melbourne University Press.

—(2003b) 'Durkheim, Vygotsky and the curriculum of the future', *London Review of Education,* 1 (2), 110–17.

The Commission for Adult and Vocational Teaching and Learning (CAVTL) (2013) *It's about Work ... Excellent Adult and Vocational Teaching and Learning.* Coventry: Learning and Skills Service.

Thomas, L., Bland, D. C. and Duckworth, V. (2012) 'Teachers as advocates for widening participation and lifelong learning'*, Journal of Widening Participation and Education,* 14 (2), 40–58.

Thomson, A. and Tuckett, A. (2010) *Lifelong Learning in Challenging Times: An Agenda for a new Government.* London. NIACE.

Tizard, B., Blatchford, D., Burke, J., Farquhar, C. and Plewis, I. (1988) *Young Children at School in the Inner City.* Hove: Lawrence Erlbaum.

Tomlinson, M. (2004) *14–19 Curriculum and Qualifications Reform.* Final Report of the Working Group on 14–19 Reform. Annesley: DfES.

University and College Union (UCU) (2013) 'Developing a National Framework for the Effective Use of Lesson Observation in Further Education'. Project report, November 2013. Available from http://www.ucu.org.uk/7105

Unwin, L (2004) 'Growing beans with Thoreau: rescuing skills and vocational education from the UK's deficit approach', *Oxford Review of Education,* 30 (1), 147–60.

Unwin, L (2009) *Sensuality, Sustainability and Social Justice: Vocational Education in Changing Times. Professorial Inaugural Lecture.* Institute of Education: University of London.

Van Manen, M. (1995) 'On the epistemology of reflective practice', *Teachers and Teaching: Theory and Practice,* 1 (1), 33–50.

—(1991) *The Tact of Teaching.* Alberta: The Althouse Press.

Vygotsky, L. S. (1978) *Mind in Society: The Development of Higher Mental Processes.* Cambridge, MA: Harvard University Press.

Warhurst, C., Grugulis, I. and Keep, E. (eds) (2004) *The Skills That Matter.* Basingstoke: Palgrave.

Watson, B., and Ashton, E. (1995) *Education, Assumptions, and Values.* London: D. Fulton.

Wells, G. (2001) *Action, Talk, and Text: Learning and Teaching Through Inquiry.* New York: Teachers College Press.

—(2008) 'Dialogue, Inquiry and the Construction of Learning Communities'. In B. Linguard, J. Nixon and S. Ranson (eds) *Transforming Learning in Schools and Communities.* London: Continuum.

Wertsch, J. (1998) *Mind as Action*. New York: Oxford University Press.

Westerhuis, A. (2007) 'The Role of the State in Vocational Education: A Political Analysis of the History of Vocational Education in the Netherlands'. In L. Clarke and C. Winch (eds) *Vocational Education. International Approaches, Developments and Systems*. London: Routledge, 21–33..

Weston, P. and Stradling, R. (1993) 'Vers L'Europe des compétences? Setting the 14–19 curriculum in a European perspective'. In H. Tomlinson (ed.) *Education and Training 14–19. Continuity and Diversity in the Curriculum*. Harlow: Longman, 3–25

Wheelahan, L. (2005) *The Pedagogic Device: The Relevance of Bernstein's Analysis for VET. 13th International Conference on Vocational Education and Training*. Griffith University, Queensland. Australia: Australian Academic Press.

—(2008) 'An analysis of vocational qualifications in Australian tertiary education: How do they mediate access to knowledge?'. Paper presented at the 5th International Basil Bernstein Symposium, University of Cardiff, July 9–12.

—(2010) *Why Knowledge Matters in Curriculum. A Social Realist Argument*. London: Routledge.

Wiliam, D. (2007) 'Assessment for Learning: Why, What and How?'. Inaugural Lecture, Institute of Education, University of London.

—(2008) 'Keeping Learning on Track: Formative Assessment and the Regulation of Learning'. In F. K. Lester Jr. (ed.) *Second Handbook of Mathematics Teaching and Learning*. Greenwich, CT: Information Age.

Williamson, S. (2006) *A New Shape for Schooling: Deep Support*. London: Specialist Schools and Academies Trust.

Wilshaw, M (2011) quoted in *Times Educational Supplement,* 13 December.

Witty, T. (1993) 'Pieces of paper. A Survey of Student Attitudes toward Accreditation in Adult Literacy and English Classes in Southwark', *RaPAL Bulletin*, 21.

Wolf, A. (2002) *Does Education Matter?* London: Penguin.

—(2011) 'Review of vocational education. London: Department of Education. Working Group on 14–19 Reform. 2004. 14–19 Curriculum and qualifications reform'. Final report of the working group on 14–19 Reform (The Tomlinson Report). Annesley: DfES Publications.

Woods, P., Jeffrey, B., Troman, G. and Boyle, M. (1997) *Restructuring Schools, Reconstructing Teachers*. Maidenhead: Open University Press.

Yates, L. and Grumet, M. (2011) 'Curriculum in Today's World: Configuring Knowledge, Identities, Work and politics'. In L. Yates and M. Grumet (eds). *World Yearbook of Education 2011. Curriculum in Today's World*. London: Routledge, 3–13.

Yin, R. K. (1994) *Case Study Research: Design and Methods*, 2nd rev. edn. Thousand Oaks, CA: Sage Publications Ltd.

Young, M. (1971) *Knowledge and Control: New Directions for the Sociology of Education*. London: Collier Macmillan.

—(1998) *The Curriculum of the Future*. London: Falmer.

—(2008) *Bringing Knowledge back in. From Social Constructivism to Social Realism in the Sociology of Education*. London: Routledge.

—(2011) 'The return to subjects: A sociological perspective on the UK coalition government's approach to the 14–19 curriculum', *The Curriculum Journal*, 22 (2), 265–78.

—(2013) *Powerful Knowledge in Education*. London: University of London, Institute of Education.

Young, M. and Gamble, J. (eds). (2006) *Knowledge, Curriculum and Qualifications in South African Further Education*. Cape Town: HSRC Press.

Zeichner, K. (2009) *Teacher Education and the Struggle for Social Justice*. London, Routledge.

Zeichner, K. and Gore, J. M. (1990) 'Teacher Socialization'. In W. R. Houston (ed.) *Handbook of Research on Teacher Education*. New York: Macmillan.

Permissions

We are grateful to the authors and publishers listed below for permission to reproduce the following extracts:

1.1 'What is education for? And what does that mean for teachers? On the role of judgement in teaching', by Gert Biesta, edited from *Good Education in an Age of Measurement: Ethics, Politics, Democracy* (2010), reproduced by permission of Paradigm Publishers.

1.2 'What is Further Education for? What freedoms do tutors have?', by Frank Coffield, edited from *Beyond Bulimic Learning* (2014), reproduced by permission of Institute of Education Press.

2.1 'The science of learning and the art of teaching', by Burrhus Skinner, edited from 'The science of learning and the art of teaching', *Harvard Education Review, 24,* (1954), reproduced by permission of Harvard Education Review.

2.2 'Mind in society and the ZPD', by Lev Vygotsky, edited from *Mind in Society: The Development of Higher Psychological Processes* (1978), reproduced by permission of Harvard University Press.

2.3 'Learning, development and schooling', by Gordon Wells, edited from 'Dialogue, inquiry and the construction of learning communities', in B. Linguard, J. Nixon, J. and S. Ranson (eds) *Transforming Learning in Schools and Communities* (2008), reproduced by permission of Bloomsbury Publishing.

2.4 'Why thinking should be taught', by Robert Fisher, edited from *Teaching Thinking: Philosophical Enquiry in the Classroom* (2013), reproduced by permission of Bloomsbury Publishing.

2.5 'Challenging the intuitive appeal of learning styles', by Lawrence Nixon, Margaret Gregson and Patricia Spedding, edited from 'Pedagogy and the intuitive appeal of learning styles in post-compulsory education in England' (2007) *Journal of Vocational Education and Training* 59 (1), reproduced by permission of Lawrence Nixon, Margaret Gregson and Patricia Spedding.

3.1 'Competence and the complexities of teaching', by James Calderhead, edited from 'Can the complexities of teaching be accounted for in terms of competences? Contrasting views of professional practice from research and policy', mimeo produced for an ESRC symposium on teacher competence (1994), reproduced by permission of James Calderhead.

3.2 'Thinking and reflective experience', by John Dewey, edited from *How We Think: A Restatement of the Relation of Reflective Thinking to the Educative Process* (1933), published by Henry Regnery, and from *Democracy and Education* (1916), reproduced by permission of the Free Press.

3.3 'The teacher as researcher', by Lawrence Stenhouse, edited from *An Introduction to Curriculum Research and Development* (1975), reproduced by permission of Heinemann.

3.4 'Action research and the development of practice', by Richard Pring, edited from *Philosophy of Educational Research* (2000), reproduced by permission of Continuum Publishing.

4.1 'Practical judgement and evidence-informed practice', by Ruth Heilbronn, edited from 'The nature of practice-based knowledge and understanding', in R. Heilbronn and J. Yandell,

8.2   'Environment, affordance and new technology', by Anthony Edwards, edited from
        New Technology and Education (2012), reproduced by permission of Bloomsbury
        Publishing.

8.3   'The profound shift of digital literacies', by Guther Kress, edited from J. Gillen and D.
        Barton (eds) *Digital Literacies* (2010), reproduced by permission of IOE Press.

8.4   'Improving learning cultures in further education: Understanding how students learn',
        by Gert Biesta and David James, edited from *Improving Learning Cultures in Further
        Education* (2007), reproduced by permission of Routledge.

9.1   'Curriculum and method in a student-centred field', by Mary Hamilton and Yvonne Hillier,
        edited from *Changing Faces of Adult Literacy, Numeracy and Language* (2006), reproduced
        by permission of IOE Press.

9.2   'Powerful knowledge' by Michael Young, edited from *Powerful Knowledge in Education*
        (2013), reproduced by permission of University of London, Institute of Education.

9.3   'Vocational education matters', by Lorna Unwin, edited from *Sensuality, Sustainability and
        Social Justice Vocational Education in Changing Times* (2009), reproduced by permission
        of IOE Press.

10.1   'Outstanding teaching – the reality', by Harriet Harper, edited from *Outstanding
        Teaching in Lifelong Learning* (2013), reproduced by permission of OUP Press/
        McGraw-Hill Education.

10.2   'Instructional time – and where it goes', by David Berliner, edited from M. Ben-Peretz
        and R. Bromme (eds), *The Nature of Time in Schools* (1990), reproduced by permission of
        Teachers' College Press.

10.3   'Progression and differentiation', by Anthony Haynes, edited from *The Complete Guide
        to Lesson Planning and Preparation* (2010), reproduced by permission of Bloomsbury
        Publishing.

10.4   'Mind frames for visible learning', by John Hattie, edited from *Visible Learning for
        Teachers* (2012), reproduced by permission of Taylor & Francis.

10.5   'A clear line of sight to work', by Frank McLaughlin, edited from *It's about work...
        Excellent adult vocational teaching and learning* (2013), reproduced by permission of
        Learning and Skills Improvement Service (LSIS).

11.1   'Folk pedagogy', by Jerome Bruner, edited from *The Culture of Education* (1996),
        reproduced by permission of Harvard University Press.

11.2   'Why no pedagogy in England?', by Brian Simon, edited from 'Why no pedagogy in
        England?', in B. Simon and W. Taylor (eds) *Education in the Eighties: The Central Issues*
        (1981), reproduced by permission of Pavilion Books.

11.3   'The role of Higher Education institutions in supporting the development of pedagogic
        practice in Further Adult and Vocational Education (FAVE) sector in England', by Margaret
        Gregson and Lawrence Nixon, edited from invited papers and evidence presented to the
        Commission on Adult and Vocational Teaching and Learning (CAVTL) (2013), reproduced
        by permission of CAVTL and Margaret Gregson and Lawrence Nixon.

11.4   'The nature of pedagogic repertoire', by Robin Alexander, edited from *Essays on Pedagogy*
        (2008), reproduced by permission of Taylor & Francis.

11.5   'Using questions in classroom discussion', by Elizabeth Perrot, edited from *Effective
        Teaching: A Practical Guide to Improving Your Teaching* (1982), reproduced by permission
        of Pearson.

12.1   'Foregrounding in adult literacy', by Sam Duncan, edited from *Reading Circles, Novels and
        Adult Reading Development* (2012) Chapter 2, reproduced by permission of Continuum/
        Bloomsbury.

12.2   'Unlocking the potential for improvement in Skills for Life teaching and learning at
        the local level', by Margaret Gregson and Lawrence Nixon, edited from 'Unlocking
        the potential of Skills for Life (SfL) tutors and learners: A critical evaluation of the

implementation of SfL policy in England', (2011) *Teaching in Lifelong Learning* Vol. 3, Issue 1, reproduced by permission of University of Huddersfield Press.

12.3 'Lifelong learning in challenging times; an agenda for a new government', by Alastair Thomson and Alan Tuckett, edited from *Lifelong Learning in Challenging Times: An Agenda for a New Government* (2010), reproduced by permission of National Institute of Adult Continuing Education (NIACE).

13.1 'Mapping and tracking: assessment and accreditation', by Mary Hamilton and Yvonne Hillier, edited from *Changing Faces of Adult Literacy, Numeracy and Language* (2006), reproduced by permission of Trentham Books.

13.2 'Assessment purposes and principles', by Wynne Harlen, Caroline Gipps, Patricia Broadfoot and Desmond Nuttall, edited from *Assessment and the Improvement of Education Curriculum Journal* Vol. 3, No. 3 (1992), reproduced by permission of Taylor & Francis.

13.3 'Authentic assessment for learning', by Sue Swaffield, edited from *Assessment in Education: Principles, Policy and Practice* 18 (4) (2011), reproduced by permission of Taylor & Francis.

13.4 'Assessment for learning', by Assessment Reform Group, edited from *Assessment for Learning: Beyond the Black Box* (1999), reproduced by permission of Assessment Reform Group.

14.1 'Ways of seeing impact', by Margaret Gregson and Lawrence Nixon, edited from 'Assessing effectiveness: Ways of seeing impact', *International Journal of Interdisciplinary Social Sciences* 21(3) (2009), reproduced by permission of Margaret Gregson and Lawrence Nixon.

14.2 'Students as learning partners within a community of learning', by Frank Coffield, edited from *Beyond Bulimic Learning* (2014), reproduced by permission of IOE Press.

14.3 'Under new management: Changing conceptions of teacher professionalism and policy in the further education sector', by Farzana Shain and Denis Gleeson, edited from 'Under new management: Changing conceptions of teacher professionalism and policy in the further education sector' (2010) *Journal of Education Policy* 14 (4), reproduced by permission of Routledge.

15.1 'Principles for equality and diversity', by Robin Richardson, edited from *Holding Together* (2009), reproduced by permission of IOE Press.

15.2 'Learning through life', by Tom Schuller, edited from *Inquiry into the Future for Lifelong Learning. A Summary* (2009), reproduced by permission of National Institute of Adult Continuing Education (NIACE).

15.3 'Tackling prejudice together: What are trainee teachers' experiences of prejudice in educational contexts?', by Margaret Gregson, Lawrence Nixon and Patricia Spedding, edited from *Tackling Prejudice Together* (2011), presentation at University of Sunderland, Faculty of Education and Society Conference, 5 September, reproduced by permission of Margaret Gregson, Lawrence Nixon and Patricia Spedding.

15.4 'Who are the learners?', by Yvon Appleby, edited from N. Hughes and I. Schwab (eds) *Teaching Adult Literacy: Principles and Practice* (2010), reproduced by permission of Open University Press.

16.1 'Helping good ideas to become good practice: Enhancing your professional practice through Joint Practice Development (JPD)', by Margaret Gregson, Patricia Spedding and Lawrence Nixon, edited from *Helping Good Ideas Become Good Practice: Enhancing Professionalism through Joint Practice Development (JPD)* (Forthcoming 2015), reproduced by permission of Bloomsbury Publishing.

16.2 'Small-scale research: Action research and reflective practice', by Jill Jameson and Yvonne Hillier, edited from *Empowering Researchers in Further Education* (2003), reproduced by permission of Trentham Books.

16.3 'Contemporary change and professional inertia', by Andy Hargreaves, edited from *The*

Persistence of Presentism and the Struggle for Lasting Improvement (2008). Inaugural Professorial Lecture, reproduced by permission of Andy Hargreaves and IOE Press.

16.4 'Measurement as an obstacle to improvement: moving beyond the limitations of graded lesson observations', by Matt O'Leary, edited from *Classroom Observation: A Guide to the Effective Observation of Teaching and Learning* (2014), reproduced by permission of Routledge.

17.1 'Improving teacher expertise', by Dylan Wiliam, edited from *Assessment for Learning: Why, What and How?* (2009). Inaugural Professorial Lecture, Institute of Education, University of London, reproduced by permission of Dylan Wiliam.

17.2 'Combining research and practice in teaching', by Pasi Sahlberg, John Furlong and Pamela Munn, edited from *Report of the International Review Panel on the Structure of Initial Teacher Education Provision in Ireland* (2012). Review conducted on behalf of the Department of Education and Skills, reproduced by permission of the Government of Ireland.

17.3 'Teacher education and professionalism', by Ian Menter, Moira Hulme, Dely Eliot and Jon Lewin, edited from *Teacher Education in the 21st Century* (2010), Crown copyright, reproduced by permission of Ian Menter and under Open Government Licence.

17.4 'Towards a universal upper secondary education system in England. A unified and ecosystem vision', by Ann Hodgson and Ken Spours, edited from *Towards a universal upper secondary education system in England. A unified and ecosystem vision* (2012). Inaugural professorial lecture, 27 June, reproduced by permission of Institute of Education, University of London.

Index

This index categorises reflective schools, classrooms, teachers, pupils, teaching and learning, and related concepts under different headings; it covers Chapters 1–17 but not personal names. An 'f' after a page number indicates a figure.

The reflective teaching series

This book is one of the *Reflective Teaching Series* – applying principles of reflective practice in early, school, further, higher, adult and vocational education. Developed over three decades, the series books, companion readers and website represent the accumulated understanding of generations of teachers and educationalists. Uniquely, they offer *two* levels of support in the development of teacher expertise:

- *Comprehensive, practical guidance* on key issues – including learning, relationships, curriculum, teaching, assessment and evaluation.

- *Evidence-informed principles* to support deeper understanding.

The Reflective Teaching Series thus supports both initial steps in teaching and the development of career-long professionalism.

The series is supported by a website, **reflectiveteaching.co.uk**. For each book, this site is being developed to offer a range of resources including reflective activities, research briefings, advice on further reading and additional chapters. The site also offers generic resources such as a compendium of educational terms, links to other useful websites, and a conceptual framework for 'deepening expertise'. The latter draws on and showcases some of the UK's best educational research.

Underlying these materials, there are three key messages.

- It *is* now possible to identify teaching strategies which are more effective than others in most circumstances. Whatever the age of the learners for whom we have responsibility, we now need to be able to develop, improve, promote and defend our expertise by marshalling such evidence and by embedding enquiry, evaluation and improvement within our routine practices.

- All evidence has to be interpreted – and we do this by 'making sense'. In other words, as well as deploying effective strategies, we need to be able to pick out the underlying principles of learning and teaching to which specific policies and practices relate. As well as being practically competent, we need to be able to *understand* what is going on.

- Finally, we need to remember that education has moral purposes and social consequences. The provision we make is connected to our future as societies and to the life-chances of those in our care. The issues require very careful consideration.

The series is coordinated through meetings of the volume and series editors: Paul Ashwin, Jennifer Colwell, Margaret Gregson, Yvonne Hillier, Amy Pollard and Andrew Pollard. Each volume has an editorial team of contributors whose collective expertise and experience enable research and practice to be reviewed and applied in relation to early, school, further, higher, adult and vocational education.

The series is the first product of the Pollard Partnership, a collaboration between Andrew and Amy Pollard to maximise the beneficial use of research and evidence on public life, policy-making and professional practice.

Andrew Pollard, Bristol, February 2015